LONDON VILLAGES

By the same author

MEMOIRS AND BIOGRAPHY
We Mixed Our Drinks
Come into the Sunlight
The Escapist Generations

NOVELS
Another Man's Poison
Georgian Lady
  (Fanny Burney)
Poet Pursued
  (Shelley)
Victorian Love Story
  (Dante Gabriel Rossetti)
Malady of Love

FOR SCHOOLS AND PARENTS
Favourite Books for Boys and Girls

NERINA SHUTE

London Villages

ROBERT HALE LIMITED
LONDON

ST. MARTIN'S PRESS
NEW YORK

ISBN 0 7091 5812 2

Robert Hale Limited
Clerkenwell House
Clerkenwell Green
London EC1R 0HT

St. Martin's Press, Inc.
175 Fifth Avenue
New York, N.Y. 10010

Library of Congress Catalog Card Number 76-46673

ISBN 312-496125

Printed in Great Britain by
Lowe & Brydone Printers Limited, Thetford, Norfolk
and bound by Redwood Burn Limited, Esher, Surrey

Contents

To

IVY HOBDAY

my critic and friend, who might be described as a
literary osteopath. Her gift for immediately finding
a writer's weakness, and placing a ruthless but
dedicated finger on the place which hurts most,
helped me greatly in preparing this book.

N.S.

Illustrations

ILLUSTRATIONS

PICTURE CREDITS

Kensington and Chelsea Borough Library, 1
Museum of London, 3
National Portrait Gallery, London, 4, 5, 6, 7, 10,
    11, 17, 19, 20, 24, 26, 29, 30, 31, 32, 33, 34
London Borough of Wandsworth, 12
Westminster City Council, 15
Christopher Oxford, 16, 18
London Borough of Islington, 22
Dulwich College Gallery, 25
Radio Times Hulton Picture Library, 27, 28

Acknowledgements

I am beginning to think that librarians and local historians must be among the kindest and most helpful people in the turbulent world we Londoners live in today. Certainly they have given me so much help in writing this book that I hardly know how to thank them. Each chapter has been checked and corrected by a local historian, using up his or her valuable time, and I, the grateful author, am surprised to receive letters of thanks from my helpers and advisers.

There seems to be a bond between those who love London villages as there is between gardeners, or musicians, or dancers. We quickly understand one another. At any rate, I wish with all my heart to thank the following knowledgeable people for the trouble they have taken and the time they have all so generously given.

Mrs Patricia Pratt, when in charge of the Chelsea Reference Library, supplied me with numerous books, and as local historian has checked the Chelsea chapter, in addition to many other services from her colleagues in the Reference Library where I have so often worked. Miss W. M. Heard, as Chiswick local historian, has helped with the Chiswick chapter. Mr Philip D. Whitting, local historian, and Mr Usher, the Mayor's secretary, have both helped with the Hammersmith chapter. Mr A. J. D. Stonebridge, local historian, and Mr Richard Bowden, archivist at the Marylebone Reference Library, have both helped with the Marylebone chapter. Mr Tony Shaw, local historian, working at the West Hill Library in Wandsworth, helped with the chapter on Putney and Fulham. Mr Harold Smith, local historian, and also Mr Tony Shaw, (mentioned above) helped with the Battersea chapter. Mrs Christina Gee, local historian, working at Keats House Library, helped with the Hampstead chapter. Mr W. G. Campbell, local historian, working in the Hornsey Reference Library, helped with the Highgate chapter. Mr E. A. Willats, local historian, working in the Islington Reference Library, helped with the Islington chapter. Miss Mary Boast, local historian, working at the Dulwich Reference Library, helped with the Dulwich chapter. Mr Nigel Hamilton, local historian and author of *Royal Greenwich*, helped with the Greenwich chapter.

Introduction

It has often been said that London is a collection of villages. At one time they were far away from the old city, each one separate and independent, with a small but important life of its own. Now they have been gobbled up by a growing and enormous London. Their personalities are nearly—but not quite—extinguished by modern life. Because of all this rapid expansion there seems to be a certain similarity in the outward appearance of vast areas of London today. Nevertheless, to those of us who know and love it, London is full of exciting reminders of lovely old villages and the famous men and women who once lived in them by choice, taking pride in their beauty.

In this book I have not space to include all my favourites. Richmond is beautiful and full of history. Wimbledon still has some charming old houses clustered round the common. Twickenham is greatly loved by some, and needs to be described. Barnes and Ealing are in some ways as interesting as Kensington. These, and many others, have been left out, unfortunately, for reasons of space.

My own chosen village happens to be Chelsea. As a child I lived in Cheyne Walk, not far from the strange and romantic house where Rossetti wrote his best poems and painted his best pictures. Cheyne Walk is always exciting to visit but the essence of Chelsea is the Royal Hospital where the spirit of King Charles II can be felt so strongly that he might still be alive and present.

King Charles II left his mark on Chelsea just as King George IV left his mark on Marylebone. Almost every village is dominated by at least one personality. Sometimes there are several who make themselves felt. In Chiswick, for example, we have Lord Burlington's memory, and the ghost of Georgiana, the gorgeous Duchess of Devonshire, not to mention the wicked Lady Castlemaine. In Battersea, in one of London's most beautiful small churches, we can see the exquisite face of the woman adored by Lord Bolingbroke. It brings to life an old love story. How lucky we are in Battersea to have the memorial by Roubiliac, the two faces of the lovers, traced in marble, to remind us of the past. Hampstead is dominated by the poet, Keats, Dulwich by Shakespeare's contemporary, Ned Alleyn. Hammersmith has a rakish and lovable quality which might have something to do with Queen Caroline. Highgate has memories of Coleridge. Greenwich seems to give us the whole pageant of English history from the time of the Tudors.

There are certain well known historical characters who appear in more than one village. Alexander Pope, for example, was loved in Chiswick as a friend of Lord Burlington, admired in the Pump Room at Hampstead, where he brought John Gay, author of *The Beggar's Opera*, a well known figure in Battersea, a constant visitor to Lord Bolingbroke, who at first liked him, then detested him, and in Marylebone he was mocked by Lady Mary Wortley Montagu, with whom he fell in love. The character of King Henry VIII is seen differently in the villages of Chelsea, where he was hated, in Marylebone, where he was loved, in Islington where he was greatly admired for his skill at archery, and in Greenwich, where he was born, and where, of course, the villagers understood him. Queen Elizabeth I appears in Highgate, in Putney, in Chiswick, as well as in her palace at Greenwich. King Charles II seems to belong to Chelsea but we meet him in Greenwich, also in Putney, also in Highgate with Nell Gwynne. Characters like Dr Johnson and Fanny Burney flit about from Marylebone to Chiswick. We meet John Donne in Dulwich, and hear about him in Chiswick.

To the student of local history it is fascinating to find all these kings and queens and poets and philosophers, gathered like starlings in London's villages. We see them behaving like ordinary human beings. We fit them into place like the pieces in a jig-saw puzzle. We see more clearly the history of London and sometimes, in a new light, the history of England. This is because the villages give us the background to stories of love and hate about glamorous people like Henry VIII and Anne Boleyn, Charles II and Lady Castlemaine, 'Prinny' and Mrs Fitzherbert, Lord Bolingbroke and his beautiful Marie Claire, Keats and Fanny Brawne, even Pope and Lady Mary Wortley Montagu. In almost every village there is a personal story. It adds, somehow, to the quality of history. Most of us like to see the palaces and churches and villages where exciting things have happened to the heroes and villains of the past.

I have listed works and authors for readers who may wish for more than a brief summary of local history—which is all I can manage here. Each London village deserves a full length book to do it justice. All I have tried to do is to summarize each history and to indicate some of the authors offering more detailed research. Excellent books have been written recently about Chelsea, Marylebone, Islington, and Greenwich. Other villages are still waiting for contemporary authors to love them and describe them.

I happen to be a Londoner with a great love for London. It would make me happy to share this love and therefore I have written this book. If I can manage to arouse interest in my favourite villages the reader may feel inclined to visit some of them—and afterwards, perhaps, will study local history with greater pleasure and enthusiasm.

N.S.

1

Chelsea

At the heart of noisy Chelsea we still have a little humble church, the centre of the original village, standing by the River Thames like a peaceful seabird, untouched by the crash of passing lorries, a church which was known to King Henry VIII nearly 500 years ago, and used on Sundays by his dear friend Sir Thomas More, who was criticized at the time for singing in the choir. Behind Chelsea Old Church, running north into the famous King's Road, is a narrow street, once the village High Street. It is now called Old Church Street and it still has character.

In the exciting time of Sir Thomas More, who became Henry's Lord Chancellor, and built a beautiful country house, facing the present Battersea Bridge, about 100 yards from the clear clean river which he loved, the little village of Chelsea was a place of beauty and silence. The king's friend came here in 1521, and remained here until sent to the Tower in 1534. Later his house became known as Beaufort House because bought and rebuilt by the first Duke of Beaufort.

On summer evenings he and his affectionate family were visited by Henry, who travelled by river from Whitehall or Greenwich, arriving in his gilded barge, and dined and wined and strolled on the sloping green lawns with his royal arm round the shoulders of his favourite companion.

In 1535, when Sir Thomas More was executed, these delightful visits were recalled by his family but not by the ruthless Henry. His friend had refused as a Catholic to recognize his marriage to Anne Boleyn, and therefore became her enemy, as well as Henry's enemy. Less than a year later Anne herself was executed—and the following day, 21st May 1536, Henry was secretly married to his new favourite, Jane Seymour.

These happenings are still vividly remembered in Chelsea. We now have the statue of Sir Thomas More, seated by the river, outside his little church, gazing at the passing boats with an expression of love.

By the Catholics he is honoured as a saint. (He was canonized in 1935.) Round the neck of his statue hangs a crucifix, copied from the one he carried with him to the scaffold. His last words, waiting on the scaffold to meet his death, have not been forgotten. He intended to die, he said calmly, "the King's good servant, but God's first".

It is still felt in the village of Chelsea that Sir Thomas More is to be pitied and deeply admired. How could Henry, who once loved him as a brother, allow this brave man's head to be spiked on the end of a pole and displayed for all to see at London Bridge? Indignation is still felt when the terrible story is told. Some say his headless body was buried in Chelsea Old Church, near the middle of the south wall. It is not known for certain where his body was buried. His beloved head, after the exhibition on London Bridge, was rescued by Margaret Roper, his daughter, and buried in the family vault in St Dunstan's Church, Canterbury. (The memoirs of Roper, his son-in-law, give us some valuable information.)

Sadly, Chelsea Old Church was demolished by a German mine in 1941. Of the original building only the Thomas More Chapel remains, and there it still stands, behind his statue, waiting to be visited. The rest of the church has been cleverly and lovingly restored, brick by brick, treasure by treasure, scrap by scrap, and now looks almost as interesting as it did in the past, though perhaps a bit cleaner and more sprightly.

After the death of Sir Thomas More there were many changes in the simple life of the villagers who so greatly missed him. King Henry VIII, desiring a summer palace in this lovely and romantic village, decided to confiscate the dead man's estate and reduce his family to poverty. Some thought Henry would live in the dead man's house. Instead he acquired the Manor of Chelsea, making himself the Lord of the Manor, and annoyed the family by building his summer palace, only a few hundred yards away, on the east side of the church. He chose the place which is now Cheyne Walk.

We are told it resembled St James's Palace, which he had built for Anne Boleyn. This one was intended for Jane Seymour, with orchards and gardens sloping to the river like those which had once belonged to Sir Thomas More. Perhaps he regretted his act of murder. He was punished for it when the lovable Jane Seymour died in childbirth. But the two important buildings, so near one another, so full of history, reminding Chelsea of a tragic royal friendship, were both destroyed in the eighteenth century. The villagers were sad when they disappeared.

Today we have only the chapel, and the solemn riverside statue, by which to remember the charming Sir Thomas More, the martyr, the writer, the gentle philosopher, the statesman, the twice-married family man, the gentleman who loved both his wives so devotedly that he hoped, and sometimes prayed, for a threesome up in heaven. He is very much a part of the London story. Lovers of Chelsea can no more forget him than King Charles II, Thomas Carlyle, Rossetti, Oscar Wilde, Whistler, and others who came later.

King Charles left his mark on Chelsea. In the following century it was still a beautiful and peaceful village. The two historic buildings were still standing by the river, entertained by the sight of fishing boats and barges, their flowery gardens divided by the ancient church. A country lane still wandered beside the water, close to the boats and the fishing nets, and ended near the new building, the Royal Chelsea Hospital, designed by Sir Christopher Wren, and created by Charles for his old soldiers.

In those days the King's Road was used only by Charles, who was followed as a rule by a noisy band of cheerful friends, watched by the villagers as their horses clattered in the direction of Putney. It was a private road down which they all trotted or galloped, on their way from Whitehall to Putney, and on, by river, or by road, to Hampton Court.

No doubt the villagers of Chelsea enjoyed the disturbance, and so did Charles. It must have been gay and exciting. For one thing, the church bells in Chelsea were loudly rung whenever royalty passed through the village. Indeed Chelsea was compelled to ring the bells. We are told that in 1597 the churchwardens were fined four shillings because the bells were not rung when Queen Elizabeth was carried from Kensington to Richmond.

In Chelsea he was always much loved. As we know, it was Charles who founded the Royal Hospital in 1682, and today we have a community of people who continue to dress and live much as they did in the time of Charles. What is more, they love him still.

Any one may pay these people a visit. Leave the noise of Sloane Square and discover the stately buildings in the Royal Hospital Road. Immediately the sense of noise and discord is left behind. The visitor who happens to arrive before lunch will be greeted by a dignified gentleman who might be a retired judge, in his eighties or nineties, sometimes wearing a scarlet uniform, a three-cornered hat. He bows, or nods his head, and smiles gravely. In a gentle tone, as though offering a blessing, he slowly says: "Good morning." His companions are equally dignified, and the visitor is given a feeling of importance.

These elegant old soldiers have a special quality which belongs to the colourful village of Chelsea. All of them are immaculate in appearance, self contained, as serene and stately as swans floating slowly on the Thames.

In summer their scarlet uniforms are like those worn by the soldiers of Marlborough in the eighteenth century. In winter they often wear dark blue, with peaked caps, which most of them seem to prefer, being less conspicuous and grand. For nearly 300 years men like themselves have lived in this building, peacefully sleeping, side by side, in cubicles designed for them by Sir Christopher Wren.

Today they still have their meals in the panelled dining-hall, looking up sometimes at the huge picture of Charles, the wonderful man who gave them their home, the king who continues to make himself felt, guarding them, always present, as lovable and familiar as a family ghost.

Perhaps the first thing to see at the Royal Hospital is the statue of Charles by Grinling Gibbons. He stands outside, in the middle of Figure Court, at the heart of the quiet, beautiful, sleepy buildings, surrounded on a sunny afternoon by his old soldiers who rest on benches round the grass. Charles is seen here with bare knees, dressed in the fashion of a Roman Emperor. The old soldiers admire the statue, but some say, with a touch of disapproval, that Charles does not look his best in a toga.

We are told that Charles was inspired in many ways by the French king, Louis XIV, who built Les Invalides in Paris, the first Army Hospital in the world. But Les Invalides, where Napoleon lies buried, is as different as the French language from the English. Les Invalides is a palace. The Chelsea Hospital is a stately English home. It was described by Carlyle as "quiet and dignified and the work of a gentleman".

In the eyes of most of the old soldiers, living there today, nothing could be more desirable, and Charles, who planned it for them, was truly an English gentleman. It is well known that he walked in the London streets, alone, or with his dogs, and any stranger might speak to the king. He loved the company of pretty women, and one night he was heard by Evelyn, the diarist, quarrelling in a loud voice with Nell Gwynne as they strolled together in the Mall.

Old soldiers remember such things with enjoyment. "Let not poor Nellie starve." Charles said to his brother, not long before his death. Most of them can remember the names of his numerous mistresses, including the Duchess of Cleveland, the Duchess of Portsmouth, the Duchess of Richmond, the wicked Lady Castlemaine, not to mention his faithful Queen Catherine of Braganza, who lived in Hammersmith after his death, and heard him say on his death bed, making his last joke, in a tone of apology: "I am an unconscionable time a-dying."

In the Chelsea Royal Hospital, everywhere, in the rooms and in the grounds, the personality of Charles seems to penetrate the air like a minty perfume from the past. Even in the club room, next door to the bar, where the old soldiers gather in the mornings and evenings for a glass of beer, or sherry, or whisky (cheap and good) resting pleasantly in their scarlet armchairs, there is a portrait of Charles which no one can fail to notice.

In the dining hall there is a vast allegorical mural, with Charles on horseback, a heroic Charles, apparently stamping out evil, aided by fantastic female figures, no doubt angels, who seem to be encouraging him in his battle for science, and architecture, and peace and progress. In the background can be seen the Royal Hospital as it looked then.

It seems that the spirit of Charles will never die in the village of Chelsea. The ceremony which takes place each year on or near 20th May must be seen to be believed. This is called "Founder's Day", or sometimes "Acorn Day". The old soldiers, marching magnificently to a military band, dressed in their gorgeous scarlet uniforms and three-cornered hats, parade before Charles and decorate his statue with oak leaves. Each old soldier wears an oak leaf in his button hole. This, of course, is to commemorate the day when brave Charles climbed into an oak tree and escaped from the men of Cromwell, after the Battle of Worcester, by hiding in the leafy branches. A strange ceremony! Very English!

A moment comes when the military band stops playing and the old soldiers, standing to attention, their eyes fixed on the statue of Charles, wait for the word of command. The guest of honour, usually a member of the Royal family, calls out loudly: "Three cheers for King Charles II." The response is touching and unexpectedly moving. Tears almost come to the eyes when the old soldiers, with a wave of their beautiful three-cornered hats, medals glittering in the sunlight, apparently untired by the long session of parading and marching in formation before the statue, raise their voices and call three times, in a shout of delight, as though one man: "Hip, Hip, Hooray!" Afterwards they cheer the queen, and the guest of honour, but the big moment, the supreme moment, is the cheer for King Charles II.

It is worth a visit to the wards where the old soldiers sleep. One of them will lead the visitor slowly and peacefully to the old fashioned lift, or the oak staircase, black with age, leading at last to a long corridor with windows overlooking the statue.

The panelled cubicles are polished oak. On each door is printed the name of the owner, his age, his regiment, his religion. The owner is proud of his possessions. On the shelves around his bed are the family photographs, silver trophies, regimental decorations, coloured pictures and paintings of uniforms, and helmets, and flags, souvenirs of war and peace, lovingly preserved.

One old soldier, who plays bowls (at the age of eighty) will show his gleaming collection of cups and awards. Another has a hobby. He will bring out one of the dolls' houses, fully furnished, complete with electricity and garage and petrol pumps, which he designs and builds for spastic children. Another has a shelf on which he keeps a row of highly polished shoes, taking pride in the good gleam of leather which is rubbed and shined every day.

At the time of writing the oldest pensioner is ninety-seven years of age. Many are in their eighties. The juniors are in their seventies, or late sixties. Each man receives board and lodging, clothing, a pint of beer daily, or tobacco, and sometimes a money allowance. All this he owes to Charles. Perhaps it explains the sense of dignified kindness, the day to day courtesy, the belief that God is nearly always in his Heaven, smiling, benign, which seems to greet the visitor, and to separate the old soldiers, like an invisible wall, from the instability and uncertainty of the turbulent world outside.

The old soldiers were grieved and concerned by the death of their dear Charles. They missed the cheerful clatter of trotting and galloping horses in the King's Road, the sound of church bells loudly ringing to greet the popular king when he passed through the village. His brother, James, was not a favourite. The villagers had no great love for William and Mary, and less still for the German kings from Hanover, who could not speak English.

We know that life went on, as it does today, in the Royal Hospital, but in fifty years, or so, a change was noticed outside. Almost on their doorstep the old soldiers were astonished to see a place of entertainment, a meeting place for eighteenth-century nobility and society. This was Ranelagh Gardens—where the famous Chelsea Flower Show now takes place each year, attracting visitors from all parts of England, Scotland, and Wales.

Today this romantic place is almost empty at other times, but try to imagine it in the past. Here is an animated description by a young girl in Smollett's *Humphrey Clinker*.

Ranelagh looks [she tells us] like the enchanted palace of a genius, adorned with the most exquisite performances of painting, carving, and gilding, enlighted with a thousand golden lamps, that emulate the noon-day sun; crowded with the great, the rich, the gay, the happy, and the fair; glittering with cloth of gold and silver, lace embroidery and precious stones. While these exulting sons and daughters of felicity tread this round of pleasure, or regale in different parties, and separate lodges, with fine imperial tea and other delicious refreshments, their ears are entertained with the most ravising delights of music, both instrumental and vocal.

What a picture this gives! Ranelagh Gardens, in the eighteenth century, was visited on summer evenings by everyone of interest, including Dr Johnson and Fanny Burney and Sir Horace Walpole. There were concerts and masquerades and fireworks. Mozart, aged eight, gave a concert here in 1764. In the middle of this fashionable playground was a famous building, the Rotunda. Canaletto painted it, and you can see his picture of Ranelagh Gardens in the National Gallery.

Unfortunately the average Londoner has forgotten, or perhaps never knew, the history of the place. Many of us go each year to the Chelsea Flower Show but all we see is the flowers!

No doubt the old soldiers were annoyed sometimes by the nightly sound of fireworks and strains of music when they were trying to get their sleep. Perhaps some enjoyed it and others, in their nineties, were too deaf to hear it. Ranelagh was probably considered a bit of a nuisance by the old soldiers, but the Physic Garden, on the west side of the Royal Hospital, was as silent then as it is today.

Probably there is no other garden quite like this at the heart of a busy city. Members of the public have never been admitted. It is the oldest existing botanical garden in England. Its life began in the reign of Charles when the Society of the Apothocaries were driven from Blackfriars to Chelsea by the fire of London.

Had it not been for Sir Hans Sloane (whose name has since been given to Sloane Square, Sloane Street, Hans Place, Hans Crescent, etc.) the Physic Garden might soon have been lost and forgotten by Londoners. As a medical student he used it and loved it. Thea Holme tells us that, later, as a court physician, President of the Royal Society, one of Queen Anne's doctors, he became rich enough to buy it for the Apothocaries and so keep it for Chelsea.

Sir Hans Sloane was not just a clever doctor but a man of business. Today we might call him a property developer. The Cadogan family, who own much of Chelsea, are descended from Sir Hans Sloane. He was once the owner of Beaufort House, the home of Thomas More, and this he destroyed, for which deed of vandalism it is hard to forgive him. He owned Cheyne Walk, which still exists, and the Manor House of Henry VIII, which others destroyed after his death.

This second deed of vandalism would have hurt his feelings. He loved Henry's palace, in which he housed an enormous collection of fossils, minerals, books, plant specimens, precious stones, gold, silver, stuffed animals and insects, which finally became the foundation of the British Museum.

Anyway, we still have the British Museum and we still have the Chelsea Physic Garden. Follow the wall into Swan Walk, still a country lane, green and rural and peaceful, and you will discover a magnificent iron gate, locked of course, through which you can just see between the trees a white statue of a gentleman. This is Sir Hans Sloane—standing proudly in his garden.

Thomas Carlyle came to live in Chelsea in the year 1834, and settled in a house which is now numbered 24 Cheyne Row. At that time Chelsea was turning into a village of writers and artists. Carlyle was visited by Leigh Hunt, John Stuart Mill, Tennyson, Darwin, John Ruskin, even Dickens. A few years later Rossetti moved into Cheyne Walk, and there received his numerous friends, including Swinburne, William Morris, John Ruskin, Burne-Jones, Millais.

Carlyle and Rossetti were soon the two most famous personalities in Victorian Chelsea. They could not have been more different in character, one a dour Scot, the other a romantic Italian, dominated by beautiful women.

Carlyle wrote his best and most famous book, *The French Revolution*, in the fascinating house in Cheyne Row which is almost unchanged, inside and out. The furniture, the dark painted staircase, the dingy wall paper, the books, the personal possessions, the chest of drawers, full of clothing worn by Carlyle, the hip bath, used by Jane, his wife, the kitchen downstairs in the basement, where the maid slept on the floor beneath the dresser, tell us more about Victorian life than any other house in London.

Thomas and Jane Carlyle were virtuous people who loved one another tenderly. At the same time, they were quarrelsome, unhappy, bad-tempered, trapped together in a house of tantrums and squabbles.

Upstairs, in the drawing room, prim and grim as Carlyle himself, with a pedestal for the aspidistra, a screen decorated by Jane with pictures and cuttings, an oil lamp, placed there by Jane, close to her husband's chair, with a shelf for his book, it is difficult to believe that he and she are no longer living. Visitors feel like intruders. In this room, for thirty-two years, they tortured themselves with arguments, quarrels, and partings, followed by reconciliations, followed by further quarrels and more partings. It is possible for two people who are incompatible to love one another more than anyone else. This the Carlyles did. In order to endure their troublesome marriage they were forced to part again and again, at regular intervals, like two dancers, exhausted by their strenuous dance.

Jane had numerous problems at Cheyne Row, where she lived from 1834 till 1836. Next door the neighbours kept poultry in their garden and Carlyle objected strongly to the crowing of cockrels and the triumphant clucking of hens after laying their eggs. It was Jane's job to keep the hens and the neighbours quiet. Carlyle must have total silence in order to write *The French Revolution*. For this reason Jane gave him the windowless room at the top of the house where his books and papers can be seen today. When the manuscript of *The French Revolution* (the only copy in existence) was thrown into the fire by a careless housemaid, Carlyle set himself the hideous task of writing the book all over again. Jane endured his ill temper as a good Victorian wife should. In a moment of exasperation she said later: "Only fools marry for the sake of keeping a promise."

Jane was a jealous woman. She bitterly resented her husband's innocent friendship with a witty and charming hostess, Lady Ashburton. According to James Anthony Froude, who knew them both, and wrote Carlyle's biography, Carlyle was impotent. As he was never unfaithful to Jane he could not understand her jealousy. (Any woman could understand.) Jane, who was almost as witty and charming as the celebrated Lady Ashburton, could not understand why Carlyle could not understand.

When her rival died in 1857 she began to feel better in health. In 1863 she had a serious accident while driving in her carriage. Three years later, again in her carriage, driving in Hyde Park, she quietly and mysteriously died, and her body was brought home to Carlyle by a terrified coachman. John Ruskin called to see her at just this terrible moment. He was told what had happened by a weeping maid-servant.

The heart-broken Carlyle received a message of sympathy from Queen Victoria herself. Afterwards he lived by himself in a state of loneliness and misery for fifteen years. He edited and arranged publication for Jane's letters, witty, wise, revealing, satirical, not sparing the feelings of her rude and difficult husband. In the end he died, in his drawing room, sitting in his comfortable chair—the same chair, placed in the same drawing room, in the same little house in Chelsea, just as it looks today.

Returning to Cheyne Walk, these fashionable houses have changed very little since the days of Sir Hans Sloane. The most romantic is the one called Queen's House, with imposing iron gateway, where Dante Gabriel Rossetti lived and wrote and painted pictures of beautiful women for nearly twenty years. At the time it was thought to be a wing of Henry's original palace, and was admired by Rossetti for this reason.

He came here in 1863—the year when Jane Carlyle had the first accident while driving in her carriage. The Carlyles had been living in Chelsea for twenty-nine years and the villagers were proud of Thomas Carlyle, the well-known author, who lived in their midst. His famous figure, in cape and wide brimmed hat, was frequently seen, walking up the High Street [now Old Church Street] to the King's Road.

Rossetti, the painter and poet, caused interest and disapproval. Strange stories went round the village. Rossetti believed he had caused the death of his model, the beautiful Miss Siddal (or Lizzie, or Guggums, as he called her) by neglecting her after their marriage. As an act of retribution, as though making a supreme sacrifice, he had placed the only copy of his collected poems in her coffin on the day when Lizzie was buried at the cemetery in Highgate. On that day he wrote, as though treasuring his pain:

> As much as in a hundred years she's dead
> Yet is today the day on which she died.

Rossetti seems to be the only Victorian who might have enjoyed and appreciated the permissive age in which we are now living. In Chelsea, today, the bearded boys and long-haired girls disapprove of marriage as he did. They believe, as he did, in the beauty and purity of the sexual act. He expressed their feelings, and the deep and heartfelt philosophy of his life and work, in two unforgettable lines:

> Thy soul I know not from thy body, nor
> Thee from myself, neither our love from God.

It is not surprising that Carlyle was almost as baffled as the villagers and old soldiers by the bohemian behaviour of the new arrival in Cheyne Walk. Only the critic, Mr John Ruskin (who nearly ruined another great artist, no less than Whistler) believed in the genius of Rossetti and tried to reform his morals. He bought pictures, supplied Miss Siddal with money, offered to finance their wedding.

When it was all over, and the poems placed dramatically in her coffin, beneath her golden hair, Rossetti shut himself in the great house in Cheyne Walk. There he grieved for Lizzie, spending his nights and days with Fanny Hughes, his understanding mistress. This continued for eight years, while they slept and worked at the back of the house, Rossetti painting his world famous picture of Lizzie (inspired by Dante and Beatrice) while Fanny, his Cockney lover, cooked and cleaned and consoled.

In the garden he kept some peculiar animals, including hedgehogs, wombats, peacocks, wallabies, kangaroos, a chameleon, and even a laughing jackass. Most of his undesirable pets were kept, or partly kept, in wire cages from which they nearly always managed to escape. To this day, in memory of Rossetti, there is a special clause in the lease of Cheyne Walk houses. It prevents tenants from owning wild animals to the annoyance of their neighbours.

Fanny did her shopping in the village High Street, behind the church, where she may have encountered Jane Carlyle while chatting to the baker or the grocer. Rossetti was known to Carlyle, who may have nodded without speaking, on his way to buy tobacco for his pipe in the King's Road. He disapproved of Rossetti's friends, especially Swinburne, who joined Rossetti in Cheyne Walk. For a time he occupied the ground floor room by the front door on the right hand side. This arrangement was soon ended. We are told that Swinburne, when drunk, formed the habit of throwing off his clothes and sliding down the banisters naked. Even Rossetti was annoyed.

When his best picture had at last been painted, a final tribute to Lizzie, it was decided by Rossetti's friends that the time had come to open her coffin. Others arranged for the poems to be returned to Rossetti for publication. But Mr Ruskin said indignantly: "Just like Rossetti! Unfaithful to Lizzie even in her grave!"

The villagers of Chelsea, when they heard the story, were no more sympathetic than Mr Ruskin. Nevertheless the poems were published in April 1870, and soon could be found in fashionable drawing rooms, daringly displayed beside the poems of Tennyson and Browning. Two of these poems were considered extremely shocking. One was called "Nuptial Sleep". The other was called "Jenny".

At the end of eight years with Fanny Cornforth (who became very fat and heavy) the painter found a new and more beautiful model. This was Jane Morris, the wife of his friend, William Morris, owner of the Kelmscott Press, whose writings and modern designs for furniture and wallpaper were admired by all. The beautiful Jane became a frequent visitor to the big house in Cheyne Walk, and this caused further gossip in the village. Rossetti saw her as Guinevere and himself as Lancelot. At last the poet had found the woman he could love in body as in soul.

Today we know that William Morris loved and respected his wife, also Rossetti, whom he admired, allowing them to become lovers, behaving like one of King Arthur's knights, or the noble Arthur himself. Until the year 1988 we are not allowed to read his private letters, now in the British Museum, which will probably disentangle the truth from the gossip.

But the love story ended in tragedy. At the house in Cheyne Walk, when the beautiful Jane went to Italy with her long suffering husband, Rossetti attempted suicide. We know that his mood of melancholy continued. He lost his youth and even his love for beautiful women. In the end he was like a slowly sinking ship, drawn downward by depression and drugs and deep loneliness, dosing himself daily with chloral and walking by himself in the dark rooms of his empty house. At night he went out. Then he walked alone by the river, up and down the Embankment, his face hidden by his large black hat. One night he was passed by the elderly Carlyle, almost blind, who also walked in sadness by the river, led by a young girl.

The girl recognized the famous Rossetti and felt frightened. Rossetti died on Easter Day in 1882. At the age of fifty-four he seemed almost as old as Carlyle, who died in his chair a few months earlier at the age of eighty-six.

We are reminded of Carlyle, the Puritan, one of the great Victorians, by his dark little house and his grim statue placed at the end of his narrow street. But Rossetti, the romantic escapist, belongs in a special sense to the life and thought of Chelsea today. Some of his ideals and sufferings are at last understood—though despised when he lived in Cheyne Walk.

Chelsea by this time was well known as the village of painters and poets and philosophers. Edwardian Chelsea became smart and amusing as a place to live, and the two most famous personalities, received in every fashionable drawing room, were now Whistler and Oscar Wilde, artist and author.

Tite Street was considered a good address. Unfortunately the improvers and planners have pulled down several important buildings, including the famous White House, built for Whistler by Godwin. They have left us Tower House, where Whistler once had a studio. The ugly substantial red brick home of Oscar Wilde (No. 34) still stands.

Whistler, an American, was older than Oscar Wilde. Before they quarrelled, these two were close friends, and both delighted in high society, liking to be seen with dukes and duchesses. The Edwardians did everything with style. In private all these charming stylists might be lovers and sinners and transgressors but in public they must always be seen as ladies and gentlemen. Edward insisted upon loyalty and perfect discretion. To be found out was to break the eleventh commandment. Anyone making this ill bred mistake might expect to be ostracized (like Whistler and Oscar Wilde) by his or her friends.

Whistler was known in the village of Chelsea by his eyeglass, his lock of white hair, his top hat and cane, taller than other hats and canes, his fine appearance and amusing repartee. It was Whistler who introduced Oscar Wilde to the London drawing rooms. When Oscar left university (Oxford) he was tall and clumsy, with a large head on a thin neck. Whistler recognized him as a fellow wit and taught him how to make a bow, or an entrance, or a cryptic remark. Whistler was then living with his mistress at No. 2 Lindsey Row, now 96 Cheyne Walk.

On the day of Oscar's wedding Whistler sent him a telegram to the church. It simply said: "Am detained. Don't wait."

After another such witticism Oscar enviously said: "I wish *I* had said that," and Whistler laconically replied: "You will, Oscar, you will."

Oscar became outrageously famous as a wit. Indeed he outwhistled Whistler and lost his friendship. Whistler had known poverty, had gone bankrupt, had pawned the famous portrait of his mother, also the one of Carlyle, after failing to recover from a libel case, the talk of London, caused by Mr John Ruskin, who had brutally attacked a beautiful Whistler picture.

"I have seen and heard much of Cockney impudence before now," said the great critic, "but never expected to hear a coxcomb ask two hundred guineas for flinging a pot of paint in the public's face."

Although he was ruined financially, the sufferings of Whistler were nothing compared with what happened when Oscar went to court, also claiming damages for libel. By this time the friends had quarrelled. Oscar had fallen in love with Lord Alfred Douglas. After his first appearance in court he stayed at the Cadogan Hotel in Sloane Street. He was there, in his bedroom, when arrested by the police on a charge of sodomy, and taken immediately to Holloway Prison. After his second trial in May 1895 he was sentenced to two years imprisonment with hard labour.

The unhappy Oscar was dropped by London society because he had broken the eleventh commandment. Like Whistler he soon went bankrupt. It seems that no one in the village of Chelsea had the slightest sympathy with him. He was not prepared for what happened, and cruelly punished, because, like Whistler, he failed to understand the permissive society which danced and hunted through life according to a set of rules, permitting almost anything in private, nothing in public.

He was driven into exile, and we, who admire Oscar, remember him now with sorrow. He died in Paris, in 1900, unnoticed, no longer loved. He must have looked back in bitterness at the happy and successful days in Chelsea. Homosexuality was still considered a crime, "the love that dare not speak its name", condemned among gentlemen who sternly said: "He's a cad, sir", and well bred young ladies still blushed, without knowing why, at the mention of Oscar Wilde's name. The author's mother did this. Even at the end of her life she was not quite sure why she blushed.

The story of Whistler has a happier ending for the painter struggled back into London society. In 1891 (the year when Oscar met Lord Alfred Douglas) the Glasgow Corporation paid him the enormous sum of one thousand guineas for his portrait of Carlyle. Soon after that the portrait of his mother was bought for the Musée de Luxembourg. He was even awarded the *Legion d'Honneur*.

The picture despised by Mr Ruskin was eventually sold, not for 200 guineas, as at first proposed, but for 800 guineas. So rich and successful was the painter by the end of his life that in London and Paris there was even a trade in fake Whistler pictures painted by unknown artists and sold sometimes to Americans.

When his wife died of cancer in 1896 he returned to his beloved Chelsea. He died in the summer of 1903. His illegitimate son, and a pretty woman called Jo, his first model, attended the funeral service at Chelsea Old Church. He was buried at Chiswick, beside his wife, close to the river he had loved so much and painted so often.

But where is the link between modern Chelsea and the colourful collection of kings, courtiers, painters, poets, and philosophers, who belonged to Chelsea in the past?

Rightly or wrongly, the King's Road has been taken over by the cult of the young society, teenagers, pot smokers, hairy boys and girls who faithfully follow each fashion or trend. It is like a theatre. It belongs to Chelsea as a visiting circus belongs to a country village, but this one, it seems, has come to stay.

The antique shops remain but most of the artists and authors have disappeared like rabbits into their holes. The cafes and clubs and coffee bars and small expensive restaurants are still there but have changed in appearance. Teenagers use them and sometimes own them. Teenagers stroll in and out of open doors, welcomed inside the shops by pop music and wild selections of feathered hats, fancy boots, cowboy costumes, dresses and pants and shirts and pullovers, in flashy colours, for boys and girls with money to spend on dressing up for the King's Road parade. This takes place on Saturday afternoons, when they come from the suburbs to show themselves. Boy meets girl on Saturday afternoon. Boy beds girl on Saturday evening.

Sometimes you might see one of the old soldiers from the Chelsea Royal Hospital, smart in his scarlet uniform, walking down the King's Road with a teenage girl wearing a bikini. You might walk behind two bearded young men, their arms entwined, who stop to kiss one another.

At the time of writing the boys who parade on Saturday afternoons are better dressed than the girls and some of them seem to have a sense of purpose. They are beginning to dress and behave with a touch of style, more sophisticated, as if attempting to copy the Edwardians.

Much has been said about their drugs and clubs and bad habits. In the King's Road there are well known clubs for homosexuals, both male and female. Sometimes there are signals of distress. When a teenager has taken a 'trip' for the first time there might be a call for help. Sometimes a message is scribbled on a wall giving the address and phone number of those who understand drugs and offer advice without charge. It is indeed a world within a world. And yet the King's Road of the teenagers and pot smokers is something which belongs to Chelsea and is now understood in Chelsea, as familiar as the old soldiers in their scarlet uniforms.

It is difficult to believe that the King's Road was little more than a country lane until 1830. The king who used it so often was as permissive as anybody else. To tell the truth, the uninhibited outlook of boys and girls in the new society has much in common with the frankness and freedom of the Restoration period. King Charles, like Rossetti, would have understood and sometimes admired the youthful Chelsea of today.

CHELSEA LOCAL HISTORY
Recommended Books

Chelsea, Thomas Faulkner (1829)
Chelsea, Thea Holme (Hamish Hamilton, 1972)
Memorials of Old Chelsea, Alfred Beaver (1892) (S. R. Publishers Ltd, reprinted 1971)
Chelsea, William Gaunt (Batsford, 1954)
Two Villages, Mary Cathcart Borer (W. H. Allen, 1973)

2

Hammersmith

The Hammersmith Parish Church has a faintly surprised expression on its dignified Victorian face for it now stands by itself amid a deafening maelstrom of traffic, a centre point of silence within a web of noisy thoroughfares and cross roads and roundabouts and fly-overs and fly-unders which intimidate the insecure pedestrian and even the experienced motorist, weakening his or her nervous system and reducing belief in survival.

Speaking as a motorist, if you approach Hammersmith by Talgarth Road and drive your car beneath the fly-over in a determined attempt to join the traffic which thunders into Fulham Palace Road, or to join another stream of traffic which swirls round the church to cross Hammersmith Bridge, or to make a right hand turn (more difficult still) and arrive safely in Hammersmith Broad-way, you may have time to glance without death at the church clock but certainly not to observe the church. Perhaps that is why so few people know much about St Paul's Church, let alone the romantic story of Sir Nicholas Crispe. Very few Londoners have ever heard of him. You may well say: "Who is Sir Nicholas Crispe?" Such is fame!

Sir Nicholas Crispe was a remarkable man who once lived in the heart of Hammersmith, and loved the village so much that he left it his own heart to lie in the parish church for all to see. Believe it or not, the heart of Sir Nicholas Crispe has remained in Hammersmith for more than 300 years. It was placed in an urn which still stands in St Paul's Church, exactly as he wished and directed.

Sir Nicholas was born in 1598, the son of a wealthy merchant, both his parents living for several generations in the City of London, with a family home in Bread Street. He fought on the side of his friend and beloved king, Charles I, when the country was divided by the Civil War with Oliver Cromwell, and most of the people of Hammersmith took the side of their king—perhaps out of love for Sir Nicholas.

Cromwell's men were billeted in the manor house which is now the bus station opposite the church. The village was a military centre. At the time of writing, the brick wall facing the church, with steps leading up to an old and stately door, permanently closed (with buses emerging on either side of it) is all that remains of a fine old mansion called Bradmore House, a manor farm with twenty-five acres of land which stood for more than 200 years on or near the site of an Elizabethan mansion called Butterwick House.

Cromwell's officers slept in the halls where red buses now spend their nights. They emerged, as the buses do, from a door facing the church. We are told that Cromwell himself preferred to sleep in the beautiful home of Sir Nicholas, a riverside villa on the east side of Hammersmith Bridge.

Sir Nicholas was, as we know, an extremely rich man, and much of his great fortune was given to his beloved king. During the whole of the Civil War he raised money for Charles and carried supplies to him and his soldiers. As a man of the City, he carried on trade which produced for Charles £100,000 per annum, besides keeping the ports open and the ships ready for service.

His magnificent riverside villa, known to us as Brandenburgh House, on which he spent £23,000, was later confiscated by Parliament, and Sir Nicholas was heavily fined for some of his courageous activities. At one time he was imprisoned. Among other things we are told that he acted as a spy for Charles and passed between London and Oxford in the dress of a butter-woman on horseback, between a pair of panniers. At his own expense he managed to raise a regiment of horse for the king and put himself at the head of it. During the siege of Gloucester, Sir Nicholas and his regiment acted as escort for the king's train of artillery from Oxford.

There seems to be no doubt that the villagers of Hammersmith loved their king as Sir Nicholas did, and hated the dictator Cromwell for the same reason. They did their best to please and gratify Sir Nicholas. In Shepherd's Bush, for example, a plan was made to murder Cromwell by a somewhat inefficient citizen called Miles Sindecombe (under the orders of Colonel Sexby) but the plan failed. Cromwell always passed Shepherd's Bush Green on his way to and from Hampton Court, but when the moment came to strike him down, the conspirators, unfortunately, lost their nerve.

By Sir Nicholas and those who followed his lead in the fight against Cromwell, the king was not only loved and pitied but admired by many as a saint. Sir Nicholas, and most of the villagers, were broken hearted on that bitter cold day, 30th January 1649, when Charles walked across St James's Park, stopping to admire a tree planted there by his brother, stopping again to say his prayers and drink a glass of wine to keep out the cold, and then, with no sign of fear, climbed the scaffold outside his Whitehall Palace where the crowds were waiting to see him beheaded.

After this tragic event Sir Nicholas was forced to leave England, and he stayed for a while in France. Most of the villagers, loving their leader, longed for Sir Nicholas to return, and this he did. Times changed. He lived quietly in his riverside villa, and later, following the death of Cromwell, he was sent by the City of London with a message for Charles II, then living at Bude, in Holland. The new king was the son of his greatest friend, and Sir Nicholas was embraced when he gave the message.

"Surely the City has a mind to oblige me," Charles said, "by sending even my father's old friend to invite me."

When the news reached Hammersmith the villagers were delighted, and Sir Nicholas was rewarded for his loyalty and bravery. He was created a baronet, and continued to help and protect the people of Hammersmith, where he lived happily until his death in 1666.

It was Sir Nicholas who contributed £700 towards the building of a new chapel for Hammersmith (now replaced by the Victorian church crouching under the fly-over) and here he went every Sunday to worship God. It was the good Sir Nicholas who left a sum of £100 (to increase through the years) to be invested in land and buildings for the benefit of poor people living in Hammersmith.

Finally, and best of all, it was Sir Nicholas who left instructions that after his death his body should be buried in the tomb of his ancestors in the City Church of St Mildred's, in Bread Street, but his heart must be sent to the Hammersmith chapel.

The villagers were touched by this unusual mark of affection. By Thomas Faulkner we are told: "It was the custom to take out the heart on the anniversary of its entombment, and to refresh it with a glass of wine; at length, after the expiration of more than a century and a half it became decayed, and it was finally enclosed in a leaden case and deposited agreeably to his direction." The leaden case is still there, hidden beneath the lid of the urn, and so, no doubt, is the dust of the romantic heart of Sir Nicholas.

In 1834 the chapel became the parish church. Today it is large and imposing, Victorian Gothic, created in the wealthy period, the 1880s, but inside the church there is still a most moving reminder of

Sir Nicholas, the Hammersmith hero, and his great love for his saintly, sensitive, and stubborn king. For some reason it is placed behind the door, so high you can hardly see it, on a monument of black and white marble. It is a beautiful bronze head of King Charles I, and Sir Nicholas wrote the humble and charming inscription.

This effigies was
created by the special appointment
of Sir Nicholas Crispe, Knight and Baronet,
as a grateful commemoration of that
Glorious Martyr, King Charles
the first of blessed
Memory.

The urn is placed beneath, on a pedestal of black marble. As we know, it contains his heart, and the owner, Sir Nicholas, is humbly described as: "a loyall sharer in the sufferings of His Late and Present Majesty".

Soon after the present church was built his body was lovingly removed from the family vault in the City and brought back to Hammersmith. The villagers felt this was right and proper. He now lies in a Victorian tomb, and his headstone leans on the outside wall of St Paul's Church, only divided by the black railings and the many streams of traffic from the old manor house, once used by the soldiers of Oliver Cromwell, which today is the bus station.

At the time when he died, Hammersmith was a pretty and patriotic little village. The great main roads to Bath and Bristol, Exeter and Plymouth, passed through it, and many inns were established to cater for travellers. They clattered in their coaches and carriages along the village High Street (now King Street) through which passed the Great Western Road. In Hammersmith Broadway, where The George stands today, an inn has existed for over 400 years. It was once called The White Horse and is mentioned in the will of its owner, Nathaniel Dauncer, in 1656. In 1691 a notice in the *London Gazette* offered a reward for a mare stolen from the stables of The George Inn—by which name it has been known ever since. Unfortunately the remains of the old building were pulled down in 1911.

In the time of Sir Nicholas the village cottages were gathered round the chapel, and families from the City built large houses by the river. Today the path by the river from Hammersmith Bridge to Chiswick is still considered London's most delightful walk. On the east side of the Bridge, in the place of the house once occupied by Sir Nicholas,

we now have the Distillers Company, a factory. On the west side we
have a number of eighteenth-century houses, unchanged and
beautiful, looking down as peacefully as possible on their flowery
gardens and their well-painted boats.

These riverside houses were as desirable then as they are today. We
must not forget that Hammersmith was a favourite fishing village,
and the fisheries were leased to Sir Abraham Dawes, Sir Nicholas,
and others, for the price of "three salmons". Apparently salmon
fishing began on 1st January and ended on 4th September. The
salmon caught in Hammersmith were highly esteemed and sold from
five to twelve shillings a pound.

Then as now Hammersmith was a centre for Roman Catholics.
Near the Broadway we now have the Convent of the Sacred Heart.
A nunnery has been here, we are told, since the Reformation.

That is why the villagers became so interested in Queen Catherine
of Braganza, a staunch Roman Catholic, who later visited the
convent, and bought a house by the river. She arrived from Portugal
one year after the death of Sir Nicholas, who would have wanted to
meet her. In the month of May, 1667, she was seen for the first time
in Portsmouth, unprepared, unsophisticated, innocent as a child, and
immediately fell in love with the glamorous Charles, so soon to be
her husband. As a strict Catholic she was not satisfied by the Church
of England marriage service alone. A second service was performed
in her Portsmouth bedroom. Charles explained that a Catholic
ceremony, if performed in public, would anger his people.

But in Hammersmith, even though Charles was greatly loved,
sympathy was felt for the Catholic queen in a Protestant country.
Everyone wondered how this young girl would feel about Lady
Castlemaine, the king's mistress. Without a doubt poor Catherine
had a bad time. At first Charles was much amused by the "Guarda
Infantas", in other words the huge and hideous farthingales which
protected Catherine's Portuguese ladies from *l'amour*, making it as
difficult to transport them in large numbers as to molest them or
marry them.

Charles and Catherine travelled slowly in a great state coach, the
farthingales having been shipped ahead, and arrived at Hampton
Court on his birthday, 29th May. There were banquets in the park
and water parties in the great gilded barges and other entertainments
such as cock-fights and bull- and bear-baiting. In the evenings there
were plays and dances. The king danced better than anyone at
Court. In fact the only fly in the ointment was Lady Castlemaine.

Charles was persuaded to explain his mistress to his wife, and Catherine, to his astonishment, threatened to leave him if the lovely Castlemaine joined the Court as Lady of the Bedchamber.

When they moved to Whitehall Palace the queen was advised by Lord Clarendon to give in to her husband "lest she should too late repent". At Court she was now quite lonely and neglected, as Clarendon says: "untaken notice of". Lady Castlemaine, supported by Charles, was frequently surrounded by laughing courtiers while the queen in her own palace, was found unamusing, unwanted. To make matters worse, Charles now spent his evenings with Castlemaine, taking supper at her lodgings.

Catherine was to live in England for almost thirty years. During that long and lonely time she was to endure the presence of one mistress after another. As a well taught Roman Catholic she drew strength from her religion but for this reason she was hated and despised by the Protestant people of England. Only in Hammersmith, a village overlooked by a Roman Catholic convent, frequently visited by Catherine, was the queen loved and understood.

About 1679 she bought a building in Hammersmith, situated near Cupola House (a Portuguese Embassy building) to which she retired when life at Court became too exhausting. She spent much time in Hammersmith. She joined with a community of nuns, at one time in Germany, inviting them to make Hammersmith their home, and they became known in the village as "The English Ladies".

Catherine's nuns lived in her house near Hammersmith Broadway for more than 100 years. Today, in the same place, we have the Convent of the Sacred Heart (a flourishing Catholic school) and the tombstones of some of her "English Ladies" are still to be seen in the convent grounds.

Until the end of her life she loved Charles, and when the king died, leaving no less than fifteen natural children, Catherine became a heart-broken and childless widow. It was then that she settled in her rented riverside house in her favourite village of Hammersmith, using it as her summer palace from 1686 till 1692. It was known then as Rivercourt. Today you can only see Rivercourt Road which connects King Street to the river. The famous elms at the bottom of Catherine's garden were planted in memory of Charles. They have now disappeared. Even now they are sometimes discussed in the local pub, and were called "the Braganzas".

She was often visited by her husband's brother, King James II, and in 1687 the Parish Books record that six shillings were paid to the bell ringers "when the king dined at Hammersmith" and the same "when the king returned to London".

Fortunately for Catherine she returned to Portugal, where she reigned as queen until her death, but before she left an amusing advertisement appeared in a newspaper of 1702.

Stolen out of Queen Dowager's gardens at Hammersmith the 21st instant, at night, 69 striped Hollies of divers colours, between one and two feet high; 6 striped Box of one foot and a half in height; and several Filaira striped, about three feet high. Whoever discovers the persons that stole the same giving notice thereof to Mr R. Frost at the Porter's Lodge at Somerset House shall have 30 shillings reward.

Catherine's house has disappeared but we still have some old buildings nearby which were occupied, some say, by her household. At any rate, she has not been forgotten.

It seems that Hammersmith had a weakness for queens in distress. Later in this story comes the lonely Queen Caroline of Brunswick, a bad queen if ever there was one. After Catherine's death there were no great changes in the village, or along the Hammersmith Mall, where Catherine once lived.

The Dove, for example, was and still is a much loved public house, in use by Hammersmith people since 1790. We are told it was lived in by the poet James Thompson, and in one of the little rooms upstairs some of us believe he wrote *The Seasons*, about 1726.

On the west side of Rivercourt House, approaching Chiswick, we have Linden House, now used by the London Corinthian Sailing Club (date 1733) and Hammersmith Terrace—sixteen houses, fronting the river, which were first mentioned in 1755.

Today the charm of all this is the countrified atmosphere, so unexpected, here in the heart of London, a gathering of ancient houses, protected from noise and ugliness by riverside gardens and boats and memories of the past. This is old Hammersmith. It reminds us that 200 years ago this was part of a proud little village, used by kings and queens, but concerned mainly with market gardens and small farms and fishing—producing, as they still remind us, the best strawberries and raspberries and salmon.

The original village lay between the river and the market gardens which stretched from Brook Green, on the north side of Hammersmith Road, to the site now covered by the Olympia building. The most famous nursery was that of Lee and Kennedy, called the

Vineyard Nursery. It was founded by Lewis Kennedy and James Lee about 1745. Before they took over the ground it had been a vineyard which, Faulkner tells us, "produced annually a considerable quantity of Burgundy wine". This wonderful garden became world famous in the eighteenth century because Lee was a distinguished botanist. He was the first nursery man to grow seeds from Australia. The plant which made Lee's name was the fuchsia.

The partnership became a family business which continued for several generations. Lewis Kennedy died in 1783 but John, his son, became equally famous. He was advisor to the Empress Josephine (wife of Napoleon) and helped her to plan and stock her garden at Malmaison.

Enormous sums were spent on plants from the Hammersmith garden. Josephine purchased plants from Lee and Kennedy for £2,600 in the year 1803, and £700 in 1811. It is said that the Marquis of Blandford was at one time in debt to the firm for £10,000.

Sir Walter Scott visited the Nursery on 3rd May 1828 and noted in his journal: "I drove to Lee and Kennedy's and commissioned seeds and flowers for about £10, including some specimens of the Corsica and other pines. Their collection is very splendid, but wants, I think, the neatness that I would have expected in the first nursery garden in or near London. The essentials were admirably cared for."

Today we have a mystery house on the north side of Hammersmith Road (No. 188). It is a Georgian building which was probably a small farm house with nursery gardens, perhaps twenty acres, running between Hammersmith Road and Brook Green. A pretty house, spoilt by some ugly Victorian embellishments, it is now used by the Constitutional Club and the Phyllis Haylor School of Ballroom Dancing. Unfortunately there seem to be no records, but this nice old house must have been connected with one of the numerous Hammersmith nurseries. A gentleman called William Wells is said to have come to Hammersmith to help two aunts run their farm and market garden and he is known to have been in Brook Green by 1828. Possibly the Georgian house—the only one left in this busy street—belonged to his two garden-loving aunts. Who knows?

Meanwhile the famous Brandenburgh House, the beautiful home of Sir Nicholas Crispe, had come into the possession of Lord Melcombe. Dr Johnson was a frequent visitor and greatly enjoyed Lord Melcombe's hospitality. The villagers of Hammersmith were delighted when Brandenburgh House became the residence of Queen

Caroline in 1820. Strangely enough they loved the rampageous Queen Caroline. Sir Nicholas, without a doubt, would have turned her out in the street.

By this time almost everyone in London knew the queen's extraordinary story. From the modern point of view she seems to have been a lovable schizophrenic.

The Prince of Wales had decided to marry her, without seeing her, because he had debts of £375,000 and King George III, his disapproving father, refused to appeal to Parliament for financial help unless 'Prinny' agreed to marry. For this reason the wedding was arranged for April 1795. The honeymoon, accompanied by Lady Jersey (at that time 'Prinny's' mistress) was a catastrophe. After two or three weeks they occupied separate apartments in the Brighton Pavilion. A daughter was born, nine months (almost to the day) from the date of the wedding. In April 1796 'Prinny' asked for a separation and Caroline was removed, like a piece of unwanted furniture, to a house in Blackheath where she lived unhappily for some years.

All this was very sad. Sympathy was felt for Caroline. It was no wonder that scandals and rumours about lovers and illegitimate babies blew about Blackheath like leaves in the wind. An adopted son called William Austin (who remained with her till the end of her life) was said to be her own child.

When 'Prinny' became Regent he forbade Caroline to see her daughter on moral grounds. Caroline protested. In 1814 she went abroad, taking with her a handsome allowance of £50,000 a year, and proceeded to live it up, as we say now, in Italy. She found in Milan exactly the type of lover she required. This was Bergami, her servant, a handsome Italian, who bathed Caroline, dressed her, made love to her on every possible occasion, as well as driving her horses and taking charge of her money—which he spent on all his family.

Caroline and her servant-lover, Bergami, continued to frolic round Europe until January 1820, when George III died and 'Prinny' became king—making Caroline the Queen of England. That was why she arrived in Hammersmith, on 6th June 1820, to claim her rights.

As we know, she was received with open arms by the villagers. She lived in Brandenburgh House, in the beautiful rooms overlooking the river which Sir Nicholas Crispe had loved. It now boasted a State Bedchamber with a beautifully carved and gilded State Bed, a Grand Dining Room with imperial carpet, the royal arms emblazoned in the centre, and portraits round the walls of the Brunswick family, including one by Lawrence of Caroline with her daughter. Best of all, there were balconies on which Caroline appeared many times to smile and wave and bow and kiss her hands to the cheering public, the villagers and visitors who came almost daily to Brandenburgh House. Caroline was seen as a martyr. Even the commonest people could now meet the queen of England and this they greatly enjoyed.

Lady Brownlow described the astonishing scenes at Hammersmith:

Thither to do her honour went processions of various of the Radical City Companies, and of people from the lowest classes, who were all received by Her Majesty in due form. I shall scarcely be believed when I tell of the way in which these processions were formed, and the sort of persons who composed them. Half-guinea tickets were given to those who wished to attend, presenting which at some place named, they were provided with dresses for the occasion, and I can state from my own knowledge that two next-door neighbours in South Street, Park Lane, one of them rejoicing in the aristocratic name of Manners, but keeping an open coalshed, and the other selling potatoes in an equally dignified stall, appeared in splendid dresses, Mrs Manners in a crimson satin gown with white shoes and gloves, and her friend in a white satin suit. Thus arrayed, they were picked up by a hackney coach and went on their way, their red elbows protruding out of the carriage windows.

Never before, or since, in London, have there been such delirious scenes of hysterical love for a queen of England whose crime was that she made love with her servant. Day after day the details of Caroline's sex life were revealed. Lady Brownlow gives us a vivid description of Caroline's appearance at this time: "She had exchanged her long fair hair for a black wig with a mass of long curls hanging on each side of her face, her eyebrows were painted black, her cheeks were plastered with rouge, and the expression of her countenance was most disagreeably bold and stern."

A Bill to dissolve her marriage on the grounds of adultery with Bergami (whom she had tactfully left in Italy) was brought into the House of Lords one month after the queen's arrival in Hammersmith. Her trial began on 17th August 1820, and continued for three months. Caroline's escapades in Italy were truthfully and brutally disclosed. Through it all, in Hammersmith, there were processions and demonstrations and great crowds of loyal citizens who followed the queen's carriage, shouting and cheering, and appeared daily at Brandenburgh House, by road or by river, to present an address, or a petition, or a gift, or a signed declaration of loyalty.

For example, the Watermen and Lightermen of the River Thames came to see Caroline in decorated barges. These, a floating procession of flags and banners and placards, were anchored or moored beneath Brandenburgh House. The queen appeared on her balcony to receive their address, smiling and blowing kisses, to the sound of loud and patriotic music played proudly by brass bands, and even the firing of cannon. Caroline, the people's queen, was a woman they loved.

The seamen marched to Brandenburgh House, each man with a white cockade in his hat. The brass founders marched, their men in armour, some on horseback, carrying a handsome brass crown and a flag with the words: "The queen's Guard are men of metal."

The trial of the guilty queen was at last abandoned because the bewildered ministers felt (after passing the third reading of the Bill in the House of Lords) their majority was too small to be acceptable by the people. Caroline had won her war against the king. She was allowed to keep her title. Hammersmith went mad with delight.

So now there were more processions and more deputations, not to speak of bonfires and fireworks and illuminations. The Lord Mayor himself came to Hammersmith, attended by all the City Officers in their dress robes. They were accompanied by twenty-five carriages and Caroline, of course, was as pleased as the villagers.

By the following year the people's queen was no longer so popular. Opinion was beginning to change. As the day of the Coronation approached sympathy was felt for the king—expressed for students of history in the delightful lines:

> Gracious Queen, we thee implore:
> Go away, and sin no more.
> Or, if the effort be too great,
> Go away at any rate.

The Privy Council decided the queen had no right to be crowned with her husband at Westminster Abbey. Caroline, being Caroline, determined to go as a spectator if nothing else. She was refused a ticket. When the great day came the queen was turned away from the Abbey. There were cries of: "Go home, you common disturber! Go back to Bergami!"

Weary, angry, terrified, she drove back to Brandenburgh House, the unwanted people's queen, the "Bedlam Bitch of a queen" as Walter Scott described her, adding: "I really believe she is mad."

That same evening Caroline wrote to the king asking for the favour of another coronation for herself as queen of England to take place "next Monday". To her annoyance this idea was not welcomed. Very soon afterwards, in Brandenburgh House, separated from Bergami, her servant lover (still waiting hopefully in Italy) in a mood of depression, as though mortified by the king's rejection, as though broken hearted, poor unwanted Caroline quietly and unexpectedly died, leaving all her possessions to William Austin, her adopted son. Her death took everyone by surprise. It was the most dignified thing she had done for quite a long time.

The sudden loss of Caroline brought a change of heart in the village, and everywhere in London. For a short time her popularity returned, and a great crowd assembled on the day of the funeral at Brandenburgh House. There was fighting and bloodshed. Richard Honey and George Francis, both of Hammersmith, were killed. Today their tomb can be seen by that of Sir Nicholas Crispe, outside St Paul's Church, and on it you can read an indignant description of what happened.

It is difficult not to feel sorry for Caroline. At least the people's queen has never been forgotten in Hammersmith. A patriotic memorial, or a statue, was not permitted, but we have to this day a reminder of her, close to the church, beneath the fly-over. It is only a road sign, announcing to motorists and nervous pedestrians that this is Queen Caroline Street. It leads, although few people know this, to the riverside factory building which was once Brandenburgh House, the home of Sir Nicholas Crispe, the death place of poor Caroline.

In Queen Caroline Street, still standing, unchanged by thundering traffic overhead and all around, is a fine old Georgian house which Caroline must have passed many times in her open carriage drawn by six horses. It is protected by a walled garden and a beautiful tall tree, an ash. It stands in silence, very calm and serene, at the edge of noise and chaos, bringing to mind a dignified dowager watching a pop festival.

It is called Temple Lodge, and not many Londoners know of its existence. You find it by accident, when exploring Hammersmith, for it belongs nowadays to the Christian Community and is used as a centre for religious and philosophical study as well as a place of worship by the Rudolph Steiner group.

In this lovely old house lived Brangwyn, famous artist, trained for a short time by the great William Morris during the Victorian period. Brangwyn's enormous studio is still there. When he died he left us some magnificent murals and a few amusing stories about William

Morris, his violent temper, his beautiful wife, his methods of work.

Victorian Hammersmith was still a cosy little village. After the turbulent times of the Stuarts, the wars with Oliver Cromwell, followed by the wild behaviour of 'Prinny' and Caroline, it must have been pleasant to settle down to bourgeois respectability under Queen Victoria. (Caroline and 'Prinny' had managed to discredit the delights of sex.)

At the time when Brangwyn was working for William Morris, and walking by the river, and stopping at The Dove for a drink, or a meal, as we do today, Hammersmith was countrified and friendly. In those days the Lower Mall and the Upper Mall were divided by a muddy creek, only to be crossed by an old wooden bridge. It was called Little Wapping. The watermen and fishermen were tough characters, some of them still remembered today by the old men who call at The Dove for beer and a chat. Stories are still told about Ducker Silvester who partly made a living by picking up corpses in the river. On the Surrey bank a corpse delivered safely was worth two shillings and sixpence, on the Middlesex bank only two shillings —and so Ducker always carried his corpses to Surrey.

It is easy to imagine the village life when William Morris was working by the river at Kelmscott House, still there today. The Suspension Bridge designed by W. Tierney Clerk in 1827 (the first of its kind) was replaced by the present one, an elaborate and feminine bridge, dressed with paint, decorated like a woman, as homely and pleasant in its own way as Queen Victoria, whose personality must have inspired it.

The whole village was becoming smarter, more wealthy. And William Morris, who hated capitalism, and introduced a new form of socialism to Hammersmith, stamped up and down the river path, his red beard bristling, his hair on end, his loud voice shouting with laughter, or bellowing with rage. His wife once complained that she would soon have no house linen left. "Whenever William is angry, or upset," she said, "he takes the sheets between his teeth and worries them into rags."

No wonder she preferred the romantic Rossetti, living in Chelsea. Morris and Rossetti, bohemians and socialists, belonged to a group of free-thinking people who startled the Victorians as the permissive society shocks some of us today. Jane Morris was adored by both men. She inspired their work. To the cosy Victorians, living in tight family circles, still reacting violently to the sexual extravagances of 'Prinny' and Caroline, the Pre-Raphaelite world of Morris and Rossetti was incomprehensible. How could Morris, the husband, endure the presence of Rossetti, the lover?

There was in all this romantic manoeuvring and questing a touch of the unsophisticated which annoyed and flabbergasted the Victorians. They were bored with bad behaviour. Wife sharing, if done openly, was as dangerous and disagreeable as socialism. William Morris might be a genius but he was, they considered, a silly fool.

It was easier for the villagers to understand that other Hammersmith character, a magnificent Victorian called Dr Furnivall. Today, if you walk by the river along the Hammersmith Mall, not far from the bridge, you will certainly notice the Furnivall Club, a small house which is still used as a sculling club. Upstairs there is a splendid photograph of an old gentleman with a flowing white beard. This, of course, is Dr Furnivall. Among other things, he started the Chaucer Society, the Shakespeare Society and the Browning Society. He lectured with Ruskin and Rossetti at the well known Working Man's College. He founded the Hammersmith Sculling Club for girls and men in 1896 and for this he is loved to this day.

In the club they enjoy talking about Dr Furnivall. He was, they say, the man who first taught women to scull. In the old days girls were forced to tie their skirts to their ankles but Dr Furnivall put an end to this nonsense. When the girls started wearing bloomers and stockings the village was horrified. Each young lady walked from the club house to the water and tried to hide her bloomers beneath a long dark coat. In the end, apparently, some college girls with advanced ideas decided to wear shorts, and were reported to the police!

Dr Furnivall was aged eighty-five when he died, and until the end of his life, every Sunday, wet or fine, winter or summer, he is said to have sculled from Hammersmith to Richmond, and back. He was known to everyone, even in the distance, by his long white beard.

The river-loving people who tell these stories about him are more like villagers than town folk even today. Only a stone's throw from the club by the river, started by the great Dr Furnivall, we now have the well known Hammersmith Palais, a meeting place for dance champions, and half a mile distant is the famous Queen's Club, an international centre for tennis stars.

They might both be a million miles from the club by the river which is the true Hammersmith. They make no difference at all to the village way of life which is still, in its own way, unspoilt. By the river, undisturbed, there lives a world within a world.

HAMMERSMITH LOCAL HISTORY
Recommended Books

History and Antiquities of the Parish of Hammersmith, Thomas Faulkner (1839)

Hammersmith, Fulham and Putney, G. E. Mitton & J. G. Geikie, Ed. Sir Walter Besant (Adam & Charles Black, 1903)

Hammersmith, Warwick Draper (James Chamberlain, 1913)

History of Hammersmith, Ed. Philip P. Whitting (Hammersmith Local History Group, 1965)

3

Chiswick

On a cold but exciting day in October 1602 Queen Elizabeth paid a visit to Chiswick. The villagers had seen her gilded barge many times as she travelled by river from the City of London to Richmond. Like her father she loved the river villages. On this never-to-be-forgotten day she was received by the most important family, that of Sir William Russell of Thornhaugh, ancestor of the Dukes of Bedford, who lived in the original Corney House, close to the river, at that time more interesting than Chiswick House, for of course the Russells were much the best family in Chiswick.

A pretty village, gathered round the parish church, with a pleasant riverside walk, it was more aristocratic than Hammersmith. It still is. The subtle separation between the style of the two villages can be felt even today when crossing from Hammersmith Mall and walking westward along Chiswick Mall. Somehow the atmosphere changes.

In the days of the first Queen Elizabeth the village was dominated by the Russell family. The queen's host, Sir William Russell, had the honour to be a friend of the famous Sir Philip Sidney, who bequeathed him his finest gilt armour. Sir Philip, a noble and romantic young man, was loved by the villagers and frequently seen by them, in doublet and tall beaver hat, as he rode down the lane to call upon his mother, Lady Mary, who stayed for many years in Strand-on-the-Green, living in retreat after smallpox.

The Sidneys and the Russells, and on this day the villagers, were determined to please and flatter their elderly and magnificent queen. We can imagine the scene of arrival. Smiling and scolding, a well painted face with pencilled eyebrows above beautiful silks and velvets of green and gold, she must have been helped by her courtiers into a painted cart-coach, probably drawn by four horses. No doubt all the villagers were cheering and waving, crowding to see her, some of them hanging from cottage windows, as the equipage rumbled along Chiswick Lane. Perhaps some of them ran after the carriage and trotted beside the horses, unwilling to be parted from her. This was a spirited old lady, much loved, and once she had said: "I thanke God I am enbued with such qualities that if I were turned out of the Realme in my paticote, I were able to live in any place in Christome."

In Elizabethan Chiswick the church stood where it stands today. Between the church and the river there used to be the Parish House and some small Tudor cottages. In Chiswick Mall, on the east corner of Chiswick Lane, stood the oldest building of all. It was known as the Prebendal Manor House.

This was because, for many generations, the Prebendaries of St Paul's Cathedral had held the Chiswick Manor, owning what was called affectionately "the little mansion house", and visiting their vicars as fathers of the parish.

Still more interesting, we know that one of our greatest poets, John Donne (who joined the Church unwillingly, to please King James I) became Dean of St Paul's Cathedral. As Prebend of Chiswick he must have visited the village many times, and may have brought Isaak Walton to walk with him by the river.

Later the old Manor House was taken by Dr Busby for the use of scholars from the grammar school of St Peter's in Westminster. It then became known as College House. The famous Dr Busby, still remembered with awe by the schoolboys at Westminster, was the ferocious headmaster who refused to walk bare-headed in the presence of his Sovereign in case his pupils should think him a less significant person!

In the village of Chiswick, as in Chelsea and Hammersmith, there were several river-side mansions which were occupied, or visited, by aristocrats and rich merchant families who enjoyed the beauty of the river scene. The most important, as we know, was Corney House, at the river end of Corney Road, a building which has now disappeared. Chiswick House, less impressive, was then a rambling old Tudor building, half hidden by trees.

The comings and goings at these two aristocratic houses were watched by the villagers with interest. After the death of Queen Elizabeth, the famous Russell family continued at Corney House but there were changes and scandals at Chiswick House.

About 1624, at the end of the reign of King James I, the scandals were beginning. A wicked gentleman called Robert Carr, Earl of Somerset, and his not very innocent wife, retired for private reasons from London society and settled in Chiswick House, having given their solemn promise to the king and his friends "not to go near the Court". Much gossip about the wicked earl came to the village. Apparently he and his wife were guilty of killing Sir Thomas Overbury in the Tower of London with poisoned tarts.

However this may be, the earl and countess were not well received by their neighbours. They decided to live quietly and respectably in Chiswick House, hiding their guilty heads behind their huge and well planted trees, but they did not foresee that their daughter, the beautiful Anne, would fall violently in love with their nearest and most desirable neighbour. This was young William Russell, son of the Earl of Bedford, over at Corney House by the river—the most eligible young man in Chiswick's best family.

According to Thomas Faulkner, this lovely girl, only seventeen, was sought in marriage by young Lord Russell, whose father did not approve because the girl's family were not rich enough to please him. The poor girl suffered so much from her marriage being broken off that her father made the great sacrifice of selling Chiswick House.

Here is a fascinating letter from a certain Mr Garrard to the Lord Deputy Lieutenant Wentworth, dated 23rd March 1636, which explains what happened.

The marriage betwixt the Lord Russell and Lady Anne Carr, a most fine lady, will now shortly, at Easter, be solemnized. My Lord of Bedford loved money a little too much, which, together with my Lord of Somerset's unexpected poverty, have been the cause of this long treaty, not by any diminution of the young partys' affections.

My Lord of Somerset told the Lord Chamberlain, who hath been a great mediator in his business, before his daughter, that one of them was to be undone if that marriage went on; he chose rather to undo himself than to make her unhappy, and has kept his word. For he has sold all he can make money of, even his house which he lives in at Chiswick, with all his plate, jewels, and household stuff, to raise a portion of £12,000, which my Lord of Bedford is now content to accept.

We are told that the marriage proved most happy. Perhaps the objections of the Earl of Bedford to Lady Anne's family had less to do with poverty than poisoned tarts!

The village of Chiswick was not much troubled by the Civil War, and the Russells were still the most important family at the time of the Restoration of Charles II in 1660. By then Edward Russell had parted with Corney House but we believe he built and lived for a

Cheyne Walk, 1850, by W. Parrott. This is how Chelsea appeared to Thomas Carlyle and Dante Gabriel Rossetti, whose homes are close by

Chelsea Royal Hospital, showing the Rotunda in Ranelagh Gardens, where Mozart, aged 8, gave a concert in 1764

Queen Caroline, the permissive heroine of Hammersmith, appears at the window of Brandenburgh House, 1820

(left) Queen Catherine of Braganza, wife of Charles II, loved and pitied in Catholic Hammersmith
(right) Queen Caroline, "the Bedlam Bitch of a Queen" as Walter Scott described her

time in the red brick mansion on Chiswick Mall, close to the Vicarage, which stands there now, and is known in its two parts as Bedford House and Eynham House.

A new arrival, Sir Stephen Fox, was no doubt a friend of the Russell family. Sir Stephen was the king's good friend (knighted by Charles in 1665) and had helped him more than any man alive with the financing and organizing of Chelsea's Royal Hospital.

As Paymaster General to the forces Sir Stephen had now become extremely rich and successful. He had contributed no less than £13,000 to the Chelsea Hospital. He now built himself a comfortable home close to Chiswick House (on the site of the present great conservatory) and another in Chiswick Lane, living in the village for thirty years.

He was said to be worth £200,000. As Evelyn, the diaryist, tells us, it was "honestly got and unenvied, which is next to a miracle".

One wonders how this dignified gentleman felt and behaved, and how the Russell family reacted, when the wicked Lady Castlemaine also decided to end her mis-spent life in the village of Chiswick. No longer the king's mistress, she decided to live at Walpole House, on the Chiswick Mall, a beautiful house which is still there. Did the neighbours receive her in their homes? Did they bow when walking by the river on a fine Sunday morning? Or did they pass her by with averted eyes?

Sir Stephen Fox was an elderly man by the time Lady Castlemaine arrived in the village. He had known her in the days when she had caused the poor young queen so much jealousy and suffering. By the villagers she was recognized as another aristocrat. Her father, William Villiers, second Viscount Grandison, was the son of the great Duke of Buckingham's half brother, Sir Edward Villiers. Most people knew her history. Before she was seventeen a passionate love and mutual attachment had united her in a wild and much talked-of love affair with the young Earl of Chesterfield. She discarded Chesterfield when she fell in love with Charles (although she seems to have loved them both) and quite soon Charles rewarded her husband, Roger Palmer (the second son of Sir James Palmer of Dorney Court, Bucks) with the title of Earl of Castlemaine and Baron Limerick.

There was no one in London quite like Lady Castlemaine, let alone in the village of Chiswick. Pepys tells us that she was known to have lost as much as £25,000 in a single night at the bassett table. Today we would describe her as a compulsive gambler. She was painted many times by Sir Peter Lely. Indeed he painted many ladies of fashion, giving most of them the languorous eyes of Lady Castlemaine, and quite often the same face. (He prepared nearly all his canvases with the shoulders and bosoms of beautiful ladies and is said to have added the heads, a shade too quickly, when required by customers.)

Samuel Pepys adored Lady Castlemaine. He visited the painter, Sir Peter Lely, in the Piazza, Covent Garden, in October 1662, and described it like this:

> He came forth to us, but believing that I come to bespeak a picture, he prevented us by telling us that he should not be at leasure these three weeks—and then to see in what pomp his table was laid for himself to go to dinner; and here among other pictures, saw the so much desired by me picture of my Lady Castlemaine, which is the most blessed picture and that that I must have a copy of.

On another occasion the sensual and susceptible Mr Pepys visited a famous engraver and went home in high spirits with "three of my Lady Castlemayne's heads".

Her availability does not seem to have altered the devotion of her lovers. Among her many admirers were the young Jermyn, nephew of the Earl of St Albans, and John Churchill, the future Duke of Marlborough. At one time she seems to have loved Charles deeply, but infidelities took place on a grand scale because she felt jealous, in particular of Louise de Keroualle, the king's French mistress.

In his own unfaithful way Charles loved her until the end. She received a lavish pension, and in 1670 the titles of Baroness Nonesuch, Countess of Southampton and Duchess of Cleveland were conferred upon her.

The relationship is best explained in a letter from Lady Castlemaine to Charles who objected to her scandalous behaviour while living in Paris.

"All I have to say for myself is that you know, as to love, one is no mistress of oneself, and that you ought not to be offended at me since all things of this nature is at an end with you and I, so that I could do you no prejudice." She reminded Charles of a conversation when he had unwisely said: "Madame, all that I ask of you for your own sake is, live so for the future as to make the least noise you can, and I care not who you love."

She had taken Charles at his word and had loved as many as possible as quickly as possible. Finally, when her husband died, she had married a celebrated rake known as Beau Fielding, who was married already to some other lady. When she discovered her mistake she had thankfully and hurriedly left him.

Such was the woman who settled in aristocratic Chiswick, in Walpole House, overlooking the river, to try to forget (or perhaps to remember) the extravagance of her fertile and fruitful past. She had given birth to many illegitimate children. Even when protected by Charles she had been considered an adventuress, possibly the wickedest woman in London society. In her way she was as bad as the Earl of Somerset who had once lived in Chiswick House. So what did the local people think of Lady Castlemaine, as a middle-aged lady, still beautiful, when she decided to live in Chiswick Mall?

Sir Stephen Fox, her elderly neighbour, had an eye for pretty women. In 1696 his wife had died. By now he was happily married for the second time to Mrs Margaret Hope, the companion of his daughter-in-law, and at nearly eighty years of age had managed to produce four more children. (One of them was Henry, the future Lord Holland.)

No doubt Sir Stephen would have enjoyed a visit to Lady Castlemaine at Walpole House but was he allowed to go there by his virtuous young wife? The male members of the Russell family must have had a similar problem with their wives and daughters and sisters and aunts. It seems possible that Lady Castlemaine, however well born, was left severely alone by most of her neighbours.

We only know that her last years were spent in Walpole House where she died in October 1709 at the age of sixty-nine, almost seventy. She died of dropsy. Her funeral in the parish church was attended, we are told, by two dukes and four peers, acting as pall bearers. In spite of her rank, there is no monument to record the life or death of this fabulous lady. In the village everyone knew she had bedevilled Catherine of Braganza and bewitched Charles II. The story of her life was common gossip. Was she considered too evil a person to be remembered in the church where her funeral was held?

There is said to be a ghost at Walpole House and to this day the spirit of Lady Castlemaine, wringing her hands, is said to haunt a room upstairs, presumably her bedroom. Why does she wring her hands? In the village it used to be said that the cause of her suffering was her loss of beauty. If so, Lady Castlemaine had no business to be wringing her hands, for the portrait by Kneller, in the National Gallery, shows her as she must have looked when living in Chiswick —still buxom and beautiful. Lady Castlemaine might almost be described as the Marilyn Monroe of her time, the sex symbol of the seventeenth century.

Seven years after her death a very different person appeared in the village of Chiswick, less aristocratic but equally famous. Today his name is better known than hers.

Alexander Pope, a little frail cripple of a man, aged twenty-eight, was already well on his way to success in London society as the head of the literary world. He came with his mother and father, living with them in Chiswick Lane, the corner house which is now a public house called the Fox and Hounds. The Pope family lived in this well built red brick house for two years before moving to Twickenham. They liked the dignity and comfort of Dr Mattias Mawson's New Buildings, known today as Mawson's Row.

By this time Chiswick House had returned to its proper place of importance and respectability. Alexander Pope was slightly older than the youthful Earl of Burlington, who owned it, a young man of wit and charm whose passion for architecture was admired by all in the village. Pope and Burlington became friends. The architect earl (the third Earl of Burlington) had not yet built the Palladian villa which even today is regarded with astonishment by tourists and students who come to Chiswick House from every part of the world. He was dreaming about it. He was making plans, discussing them with Pope, living with his parents in the old building where he was visited by his new friend. The two young men clearly admired one another. Pope's essay, "On Taste", was dedicated to Burlington. Here is a description of Pope by one who knew him at Chiswick.

"The pathetic figure . . . warmed by a fur doublet under his coarse linen shirt, and enclosed in a 'straight waistcoat' of canvas to hide his curvature, with three pairs of stockings to thicken his spindels, would be seen fondly escorting his mother along the river opposite Chiswick Eyot."

This little deformed genius had a venomous tongue and a vitriolic pen with which he distributed wisdom and wit and malice and hatred with equal dexterity. For example, he fell in love with Lady Mary Wortley Montagu, living in the smart village of Marylebone. When she mocked him, and others laughed, his love turned to hatred.

Pope's famous work on Homer earned him £9,000. He wrote the well known *Essay on Man*, and was able to put into simple and pleasing words a work of profound philosophy, involving a reasonable and readable view of all humanity. He had a lighter side and could write a pretty rhyme (with a typical sting in the tail!) for the collar of the dog he gave to Frederick, Prince of Wales.

> I am his Highness's dog at Kew,
> Pray tell me, Sir, whose dog are you?

In the same light mood, writing to please Burlington, he produced the following lines about the Inigo Jones Gateway, still to be seen at Chiswick House. It was a gift to Burlington from Sir Hans Sloane, in Chelsea, who kindly removed it from Beaufort House where Inigo Jones had placed it. So Pope wrote:

> Oh gate, how com'st thou here?
> I was brought from Chelsea last year,
> Battered with wind and weather:
> Inigo Jones put me together,
> Sir Hans Sloane
> Let me alone,
> Burlington brought me hither.

Pope is unforgettable. Most of us remember, without even being aware that Pope wrote them, such lines as: "A little learning is a dangerous thing." "To err is human, to forgive divine." "What oft was thought but ne'er so well expressed." "For fools rush in where angels fear to tread."

Most of us know the famous couplet from *Essay on Man*:

> Know then thyself, presume not God to scan,
> The proper study of mankind is man.

When Pope met him, Burlington had recently returned from his first trip to Italy and was burning with his new interest in Italian architecture. He had designed a garden building in the grounds of Chiswick House. He had employed Colin Campbell to improve his London home—Burlington House in Piccadilly. He had read Leoni's translation of the *Four Books of Architecture* by the sixteenth-century Italian architect, Palladio. It had been published in 1715. As Pope came to Chiswick in 1716 we can imagine the conversations between the two learned young men.

Burlington thought the feeling for Roman culture already being created in English literature by Pope and other writers might be brought to life more vividly still by a Palladian villa in an English garden. This was Burlington's dream. The two young men must have discussed his exciting idea. Why not carry it out? They must have reminded one another that a hundred years ago the Court architect of Charles I, Inigo Jones, had studied Palladio and had modelled his work on the Italian master's *Four Books of Architecture*. (As a result we now have three magnificent buildings, the Banqueting House in Whitehall, the Queen's House at Greenwich, and the Queen's Chapel at St James's Palace.) Why not, said the two young men, create another masterpiece?

So that was how Chiswick House came into existence, the wild and wonderful building which stands there today. Pope left Chiswick after two years, and went to live in the neighbouring village of Twickenham in 1718. The friendship continued. Pope knew all about Burlington's Roman villa, not so much a home but a show place, a cabinet for beautiful possessions, an art centre, a meeting place for cultured people among beautiful pictures and priceless Italian furniture. Work started in 1725. The building was completed in 1729, and the date was carved on the chimney pieces of the Red Velvet Room. It was a kind of temple, and the villagers thought it unsuitable in a country village. Burlington still lived in the old Jacobean house of his parents but the new villa was filled with his collection of books, pictures, clocks, mirrors, all his cherished works of art. Here he received his friends. The villa was intended for conversation and culture.

Today we would describe Burlington as 'trendy'. At the age of twenty he became Lord Lieutenant of the East and West Riding of Yorkshire and Lord Treasurer of Ireland. At this age he was one of our first noblemen to complete their education by a Grand Tour, a journey through France and Northern Italy to Rome.

On his second visit to Rome, at the age of twenty-four, he discovered an art student, William Kent, who returned with him to England, became his great friend, was given apartments in his lordship's house in Piccadilly, stayed there for the rest of his life, and was buried, finally, in the Burlington vault in the Chiswick churchyard. It was a long friendship, and Kent was as 'trendy' as Burlington.

The close partnership between Burlington and Kent is part of the history of English architecture, and yet, of course, they had their critics.

It was the famous Lord Hervey (friend of Lady Mary Wortley Montagu), who sarcastically remarked that Burlington's new house in Chiswick "was too little to live in, and too big to hang to a watch chain".

Another critic was the celebrated William Hogarth, who appears to have found something decadent about their style and extravagance, either in life, or architecture, or both.

Hogarth, the son of a schoolmaster, spent thirty years in the village of Chiswick. Some of his most brilliant cartoons and satirical portraits of social behaviour and moral misbehaviour were created (and can now be seen) in his little and unpretentious home, so close to Chiswick House, so different in every way.

Burlington's home probably inspired some of his pictures. Later his masterpiece entitled "Marriage à la Mode" (dated April 1745) gives a wickedly satirical picture of 'high life', including the countess's bedroom, the earl's apartment, with its lavish coronets and old masters, the grand saloon with its marble pillars and grotesque ornaments. Much of this satire might well derive from his knowledge of Chiswick House and his objection to William Kent.

Hogarth was two years younger than Burlington but he outlived him by nine years. He was buried in Chiswick churchyard (1764) and later a tomb was erected for him by his admirers. Burlington died in 1753, outliving William Kent by five years.

There is something about Chiswick which attracts intellectuals. At the centre of the new circle was Dr William Rose, from Aberdeen. An eminent scholar, who kept a school in Chiswick for nearly thirty years, he lived, like Pope, in Chiswick Lane. Dr Rose was a close friend of the celebrated Dr Johnson, whose large figure was often to be seen shambling along Chiswick Mall on his way to have a talk with his Scottish companion. They had many literary arguments. Thomas Faulkner describes a typical discussion like this:

"On Dr R's stoutly maintaining the literary fame of his countrymen, and Johnson knocking down, with very little ceremony, Hume, Adam Smith Ferguson, Blair, and Robertson, as they were successively brought forward, a pause ensued, when Johnson, looking around with an air of triumph, exclaimed: 'Well, sir, any more of your northern lights?'."

Jean Jacques Rousseau, a French intellectual, arrived in January 1766. He took lodgings in Chiswick, perhaps to be near Dr Rose—although Dr Johnson despised him, and made no secret of it. He considered Rousseau a decadent and quite understood the outcry against him in France after the publication of his *Emile* and *Le Contrat Social*.

Nevertheless his exciting belief in the superiority of "the noble savage" to civilized man, became more and more fashionable. Ladies and gentlemen in polite society were delighted with "the noble savage". It is all described in the witty diaries of Fanny Burney, whose first novel, *Evelina*, was published in the same year, taking London by storm.

We know that Dr Johnson was immediately captured by Fanny's charm, and it seems probable that she was invited to Chiswick to meet Dr Rose. Probably she joined in their numerous debates. Dr Rose had a daughter, Sarah, who married Fanny's brother, and as they assisted him in his Chiswick school for several years, Fanny became one of the circle.

The village of Chiswick was now becoming quite a social centre. In Chiswick Mall, in place of the old Manor House, stood the comfortable home of Robert Berry and his two daughters, Agnes and Mary. They became known in London society as the "twin wives" of Horace Walpole. There was plenty of gossip for the ladies and gentlemen who went to church on Sunday mornings, and walked along Chiswick Mall, peacefully watching the flight of gulls and the movement of swans. At Chiswick House, for example, surrounded by her celebrated admirers, was the famous Georgiana, Duchess of Devonshire—the woman who knew and understood the Prince of Wales, the most fascinating hostess alive.

The villagers loved Georgiana. This memorable lady has been described as the "reigning queen" of late eighteenth-century society. Charles Fox, her dear friend, died in Chiswick House. When she died herself, the central figure in a love affair between three remarkable people, the Prince of Wales sadly remarked: "Then the best natured and best bred woman in England is gone."

In the year 1788 (the year when Fanny's novel was published) the Duke of Devonshire decided to use Chiswick House as a kind of rest house for his wife, Georgiana. It was close to London, and aristocratic, a delightful retreat. For this reason he employed James Wyatt to demolish the old Jacobean mansion and enlarge the villa.

To please Georgiana and give her a comfortable home he added wings to north and south. These were designed to match the main features of the Italian building. The villa itself was kept as before—a little museum for beautiful possessions, a small summer palace for Georgiana, who loved it.

The villagers were accustomed to the comings and goings of nobility but Georgiana, and the duke, and the Prince of Wales, gave a new excitement to the life of the village.

Georgiana was the great grand-daughter of Sarah, Duchess of Marlborough. At the age of seventeen she had married William, the fifth Duke of Devonshire, who was then twenty-seven. Here is a Victorian description of the duke:

Weight he wanted not, for a heavier man never led to the altar a wife full of generous impulses and of sensibility. He was wholly incapable of strong emotion, and could only be roused by whist or faro from a sort of moral lethargy. He was, nevertheless, crammed with a learning that caused him to be a sort of oracle at Brookes's when disputes arose about passages from Roman poets or historians.

We are told that the large and lethargic duke was somehow roused by Miss Charlotte Spencer, daughter of a country curate, who inherited a small sum of money and opened a milliner's shop where the duke met her. As a result of this meeting a daughter was born to whom the name of Charlotte Williams was given.

Georgiana treated both the duke and his illegitimate child with understanding. The duke, she discovered, was not so cold as he appeared. She enjoyed the friendship of 'Prinny' and Mrs Fitzherbert and Charles Fox. She became notorious, and was criticized by some for the enormous feathers she insisted on wearing in her beautiful chestnut coloured hair. She wrote a novel about herself called *The Sylph*, which was published in 1779.

All this provided gossip in the village of Chiswick. It was known that Georgiana, like Charles Fox and 'Prinny', was an inveterate gambler. Charles Fox, the brilliant Whig statesman, could not pay the chair-men who carried him to the House of Commons. He was seen to borrow money from the waiters at his club (Brooke's) which was then the rallying point of the Opposition. Members spent the night in whist, faro, suppers, and political consultations.

Very soon Georgiana's name was coupled in a slanderous way with the dashing Mr Fox. She became known as "Fox's Duchess".

In the spring of 1782 Lady Elizabeth Foster made her first appearance upon the London scene of love and politics. It was known that she had just left her husband. Georgiana took pity on her. When the duke and duchess went to Bath, in the month of May, they were joined by Lady Elizabeth, who made a deep and lasting impression on Georgiana's lethargic duke.

The rest of this Chiswick House love story is quite astonishing. Tongues in the village continued to wag, year after year, for the curious trio were inseparable from the moment of their first introduction until the moment of death. Georgiana seemed to love Elizabeth, and they both seemed to love the duke.

In the autumn of 1782 Georgiana asked her new friend to winter abroad with little Charlotte, the duke's illegitimate child. Georgiana and the duke supplied her with money. In the summer of 1784 she decided to return to England in order to live with them, *à trois*.

It was known that Georgiana welcomed Lady Elizabeth with open arms. She was sinking more deeply into debt, involved with Charles Fox, criticized for helping the Prince of Wales in his love affair with Mrs Fitzherbert. In the small Roman Temple in the garden, which is still there today, Georgiana used to sit with 'Prinny' and Mrs Fitzherbert, entertaining her friends, drinking a cool glass of wine, sometimes having a family picnic with Lady Elizabeth, and the duke, and their children.

In the village they may have blamed 'Prinny' for what was happening, but certainly not Georgiana. The trouble started on 8th July 1784 when the love-sick Prince of Wales actually stabbed himself and Mrs Fitzherbert was called upon by the royal surgeon to visit him at once at Carlton House. Georgiana was persuaded to leave her supper and go with Mrs Fitzherbert to 'Prinny's' room, where they found him pale and blood-stained. 'Prinny' said that death was preferable to life without Mrs Fitzherbert. In a moment of high emotion a ring was borrowed from Georgiana and placed by 'Prinny' on Mrs Fitzherbert's finger, after which he seems to have felt much better.

This was by no means the end of the matter for Mrs Fitzherbert left England on the following day and 'Prinny', unable to leave without the king's permission, galloped from London to Brighton, and from Brighton back to London. He then visited Charles Fox and, it was said, "cried by the hour, rolling on the floor, striking his forehead, tearing his hair, falling into hysterics, and swearing that he would abandon the country, forego the Crown, sell his jewels and plate, and scrape together a competence to fly with the object of his affections to America".

All this happened at the time when 'Prinny' was visiting Chiswick House. He was under twenty-five. In the end, after many months of turbulent and well testified suffering, 'Prinny' wrote a letter of forty-two pages, a proposal of marriage, and Mrs Fitzherbert finally surrendered. Without the king's consent marriage was impossible, as everyone knew. In any case he would forfeit the Crown because Mrs Fitzherbert was a Catholic. Never mind, 'Prinny' was in love.

Come then, [he wrote] oh come, dearest of Wives, best and most sacred of women, come and for ever crown with bliss him who will through Life endeavour to convince you by his love and attention of his wishes to be the best of Husbands, and who will ever remain unto the latest moments of his existence *unalterably Thine.*

Georgiana could not be present at the ceremony which was not, she said, a true marriage. In spite of this, 'Prinny' was privately married on 15th December 1785, and Georgiana remained his friend.

Lady Elizabeth Foster was by this time well known in the village, and there must have been a great deal of gossip and speculation. The popular duchess was having a delightful time between Chiswick and Devonshire House, in Piccadilly, dashing up and down to receive her guests, supported on either side by the brilliant Charles Fox and the fascinating prince. Did she, or did she not, encourage her husband to make love to her friend?

A Victorian writer sees it like this: "Lady Elizabeth Foster, the daughter of the Earl of Bristol, and a contrast to her in person— large, dark, and handsome—had attracted the duke her husband, and the coldest of men had become deeply enamoured of this woman, whom he eventually married."

At the end of 1784 Lady Elizabeth went abroad (which must have made the suspicious villagers smile) in order to have a baby, and was separated from her two dearest friends until July 1786. She left in France a little daughter by the duke who was given the name of Caroline St Jules and was later allowed to join the schoolroom at Devonshire House. The little girl was supposed to be the daughter of a French friend, but most people knew the truth. Lady Elizabeth expressed her affection for Georgiana in a typical letter from Naples.

"It is a year today that I left you—even you can scarce conceive how much unhappiness to me is comprised in that reflection—but I would not pass such another to acquire millions."

Georgiana, equally affectionate, wrote to Lady Elizabeth in July 1786.

"There is no expressing my Dst life, the agitation I feel now I draw near to the time of your coming to Paris. Will you be angry at our not coming? Oh Bess . . . je ne vie pas sans toi."

The threesome at Devonshire House and Chiswick House was now established for better or for worse, and Georgiana's mother greatly disapproved. Everyone in society knew what was meant by Mr Gibbon when he referred to "the good Duchess of Devonshire and the wicked Lady Elizabeth Foster". The light-hearted way in which the languid duke had children by both ladies was now a favourite subject for discussion, especially in the village, where he and the ladies were seen to be so contented and friendly.

In February 1788 Lady Elizabeth again went abroad to have a baby—this time a boy. By July she was back in Devonshire House, as happy as ever. In July 1789 they all went to Paris for a month before going to Spa, where Georgiana fondly hoped to conceive a son and heir. This she managed to do. She seems to have talked things over with Lady Elizabeth, and the birth of a son was considered the moment for a grand confession to the duke of her gambling debts. They now amounted to more than £60,000.

About two years later the duke came reluctantly to the conclusion that Georgiana was with child by Charles Grey, the future Prime Minister, who was then only twenty-seven years old. It was now Georgiana's turn to be sent abroad to have a baby. She was accompanied by her sister and her mother, and was followed soon afterwards by the devoted Lady Elizabeth, who took charge of the birth.

Of course Georgiana returned to England, and was forgiven by the duke, and the threesome was resumed in September 1793 as though nothing had happened.

After this they all lived peacefully together, looking after their children, both legitimate and illegitimate, until 1805, when Georgiana was taken ill with gall-stones and terrible headaches caused by pain in her eye. The end of the story was sad. In February 1806 she was well enough to give a final brilliant assembly and supper. On 30th March, in her forty-ninth year, she died in her sister's arms.

A few months later Charles Fox died. Lady Elizabeth, taking Georgiana's place, was one of those by his bedside at Chiswick House.

Lady Elizabeth, as we know, had much experience in taking Georgiana's place. Three years later, still living in the duke's homes at Chiswick and London, Lady Elizabeth wrote to the Prince of Wales to announce their marriage on 19th October 1809. The prince replied in a letter of five pages expressing his "extreme pleasure".

So ended the three-cornered love story which had entertained the village of Chiswick for such a long time. The duke died two years later but his widow never married again. She went abroad, first to Paris and then to Rome, where she lived "in almost regal splendour" until her death in 1824.

Today, all summer long, we have the pleasant sight of children running about in the beautiful gardens created for Georgiana, playing in the sunlight, hiding behind the statues and bushes. Older people sit beneath the trees. Respectful tourists take photographs of her summer palace.

In some ways the gardens are as interesting as the villa. Somehow Georgiana is everywhere. When the strange story is known of our beautiful duchess it is difficult to admire the little Classic bridge across her canal without thinking of her. The bridge was created by James Wyatt especially to please Georgiana. You can imagine her lovely figure, almost hear her laughter, as she posed on her Classic bridge, throwing kisses, perhaps, to Charles Fox, or the duke, or Lady Elizabeth.

In Georgiana's day they tried to create a garden which was full of surprises and irregularities and a hint of wildness. A garden, they said, must have "prospects to excite not only the eye but the imagination".

By this they meant a Roman temple, or a Doric column, or an obelisk, or a classic bridge.

How easy it is to imagine Georgiana and Lady Elizabeth, followed by their large lethargic duke, as they walked along an avenue of urns and sphinxes placed by their gardener on the west side of the villa. This avenue leads to a group of niches, or hollows, cut in the greenery, which they chose to call an "exedra". It contains three statues, said to represent Caesar, Pompey, and Cicero, and to have come from Hadrian's Villa at Tivoli.

Georgiana belongs to Chiswick House as the statues belong to Georgiana's garden. Georgiana is the essence of the eighteenth century in England. Here in Chiswick, in this remarkable house and garden, saved for tourists, and children, and students of architecture, her presence can be felt.

In Victorian times Chiswick House was used as a place for royal receptions by the various Dukes of Devonshire who entertained the Tsars of Russia and Queen Victoria. Changes were coming. Sad to say, in 1892, the eighth duke removed the art treasures to Chatsworth and actually permitted Chiswick House to be used as a private lunatic asylum. Georgiana must have turned in her grave!

Fortunately the Middlesex County Council came to the rescue and bought the property (with a contribution from King George V, who spent holidays there when a boy), to be used as a public park.

After the Second World War there were further changes.

Georgiana's apartments were demolished. In a way this was quite a good thing for it made possible the restoration of the villa to the proportions of the original design by Lord Burlington.

Georgiana would be surprised by the scenes today in her beautiful gardens. Yet the village of Chiswick, preserved like a jewel between the river and the motorway, is not so changed as might be expected. We still have the village post office and general shop (well worth a visit) and a cluster of ancient houses between the shop and the church. We still have Chiswick Mall, unspoilt and beautiful. Finally we have the house boats.

Many artists and authors have lived and worked in the village of Chiswick, also actors and architects. Whistler is buried in the churchyard beside his wife. So is Hogarth. The ancient houses are filled with memories and the skyline is as beautiful as ever. Walpole House, where the wicked Lady Castlemaine lived, is owned at the time of writing by an architect. Once it was used as a Preparatory School for Young Gentlemen—the most famous of these being William Makepiece Thackeray, who described it in *Vanity Fair*, changing it into a school for girls.

Chiswick is still an aristocratic little village with a style of its own. Today it is probably London's most perfect village for river-loving people, young and old, from every walk of life. It is a dream village still, as it was in Georgiana's day, a village for escapists and lovers.

CHISWICK LOCAL HISTORY
Recommended Books

The History and Antiquities of Brentford, Ealing, & Chiswick, Thomas Faulkner (1845)

Queens of Society, Grace & Philip Wharton (J. W. Jarvis & Son, 1890)

Chiswick, Warwick Draper (Philip Allan & Co, 1923)

Georgiana, Duchess of Devonshire, extracts from the Correspondence, Ed. Earl of Bessborough (John Murray, 1955)

4

Battersea

A little unexpected church, of unusual beauty, standing like a pretty woman on the edge of an architectural rubbish heap, this is St Mary of Battersea—perhaps the most beautiful small church in London.

Since the time of William the Conqueror a church has been standing in exactly this place, gracefully poised on the river bank, at the heart of the village of Battersea.

The Lord of the Manor used to live close by, about a hundred yards to the east of the church. His great house was visited by kings and queens and his open velvety lawns sloped gently down to the water so that visitors could step with ease from a gilded barge into his garden. A muddy drive led from the manor house to the church and from the church to a well known public house which still exists. It is called The Raven. At one time it overlooked the village green, with a pump placed in the centre of the grass.

Today many things have altered. The little Church of St Mary is close to another public house called The Old Swan, and both have a superb view of the boats and birds on the Thames, but there is no trace left of the manor house. In its place, unfortunately, we have factories, and all around the church we have blocks of flats and offices and sheds and blackened buildings. The village green is now a small blackened centre for little shops and dilapidated dwellings with boarded windows. There is, however, a pleasant feeling of vitality. What are these workmen doing? Are they restoring the old houses instead of tearing them down?

It seems that an effort is really being made to revitalize the old village of Battersea. The man behind it is a wealthy stockbroker, Richard Harris, who came here many years ago from Australia. His dream, he says, is to make this village the Montmartre of London.

We still have the Dower House, a quarter of a mile from the church, a gift long ago from the Lord of the Manor to his ageing wife. The style is Christopher Wren. It is called Old Battersea House

(1699), and was recently leased from the London Borough of
Wandsworth by a wealthy American publisher, Malcolm Forbes,
who has spent, we are told, £150,000 on the work of restoration. The
little blackened houses in the village shopping centre are also to be
restored.

Battersea has always been a family village. The cottages were
gathered round the manor house and the villagers were devoted to
the St John family, happily dependant on the Lord of the Manor,
his wife, and his children, who cared for them and shared in their
troubles as they shared in his. In this way Battersea was different
from other London villages. The villagers continued to be lovingly
ruled by the St John family for many generations. Even today the
name of the family is greatly respected.

The first Lord of the Manor was Oliver St John. The advowson
passed to him at the end of Elizabeth's reign and he finally bought
the manor from King Charles I in 1627. Three years later the manor
passed to his nephew, Sir John St John. The second Lord of the
Manor was proud of the family connection with the Tudor kings and
decided to beautify the church with a family east window which can
be seen today. Sir John made certain that no one in the Parish of
Battersea could easily forget his royal pedigree for the east window
was painted with the faces of King Henry VII, Lady Margaret
Beaufort (Henry's mother), and Queen Elizabeth.

The villagers understood the pedigree much better than we do.
They knew that the mother of Henry VII was the daughter of a
beautiful St John widow (who was married for the second time to
John Beaufort, first Duke of Somerset, in 1437). They understood the
link with Elizabeth. Apparently Sir John St John was married in 1611
to Ann Leighton, descended from Sir Thomas Boleyn, father to
Anne Boleyn—Elizabeth's grandfather.

So when they looked up at the east window on Sunday mornings,
admiring the three familiar faces, the villagers were reminded that
one St John wife was the great grandmother of Queen Elizabeth and
another was related to Elizabeth's mother.

The original Saxon church was dated about 800. William the
Conqueror made a present of the Manor and church to the Abbey
of Westminster. At the dissolution of the monastries in 1540 by
Henry VIII the Manor of Battersea reverted to the Crown, and then,
as we know, became the property of the St John family in the reign
of King Charles I.

During the Civil War between Charles and Oliver Cromwell the

(left) Lady Castlemaine, Duchess of Cleveland, spoilt mistress of
Charles II, ended her life in Walpole House, Chiswick
(right) Lord Burlington, aided by William Kent, was the man who
created the sensational Chiswick House which startled his friends
in 1729

Chiswick House, a Palladian villa in an English garden, a fabulous
piece of architecture, still admired by students and tourists

Battersea Church looking towards Chelsea. This little church has a touching story

(left) Alexander Pope used to visit Battersea and turned into verse a brilliant work by his friend, Lord Bolingbroke, now known as his *Essay on Man*
(right) Lord Bolingbroke, exiled in France as a Jacobite, fell in love with the beautiful Marie Claire, Marquise de Villette, who became his mistress and wife

villagers were divided in loyalty because the St John family was divided. Sir John, the elder son, was a Cavalier, and Oliver, the younger son, was a Roundhead. At the death of Sir John, the Cavalier (in 1646), he was succeeded by his son, a most remarkable man who is loved in Battersea to this day. His name was Sir Walter St John.

The good Sir Walter managed to unite his divided family by his marriage to Johanna, his cousin, who was the daughter of the Roundhead, Oliver. The villagers were as pleased as his family. Sir Walter and his young wife, after burying old Sir John in Battersea Church, settled down together, as Lord and Lady of the Manor, and lived for many years an exemplary life as lovers and benefactors of Battersea village. We are told they were treated with a mixture of respect and affection by the villagers who took a deep interest in all their family affairs.

This was a happy period for the village. Johanna was a strict Puritan and her favourite subject of conversation, apart from her husband, was her garden. Johanna created the beautiful flower beds and terraces, the lawns of emerald green sloping down to the River Thames, admired from passing barges and even, on a clear day, from the village of Chelsea. The manor house was a spacious building. It was shared by Sir Walter with his brother Henry and all their children and grandchildren. They lived a communal life, attending church, of course, every Sunday. On one side of their house was the stretch of fields and marshy lands (with a footpath to London) which is now Battersea Park. On the other side lay their pretty little village, with its cottages and village green.

We are told that the second King Charles and his brother, James, used to come, in a friendly way, to bathe at the landing stage by the church on summer evenings.

When Sir Walter reached the age of seventy-seven he decided to build a Dower House for Johanna, his saintly wife. According to Mrs Stirling, author of *The Merry Wives of Battersea* (published by Robert Hale in 1956) it was a Golden Wedding present. At that time, apparently he was employing Christopher Wren to renovate No. 10 Downing Street for his great-nephew, Lord Litchfield. He probably employed Wren, or Wren's assistant, to build the Dower House, now called Old Battersea House. At any rate, the style is that of Christopher Wren.

At that time it had six and a half acres of what was called 'pleasaunce' for Johanna to make a garden. It overlooked the river.

It had also a private ferry (between Chelsea and Battersea) and the fortunate St John family could land in their own garden when returning on a summer evening from a visit to friends. They had another precious possession, a bronze sundial (still existing) with the date of the house, 1699, and the legend *"Perunt et imputantar"*, meaning "The hours pass and are set down to our account".

It is easy to imagine the sorrow of the villagers when Johanna died on 15th January 1704. In her will occurs the following pathetic passage:

"I desire if Sir Walter outlive me his old servants may continue about him and that he be not removed to Liddard, London, or any other place from Battersea where he has lived so long, lest it hasten his death."

She further desired that the vicar should deliver her funeral oration in the house she had loved. "I would have," she wrote, "an exhortation to my children and my grandchildren to be said by Mr Gower in my own house before my being carried out of the house on that solemn occasion."

We are told she was carried to the church in a coach and six, and buried in the crypt, "Ye coffin quilt with silk", for which luxury her executors had to pay a fine of fifty shillings as it was against the law which decreed that everyone should be buried in wool in order to help the wool trade.

Sir Walter had a nephew, the Earl of Rochester, said to be the most shameless rake at the Court of Charles. The villagers felt sorry for Sir Walter because Rochester was the son of his devoted sister, Anne, and the family was given much trouble and distress. Sir Walter and his Puritan lady were not amused by Rochester's famous lampoon, which was hung, we are told, outside the king's bed-chamber.

> Here lies a great and mighty King
> Whose promise none relies on;
> Who never said a foolish thing
> Nor ever did a wise one.

If the villagers knew these lines they probably laughed, but not Sir Walter. He found it difficult to forgive his dissolute nephew. Incidentally, the wicked Lady Castlemaine, mistress of Charles II (who ended her life in the village of Chiswick) was grand-daughter of Sir Walter's aunt, Barbara St John. Poor Sir Walter! What a blow to his family pride!

The behaviour of his nephew was bad enough, but the villagers considered that his own son was more of a villain than Rochester. How could the good Sir Walter and his saintly Johanna manage to produce such an evil man?

In the village many stories were told about Henry, the black sheep of the family. At first he lived with his wife and his parents in the Manor House. A baby son was born. Unfortunately the child's mother died, and Henry, from that moment, turned against his family and refused to behave like a gentleman.

Swift described him as a "man of pleasure, who walks the Mall and frequents St James's House, and the Chocolate Houses".

On one of these occasions, in a drunken brawl, he managed to kill one of the fashionable young rakes he called his friends. It happened in the Mall, and his victim was Sir William Escourt. The headstrong Henry was forced to leave the country in order to escape being hanged. In the end, luckily, he obtained a pardon from Charles II, but only by paying the king the enormous sum of £16,000. While abroad he consoled himself by marrying a handsome French woman, Angelica Magdalina.

Meanwhile, at home in Battersea, feeling lonely and misunderstood, and pitied by the villagers, a little boy was left behind to live in the old Manor House with his grandfather and grandmother, who certainly did not spoil him. This was the future Lord Bolingbroke. In fact he was frequently scolded by Sir Walter and Lady Johanna, and complained later of the discipline they gave him, especially of a nonconformist tutor called Dr Manton, described by Bolingbroke as "a Puritanical parson, who taught my youth to yawn and prepared me to be a high Churchman that I might never hear him nor read him any more".

Every Sunday the unhappy little boy, watched by the villagers, was taken by his grandparents to say his prayers in Battersea church. The villagers must have noticed his naughty behaviour. Later he called himself a "Freethinker". He seemed to despise the forms and dogmas of religion stuffed into him by the Puritanical Lady Johanna and the gentle but inflexible Sir Walter. His mother was dead, his father in exile, his step-mother an unknown foreigner, his tutor a man he detested. Sir Walter decided to send him to the College of Eton.

The villagers were glad when he returned to the family. In the year 1700, at the age of twenty-two, he married a pretty girl called Frances Winchcombe, and proceeded to make this innocent young lady as unhappy as himself. Like his father, the black sheep of the family, he became notorious for his dissipation and extravagance. The villagers shook their heads.

They were all greatly surprised when this difficult young man, the future Lord Bolingbroke, at the age of twenty-three, entered Parliament and made himself known, in the reign of Queen Anne, as a famous statesman. Now the villagers were delighted. After all, he was a credit to the family!

The year he married Frances Winchcombe was 1700, and this was the year when Sir Walter made a remarkable decision. Sir Walter wished to endow a school for twenty scholars, poor boys from Battersea. He decided to create a trust, and he gave the boys a house and garden to be used in future as their schoolhouse.

At the time of writing there are 500 students in the Sir Walter St John School, which is now one of London's most interesting grammar schools. It was rebuilt in 1859, extended later, and still flourishes on the original site, chosen by Sir Walter, in the Battersea High Street. After nearly 300 years the students are still known in Battersea as 'Sinjins'.

In 1704, when so many important things were happening to them and their family, the villagers were shocked by the death of Lady Johanna. All her grandchildren came to the funeral. The future Lord Bolingbroke brought his wife. They gathered in the Battersea church, and the villagers, sitting in the back pews, dressed in black, many with tears on their faces, could see that Sir Walter was deeply distressed. Four years later, at the age of eighty-seven, he died also. Again the family gathered in the Battersea church, and again the rebellious grandson knelt in the family pew to say his prayers, this time for dear Sir Walter. The villagers in the back pews had lost their best friend.

In the years which followed there were many changes in the village and the scapegoat of the St John family became the Lord of the Manor. This was, as we know, Bolingbroke's father. In 1716 the scapegoat contrived to be created Viscount St John and Baron St John of Battersea. To the great pleasure and surprise of the villagers he managed to sit in Parliament for twenty-one years. He seems to have had a sense of humour. Having himself narrowly escaped hanging, he said cynically to his eldest son, now Lord Bolingbroke, "Ah, Harry, I always said you would be hanged, but now I find you will be beheaded!"

There was a family likeness between these two men and the

villagers wondered what would happen to the famous and fascinating Bolingbroke, known to be a Jacobite, and now exiled in France as his father had been before him. His wife died in 1718. She knew, poor woman, that Bolingbroke was living quite openly with Marie Claire, Marquise de Vilette, a niece of Madame de Maintenant, who was said to be the most enticing and beautiful lady in the Court of Louis XIV. Bolingbroke had once been Privy Councillor, and Secretary of State, and leader of the Conservative Party, but now, dismissed from office, he was quite in disgrace, no longer wanted—except by Marie Claire.

His wife knew, and of course the villagers knew, that Bolingbroke, who loved all the Stuart kings, had been plotting for the return of James, known as "the king over the water". Unfortunately James was a Roman Catholic. For this reason the British throne was eventually given to a German who could speak no English, King George I, and Bolingbroke fled to France. A Bill of Attainder was issued against him. The beautiful Marie Claire offered him a refuge in her home.

Most of us enjoy a good love story. How many people know the touching little tale of Bolingbroke and Marie Claire? Even in the village of Battersea it has now been forgotten. Marie Claire adored him, and he adored her, and the romance continued for more than thirty years. Marriage was not possible. Bolingbroke was a proscribed man, a 'wanted man' as we now say, and by law the Crown might seize her fortune if Marie Claire became his wife. Therefore she became his devoted mistress.

We find Bolingbroke writing from France without embarrassment to a young girl, his half sister, now living with his father in Battersea. His father, as we know, had a French wife, and the girl's name was Henrietta. In 1719 he is writing about his French mistress to his partly French half-sister: "She is a person who, although she does not yet know you, loves you very much because of all I have told her about you and the letters which have come from you."

Henrietta received pretty dresses and beautiful presents from Bolingbroke's mistress. No doubt she wore her Parisian clothes in the Battersea church on Sunday mornings and they were admired by the villagers. Later this unfortunate girl had a most unhappy marriage with Robert Knight, a friend of Bolingbroke's, to whom she was unfaithful. A letter was found from the faithless Henrietta to her lover, and she wrote as follows to her outraged husband:

I have read this over, [meaning the letter to her lover] which in my first surprise I did do and am now sure more than ever that I never wrote it as ye dictates of my own heart, and little thinking I should be thus accused. I was so imprudent as to translate and copy a large bundle of such foolish letters, thirteen of which I burnt last week to make room for things I was placing, and before God I swear that not one was other than copys or translations, I yet flatter myself I shall find the originals of this, which I would have kept had I known it could ever be of consequence. I again repeat, ye most I ever granted to ye Person I am suspected of was Compassion, which I have often accused myself of as a Crime, though I am now accused of worse.

Henrietta's husband was not at all impressed by this ingenious declaration of innocence. He knew she had been unfaithful, and therefore her children were taken from her.

The strange thing is that neither Bolingbroke, nor her father, whose morals had once been as lax as possible, had the slightest sympathy for poor Henrietta. There was one law for the male and another for the female. When the separation was finally settled, and Henrietta had given birth to a daughter (of whom we hear nothing more) Bolingbroke wrote to Henrietta's husband, who remained his friend: "I say nothing to you about the unhappy affair which has given us all so much concern. I endeavour to forget it, and hope you will do the same."

Henrietta was banished by her family, though not forgotten by her disappointed French mother and those in the village who remembered her pretty dresses from Paris. Bolingbroke's long exile in France finally ended. When his father died he was able to return to Battersea with Marie Claire, at last making her his legal wife, and to live with her in the manor house, the home of his childhood.

Today, in the Battersea church, we can see and study the portrait of Marie Claire in the form of a medallion which looks even now like a delicate cameo. We can see for ourselves that Marie Claire was a beautiful woman and the love of Bolingbroke is easy to understand.

What the villagers thought of her when she became the Lady of the Manor is another matter. No doubt they compared her with the saintly Lady Johanna—much to her disadvantage.

Marie Claire was without doubt a wonderful woman, of great charm, and had renounced her Roman Catholic faith to marry Bolingbroke, but she found the village of Battersea rather dull when she first arrived.

"Amusement is as necessary to her as food," he wrote, "nay, more than food," and the manor house was, he admitted, "an old and decayed habitation" which had been grievously neglected by his father.

"As fast as we build it up on one side," wrote Marie Claire indignantly, "it falls down on the other."

Nevertheless they were visited by numerous celebrities, including the poet, Alexander Pope, who frequently stayed in their house, although Marie Claire was less pleased with him than his friend Lord Burlington, over in the village of Chiswick. In fact she disliked the poet. Pope had recently turned into verse a brilliant work by Bolingbroke called *Essay on Man*. Lord Bathurst had said (according to Boswell) that he "did not know which to admire most, the elegance of Bolingbroke's prose or the beauty of Pope's poetry".

But Marie Claire did not trust the poet. "He would be a politician to cabbages and turnips," she said pointedly, and was not surprised by what happened later. Bolingbroke sat by his bedside when he lay dying, in 1744, and was moved to tears. At that moment he did not realize that Pope had taken possession of his own book, *The Patriot King*, and had tampered with the text, and had actually received money from the publisher for the whole edition of 1,500 copies.

When he discovered what Pope had done he was furious with his friend. On 2nd October 1744 he wrote indignantly to Lord Marchmont, to whom he had lent the Dower House, requesting him to buy the entire edition of Pope's version of *The Patriot King*.

"Be so good," he said with annoyance, "as to see it burnt at your house to keep it dry, which is the best use it can be put to."

In the village there was much interest in anything which happened at the Dower House, and everyone wished to see the great bonfire ordered by Bolingbroke. It burned one night in the garden of the Dower House—astonishing the villagers at Chelsea, across the river, and delighting the villagers of Battersea.

Bolingbroke, as we know, was a freethinker, but as Lord of the Manor he wished to create a good impression. For this reason he begged Lord Marchmont to procure a large prayer book to exhibit in church on Sundays. "Such a one," he said, "as the Lord of the Manor may hold forth to the edification of the parish. Let it be a quarto."

The villagers had known him since childhood, a naughty boy who disobeyed Sir Walter, and they must have smiled at the sight of his large new prayer book. He now lived a quiet life, more concerned with books than politics, for another German king, George II, was settled like a hen on the British throne and the "king across the water" was finally defeated in the Battle of Culloden in 1746.

The years which followed at Battersea were not easy for Bolingbroke and his Marie Claire, much as they loved one another. In March 1749 he wrote: "Battersea is much further from London than it ever was before. We have four feet of snow; the wind howls round the house, and no one ever comes near us."

Nine months later, in December, Marie Claire wrote to her great friend, Lady Denbigh, a little note which brings them both to life.

"My hermit and I go to bed before six o'clock," she wrote. "He gives himself up entirely to looking after me, in fact that is his only occupation. It is enough to give him the spleen but he shows no sign of it. I cannot tell you how touched I am by his love and care."

For thirty-five years, as mistress and wife, she had devoted herself to Bolingbroke. When she died on 18th March 1750, Bolingbroke was inconsolable. "My heart is broken, my spirit crushed and my body crippled," he wrote. "I am the most miserable of all men."

The villagers were unable to help him although by now they felt sorry for the poor old man who appeared in church on Sunday mornings with his large prayer book. On 12th December 1751 he died also, and was laid beside his dear Marie Claire in Battersea church. The memorial to Henry St John, Viscount Bolingbroke, and his second wife, Mary Clara des Champs de Marcilly, Marchioness of Villette, is there today, and is a beautiful monument by Roubilliac. The name "Mary Clara" is the Battersea translation of the French 'Marie Claire'.

The epitaphs were written by Bolingbroke himself. The one for the beautiful Marie Claire can still bring a lump to the throat when her story is known and his great love is remembered.

Today there are many living in the large area known as Battersea who still have no idea that the old village exists, or where it is. From Chelsea the best approach is across Battersea Bridge, then take the first right turning by the factories, a bleak road to the beautiful church.

Until the end of the eighteenth century Battersea was only a village, in other words a group of cottages round the church and the manor house—which lay between the church and the present bridge.

The greater part of the manor house was pulled down in 1778. For some reason a small portion was left standing and this included the famous Cedar Room, known as Pope's Parlour (used by Alexander Pope and Bolingbroke as their study) which presently became an office, and was used by the miller who owned it. Later a strange thing happened. In 1951 an enterprising American lady, Mrs Wharton Sinkler, of Philadelphia, decided to purchase Pope's Parlour. So then the last little bit of the manor house was shipped from Battersea to Philadelphia. It was re-created for this American lady with the help of photographs taken in 1911.

Fortunately for us, the Battersea church was rebuilt when the manor house was pulled down. Battersea was now becoming a fashionable suburb. The church was said to have the "second best carriage congregation in London". The Archbishop of York had a home in what is now York Road. City merchants came to live here and in 1766 Earl Spencer obtained permission to build a fine new bridge.

The decision was taken to rebuild the church in 1771. A village meeting was held at The Raven, always a gathering place for the villagers of Battersea. (It is still popular, a public house with Dutch gables, at the corner of Westbridge Road.) The local architect, Joseph Dixon, drew up some plans. The church as it now stands is almost entirely to Dixon's design and it follows the exact ground line of the old building.

The architect did a magnificent job and today the little eighteenth-century church is as charming inside as out. The original frame of the east window with its glass and tracery—the faces of Henry VII and his mother and Queen Elizabeth—are left to us unspoilt. So are the monuments from the famous St John family. And the Church Registers, which is very pleasing indeed, are almost complete from the year 1559.

It is interesting to find an entry dated 4th February 1631 which shows the first marriage of Edward Hyde, afterwards Earl of Clarendon. The baptism of Henry St John (Lord Bolingbroke) is dated 10th October 1678 and his burial 1751. There is the signature of Edmund Burke as a witness to a wedding on 4th October 1757. Still more interesting is the marriage of William Blake, poet and artist, to Catherine Boucher, daughter of a Battersea market gardener. The date is 18th August 1782.

At that time the village of Battersea was a centre for market gardening, like the village of Hammersmith. Battersea was famous for asparagus and lavender. That is why Lavender Hill was given its name.

When Catherine Boucher married the great William Blake she was a girl of twenty, from a typical working-class family, born in Battersea, unable to read or write. Her parents went to church like most villagers on Sundays, and could remember Lord Bolingbroke as an old man.

Even if the St John family was now disappearing, and ladies and gentlemen with strange faces arrived by carriage on Sunday mornings, Battersea was still a family village, and proud of the church. Catherine persuaded Blake to marry her in the building she had known all her life. Blake's signature is there in the Church Register for all to see. Catherine, who could not write, just made a cross.

It seems that Catherine was an ideal wife for William Blake. He later taught her to write and she learnt to draw and paint well enough to help him with his work. She was probably the only human being who understood him as a man if not as an artist and poet and mystic.

Blake now holds a position as one of the greatest figures in English poetry and art. He was the son of a hosier living at 28 Broad Street, Golden Square.

When he met Catherine he was only twenty-four. At the time he was suffering from a fit of jealousy, for which he despised himself, and said to Catherine, his listener, "Do you pity me?" She replied: "Yes, indeed I do," and Blake said: "Then I love you."

A year later they were married at Battersea church among the villagers, returning to Catherine's home, no doubt, for a meal. They then went to live at 23 Green Street, Leicester Fields. With Catherine's help, William Blake began to experiment with a new method of printing from etched copper-plates. For example, his beautiful *Songs of Innocence* was etched on copper with decorations coloured by hand. It was published in 1788 and was sold for a few shillings. This was the first of a series of 'illuminated printing' which occupied Blake for the rest of his life.

The artist William Turner was born in 1775, only two years before William Blake, and he too has left his mark on the Battersea church. He loved this little peaceful village of cottages and market gardens, surrounded by lavender fields and acres of green asparagus. Above all he loved the church, and he came here frequently to paint the river and the sunlit sky, especially at sunset. The chair in which he always sat by the window, in the vestry, is lovingly preserved to this day. It now stands in a special place by the east window—Turner's chair. The pictures he painted while sitting in his Battersea chair can be seen in the Tate Gallery.

Turner, like Blake, had a working-class background. His father was a barber who lived in a dark little shop, 26 Maiden Lane, near Covent Garden. His work was discovered by John Ruskin, the great Victorian critic, who made him a much more famous man. Today, in the Tate Gallery, we have about 300 pictures by Turner.

In character he was not at all like William Blake. He was unmarried and unloved, a not very lovable bachelor who happened to be a genius, a man who became rich and successful, but always a miser.

Turner lived for many years in the village of Marylebone, and the housekeeper, Mrs Danby, was his mistress. His four illegitimate children were not neglected, nor were his other mistresses abandoned. In his old age he was said by the gossips to spend his time from Saturday to Monday in low haunts, used by sailors, in Wapping or Rotherhithe. Probably not true.

Ruskin, his greatest admirer, wrote: "Respect and affection, if they came at all, came too late. Naturally irritable, though kind—naturally suspicious, though generous—the gold gradually became dim. . . ."

Obviously Turner had his faults, but he loved the River Thames, which he painted continuously from Battersea and Chelsea, and he gave us a huge collection of paintings of river and sea and sky, both beautiful and mystical.

When Turner was dying in Chelsea, nursed by Mrs Booth, he sent for a well-known doctor. When told that death was near he said: "Go downstairs, take a glass of sherry, and then look at me again." The doctor did so, and failed to make Turner believe that his end was so close. Finally Mrs Booth wheeled his chair to the window so that he might look for the last time at the River Thames, lit by the sun, between Chelsea and Battersea.

This was the man who painted the notorious picture called "Snowstorm". To do so, at the age of sixty-seven, he put to sea in a heavy snowstorm and made the sailors lash him down so that he could watch the great waves and feel fear during four hours between life and death. The critics (with the exception of Ruskin) laughed at Turner, and called his remarkable picture "soapsuds and whitewash". They failed to understand his later work, full of colour, strangely impressionistic. Indeed this brilliant old man, this early Victorian, might be called the first of the impressionists.

Turner died on 19th December 1851, and was buried in a vault beside that of Sir Joshua Reynolds in St Paul's Cathedral. How different from the unmarked grave, in Bunhill Fields, of William Blake!

It was Whistler, another impressionist painter, who gave us the famous picture of old Battersea Bridge—a wooden bridge, built in 1772, lighted by oil lamps and later by gas lamps. Its upkeep was provided by tolls. Pedestrians were charged a halfpenny, a chaise fourpence, a waggon with two horses sixpence, a coach and two horses eightpence, vehicles with more than two horses one shilling.

At the time when Turner died the beauty of Battersea village was beginning to be hidden, or forgotten, owing to the new need for factories and railways. Clapham Junction Station was built in 1845. The market gardens of Battersea were soon swallowed up by the railway, by the rows of artisan houses, the new working-class settlements. Many well-known industries which started during this period are still flourishing, ugly but successful, like Victorian aristocrats, and among them we still have Price's Candle Factory, and the Gas, Light & Coke Company.

It is pleasing to remember that Battersea Fields, now Battersea Park, used to be a marshy common fronting the river, and, needless to say, was frequented by highwaymen. It was here that a duel was fought between the Duke of Wellington and Lord Winchelsea. Apparently the cause of the bother was a disagreement about the Catholic Emancipation Bill!

In 1843 Thomas Cubitt suggested a park for the people of Battersea, protesting against the rowdy and indecent conduct of those who used Battersea Fields. The park was opened in 1858.

In the eyes of the Victorians, Battersea was still a fashionable suburb, even though spoilt by railways and factories. The Victorians knew that William Wilberforce had lived here for five years, at Battersea Rise, in Lubbock House, belonging to his friend Henry Thornton, where he stayed from 1792 until 1797, and was visited by many celebrities, including Fox, Pitt, and Gray, and the poet Southey. Later he moved to Broomfield, a house in Broomwood Road, in the parish of Battersea. His name can be seen in the Church Register as witness to a wedding.

It was Wilberforce who exposed the evils of the slave trade. John Wesley, during his last illness, wrote to him: "God be with you, may you succeed in your glorious work against this scandal of religion, of England, and of human nature. Unless God has raised you up for this work you will be worn out by the opposition of men and devils. Go on in the name of God is the prayer of your servant, John Wesley." It was the last letter he ever wrote.

Wilberforce did go on, obedient to John Wesley, and the Slave Trade was finally abolished as a result of his work while living in Battersea. Finally he moved to Cadogan Place, and was buried in Westminster Abbey (1833).

Today there are signs that the suburb of Battersea might some day become again the fashionable suburb so much loved by Wilberforce and his friends. As for the village of Battersea, it remains a family village. We still have the beautiful Battersea church which seems to have grown from the river like a reed. We still have Old Battersea House, also the vicarage, and Devonshire House, next door to the vicarage, and a strong trace of the village centre.

The villagers remember—and so does the author—the last of the great ladies of Battersea. She lived for thirty years, perhaps longer, in Old Battersea House, using the rooms which were used long ago by Sir Walter and Lady Johanna at the time of their Golden Wedding. She published many books, among others *The Merry Wives of Battersea*, full of good stories. She was known to everyone as "old Mrs Stirling".

At the time when she died the old lady was extremely frail and pathetic, within a few weeks of her hundredth birthday. She had been friendly with everyone, including Queen Mary, who came to her house quite often for afternoon tea. At home she was faithfully looked after by Mr Peters, an elderly villager, who loved her.

Here is a personal memory of old Mrs Stirling, written a few months before she died on 11th August 1965.

It is visiting day at Old Battersea House. The fabulous old lady of Battersea is arranged on the sofa like a vase of orchids, or a case of jewels, or a set of priceless ivories, or a Dresden china teaset, in her own way more unique and more inspiring, as though from another world, than all the treasures in her crowded house.

I love the glitter from her dangling earrings, the sparkle from her strings of pearls and crystals, her bracelets and rings.

It is very cold in this drawing room but the old lady does not feel it, wearing a long dress in flowered velvet, pretty black shoes, nylon stockings, and round her neck, just as my mother used to wear them, her nice shabby old furs. She is not only brightly rouged but brightly smiling, her back to the window, and behind this courageous little figure with tidy well-pinned grey hair, stretched on the sofa, half sitting, supported by gaily coloured cushions, I see the silvery gleam of the cold and disagreeable River Thames.

"Do come in. Won't you sit down?"

I can still hear the smooth voice of confidence and courtesy, see the outstretched hand glittering with rings.

"I have not been very well. Laryngitis, you know. I lost my voice. That was why Mr Peters took my place as your host."

We all shake hands with the old lady, rather nervously sit down, and now she proceeds with a bright smile to entertain us.

"Show them my scrap book, Mr Peters."

The old lady's scrap book is passed from hand to hand. It is filled with her jokes. Beneath press cuttings and photographs to do with modern art, Picasso, Epstein, sculpture, etc., the old lady has written light-hearted scornful comments, little wisecracks which make us laugh.

"Have they all seen my scrap book, Mr Peters?"

The old lady chuckles with delight. Mr Peters gives her a smile of adoration.

"Will you tell them your ghost story, Madam?"

The old lady, encouraged by Mr Peters, gives us the ghost story, then points to the pictures on the wall by Evelyn de Morgan, her sister, explaining to us their special brilliance of beauty, not quite so good in the evening light.

"It's the colour which gives me so much pleasure. Such a perfect blue . . . such a fine red . . . I wish you could all see these pictures on a beautiful morning. The light, you know. . . ."

When the old lady is feeling well she leads her visitors into each room, sometimes half carried by Mr Peters, and the tour of her house takes all of four hours. Today she is not feeling well so she stays on the sofa. At the age of ninety-nine you do feel tired.

Mr Peters tells me, in a whisper, she has just finished writing another book.

"Does she write or dictate, Mr Peters?"

"Oh, no, she types with two fingers. Then the secretary makes a clean copy."

"Does she enjoy life, Mr Peters?"

"Oh, yes, I think she does. You see, she's a lady with a strong sense of humour. But sometimes she says to me in a sad voice: 'Today I feel lonely. Please telephone for someone to come'."

I think the old lady of Battersea is the loneliest woman I have ever met. She reminds me of my Edwardian mother. I can still see that smiling, carefully rouged face and I can still hear that smooth voice, full of confidence and courtesy, saying to her almost dumbfounded guests:

"Thank you for coming. Do forgive me. I am so sorry I failed you today. Goodbye, goodbye."

"Goodbye, dear Mrs Stirling, goodbye."

That was Old Battersea House in 1965, and Mr Peters is remembered almost as vividly as old Mrs Stirling. About Queen Mary he used to say: "She was ever such a dignified lady. Mrs Stirling is one for antiques, see, her house is full of pots and plates and pictures. So Queen Mary used to call for a cup of tea in the hopes of receiving one of them pots or plates as a present, see? But there ain't no flies on old Mrs Stirling," he added with a smile. "Queen Mary used to say to Mrs Stirling: 'I do like that blue plate. Do you know, blue is my favourite colour?' And Mrs Stirling used to say, ever so politely: 'What a coincidence, Ma'am, it is my favourite colour, too!' "

According to Mr Peters, not even Queen Mary could induce Mrs Stirling to give her that blue plate. For Queen Mary, who collected so many antiques in this simple way, it must have been the first and only refusal!

Since then we have seen some changes, but old Mrs Stirling would be delighted and surprised at the way things are now happening in the village of Battersea. Not far from her home the Royal Academy Of Dancing has actually moved into what used to be a granary. On 6th November 1974 it was opened officially by Queen Elizabeth II. Old Mrs Stirling would have shared the excitement of the villagers on that wonderful day. The queen's visit to Battersea would have pleased the old lady almost as much as a visit from her friend, Queen Mary . . . or the gift of another blue plate by William de Morgan.

BATTERSEA LOCAL HISTORY
Recommended Books

Historic Battersea, Sheawood Ramsey (G. Rangecroft, 1913)
The Merry Wives of Battersea, A. M. W. Stirling (Robert Hale, 1956)
Historic Battersea, Booklet from West Hill Library
Our Lady of Battersea, J. G. Taylor (George White, 1925)

5

Putney and Fulham

There are two little churches which stand on either side of the River Thames at Putney Bridge. They seem to smile in the sunlight and scowl when it rains, two grey-headed sisters, one a bit bigger and more important, the other with a faintly rakish air. In sun or storm they face one another sturdily across the water. They have been doing so for more than 700 years. The smaller one is the parish church of Putney, known as St Mary the Virgin. Her sister is the parish church of Fulham, known as All Saints.

At the time of writing poor little St Mary the Virgin, after all these years, has recently suffered the indignity of being raped and assaulted by vandals. They broke into the church, found nothing worth stealing, and then, to amuse themselves, set the ancient building on fire. St Mary the Virgin looks sorry for herself. Her windows are broken and boarded, her roof is gaping open, so that her burnt black interior can be seen by all, her doors and gates are locked and chained so that no one can enter.

Fortunately the grey square tower looks just the same. Inside, untouched by fire, the beautiful chapel built by Bishop West in the reign of Henry VIII (about 1530) has escaped by a miracle.

By the time this appears in print no doubt the church will be partly restored. At present the diggers are at work and they have found some medieval foundations which will add to the importance of the building. In the end St Mary will recover from her dreadful experience.

The exact age of the two buildings is difficult to discover. We know that St Mary goes back to the thirteenth century because a public ordination was held here in the year 1302 by Archbishop Winchelsea. All Saints is believed to be older still. Both churches were restored by the Victorians. Today the parish church of Fulham has a very fine appearance, solid and prosperous, belonging as proudly to the ancient village of Fulham as the little and lovable St Mary belongs to Putney.

As we pass over Putney Bridge today, driving slowly, in a stream of traffic, it is pleasant to remember that both churches were in their places by the river, belonging to their separate villages, their grey heads divided by the water, when Henry VII and Henry VIII were building Fulham Palace for the bishops of London. It cannot be seen from Putney Bridge but this is a magnificent red brick Tudor building, sheltered by tall trees, surrounded at one time by a moat, which still stands at the back of the Fulham church.

The land on which the palace stands has belonged to the bishops of London since the seventh century. (It was given to them in the year 691 with the consent of Sigehard, King of the East Saxons and the King of the Mercians.) The only Gothic stones still visible are the gate posts at the entrance, rather close together from the motorist's point of view, which were left for us to admire when the medieval building was pulled down at the beginning of the sixteenth century.

Today there is still something sinister and faintly threatening about Fulham Palace. It is said to be haunted, and some of us are inclined to believe it. The Tudor courtyard is unchanged apart from the south side which was restored in 1858. At the time of writing the palace is standing empty, deserted by the bishops of London, a lonely and desolate place, with memories of evil in some of its ancient rooms. Inside the imposing front door we still have the original Great Hall which was used by Henry VIII and built by his father.

Henry quite frequently visited his bishops at Fulham Palace, and so did his daughter, Queen Elizabeth, from time to time. The great Cardinal Wolsey must have been here too. In the garden, strangely enough, their presence can be felt as strongly as in the palace.

This is because, on the south side, across a wide and well cut lawn, overlooked by the drawing-room windows, there is an ancient wall with a wonderful red brick Tudor gateway which was used, no doubt, by Henry, and most likely by Elizabeth. It must have been touched by their hands and clothing, because the opening is so small. The red arch of brick is enormously thick and solid, not unlike Henry himself, built as if intended to last forever, with a hale and hearty dignity of its own, and yet so low that the gardener remarked: "Them Tudors must have been dwarfs!"

The Palace of Fulham, like the Tower of London, was for many years a place to be feared and avoided by the men and women who dreaded religious persecution. Murders took place at the Tower but were planned very often at the palace. That is why Henry and Cardinal Wolsey and Thomas Cromwell were by turns loved, feared and hated in the two little villages of Fulham and Putney, so close to the palace.

Cardinal Wolsey, like most of Henry's friends, lost favour when he became less useful. When it happened he ceased to be the holder of the Great Seal of England and removed himself, like a dismissed servant, to his palace at Esher. On that day he went by water from Whitehall to Putney. (There was no bridge across the river, only a ferry for villagers and travellers.) He then started up Putney Hill, passing the church, an elderly man riding on a mule, his head bent, a proud man who was suffering greatly from indignation and humiliation.

Half way up the hill he was overtaken by one of the Royal Chamberlains, Sir John Norris, who presented him with a ring as a token of the king's regard.

We are told by Stowe how the great cardinal at once dismounted from his mule, refusing aid, and then knelt down in the dirt on both knees, holding up his hands for joy at the king's "most comfortable message".

It is said that Wolsey made servants attend him upon their knees, compelled the bishops to tie up his shoes, and dukes to hold the basin while he washed his hands. In egotism he was a match for Henry VIII. His morals were non-existent. He had many illegitimate children, and Henry, who grew up from boyhood under his influence, probably copied the cardinal in more ways than one.

This was the man who wrote, as Shakespeare reminds us, "*Ego et meus rex*". Probably no Latin scholar could put the words in any other order and yet it clearly reflected his mental attitude to Henry.

During the first half of his government he had greatly strengthened the Tudor monarchy both at home and abroad. He made the mistake of encouraging a marriage between Henry and Anne of Cleves, to whom, as we know, Henry took a quick and violent dislike. He was charged with treason and summoned to London. Fortunately for him, he died on the journey, and was buried at Leicester Abbey on 20th November 1530.

The cardinal was loved in quite a personal way by some of the villagers in Putney, especially by Nicholas West, who became the Bishop of Ely, and the wicked Thomas Cromwell, who became the Earl of Essex.

Nicholas West was born and bred in Putney. He was educated at Eton, and then King's College, Cambridge, where he got into serious trouble for stealing some silver spoons and setting fire to the provost's lodgings. For the last offence he was expelled from the university. This, it seems, brought him to his senses for he became a hard student, was re-admitted to King's College, and later became a splendid scholar and able statesman—a credit to Putney.

Nicholas West owed much to Cardinal Wolsey. With the cardinal's help he became Bishop of Kingston, Dean of Windsor, and chaplain to Henry's first wife, the charming Queen Catherine of Aragon. In 1515, the final honour, he was made Bishop of Ely, but Henry, having quarrelled with Catherine, turned against him over the question of divorce.

It is said that Nicholas West, the son of a Putney baker, kept no fewer than 100 servants during his time of favour. The change in his royal master is said to have caused his death, but at least he was not executed like so many others who offended Henry.

Today we have in Putney something beautiful to remind us of Nicholas West. Inside the little Church of St Mary the Virgin, where he worshipped as a boy, he created a chapel. Its great feature was, and is, the fan-vaulted ceiling—a feature seen to perfection in King's College Chapel, Cambridge. (The ribs are really carved on plaster or slabs of stone, and for this reason they are not structural, only ornamental.)

In the same little church we still have another treasure. It is a brass plate, fixed to the north wall, inscribed in Latin, with two figures in brass, the man in armour (armiger) and his lady. Translated into English the words are: "Here lies John Welbeck, armiger, and Agnes his wife, the which John died the twelfth day of March A.D. 1478, and the aforesaid Agnes died the eighth day of October, A.D. 1478, on whose souls may God have mercy."

This interesting brass plate must have been noticed many times by Nicholas West, and also by the hated Thomas Cromwell, for they both worshipped, perhaps at the same time, in the church by the river. Thomas Cromwell was born in Putney, and they must have been known to one another as boys, though never as friends.

It was said in the village that young Thomas had a bad start in life. His father was a brewer, smith, and fuller, and seems to have been trusted by nobody in Putney. Thomas, his only son, ran away from home. In 1512 he was working in London as a merchant, later a solicitor, and was admitted to Gray's Inn.

He married Elizabeth Wykes, daughter of a wealthy sheerman, living in Putney, and took over his father-in-law's business in addition to numerous undertakings of his own. The next step was to meet and try to impress Cardinal Wolsey.

In 1523 Thomas became a Member of Parliament and the villagers of Putney began to feel proud of him. He was by now the most confidential servant of the great cardinal. In 1525 he became Wolsey's agent in the dissolution of the smaller monasteries.

It was said in the village that Thomas was as ruthless as his father and as easy to bribe. Many were grieved when his wife died in 1528 for she and her family were well known in Putney as good honest folk. After her death Thomas made his will. It is fascinating to know that his chief beneficiary was his nephew Richard—the great grand-father of the Protector, Oliver Cromwell.

The villagers, who had nothing against Cardinal Wolsey, were pleased when the ruthless Cromwell showed signs of loyalty to his master. Wolsey's disgrace reduced him to despair. He was found in tears, and at his prayers, "which had been a strange sight in him afore".

In the years which followed this terrible young man became known in Roman Catholic circles as an "emissary of Satan". It was said in the village that he had studied Machiavelli's *The Prince*. He was blamed in Putney and Fulham (and most other places) for the misdeeds of Henry.

What must the villagers have thought when Thomas, the bad boy of Putney, became Henry's right-hand man? It was Thomas, the village villain, who set the divine right of kings against the divine right of the Pope. It was Thomas who set law above justice, and law to him was the will of the State. It was Thomas who boasted he would make Henry the richest prince in Christendom, and confiscate the property of the Church. As a result, three abbots were hanged. Monastic shrines and treasures were sacked and the spoil sent to the king.

In the villages of Putney and Fulham this man was now hated and feared. As a reward for ruthlessness he was knighted in July 1536, created Lord Privy Seal, Baron Cromwell, and Vicar-General and Vice-Regent of the king, in "spirituals". He then issued his famous Injunction. A bible was now to be provided in every church, big or small, and the Paternoster, Creed, and Ten Commandments, were to be recited in English. The preacher was to preach at least once a quarter, and each church was to start a register of births, marriages and deaths.

He was still not trusted by the people, least of all in Putney and Fulham, but now it began to seem that good might come out of evil. In April 1540 the "emissary of Satan" was created Earl of Essex, and Lord Great Chamberlain. The villagers could hardly believe it. Then he made his great mistake, actually sending a bishop to the Tower of London, and threatening to send five others to join him.

On 10th June Thomas Cromwell was accused of treason and himself sent to the Tower of London. The villagers were not sorry for the man they had so much feared. He was beheaded on Tower Hill on 28th July 1540—repudiating all heresy and declaring that he died in the Catholic faith.

This, perhaps, was our worst period of religious persecution. Living in the village of Fulham was a second obnoxious character, almost as bad as Thomas Cromwell, some say worse. This was Edmund Bonner, Bishop of London, and he lived in the hateful palace where so many crimes were planned and accomplished. It is his ghost, we are told, which haunts Fulham Palace to this day!

Bonner became Bishop of London in 1539. During the last years of Henry's reign, under the orders of Thomas Cromwell, he inflicted constant punishment to Catholics by the "whip with six strings". The villagers were frightened of him, and dared not go near the palace. He was deprived of his bishopric during the reign of Edward VI and sent to Marshalsea. Queen Mary (on her accession) released him. He was able to restore the Catholics in his diocese, which he did, and in 1555 he began the burning and whipping of Protestants. Bloody Mary was pleased with Bishop Bonner for changing his faith. Neither Mary, as a Catholic, nor Henry, as a Protestant, should ever have admitted him to the privy council, but they both did, for he seems to have pleased them both as a useful instrument for torturing and burning their enemies. Elizabeth later became queen, and refused to allow the perfidious Bishop of London to kiss her hand. He, in his turn, refused to take the oath of supremacy. In the end he was sent back to Marshalsea, where he died in 1569, and no doubt the villagers of Fulham and Putney breathed a sigh of relief.

Today, when most of the London churches are sadly empty on Sundays, it is difficult to imagine the religious frenzy which drove through the English people in Tudor times like a cyclone. The two little churches, on either side of the river, must both have been filled with trembling villagers, afraid to displease Henry, the Protestant king, or Mary the Catholic queen, by saying their prayers and worshipping God in a wrong or disloyal or disrespectful way.

In the reign of Bloody Mary nearly 300 persons were burned to death as heretics, among them five bishops, including Ridley of London. The Palace of Fulham, always at the heart of things, again the home of Bishop Bonner, became a house of horror, a crime centre, an evil place, to be avoided by all in the village. On the opposite bank was the other little church, St Mary the Virgin, not quite so close to the monstrous bishop in the red brick building, and yet the villagers of Putney were as frightened as the villagers of Fulham. Who would be the next to die?

The villagers had little respect for Bloody Mary. When Elizabeth came to the throne, at Mary's death on 17th November 1558, there were great rejoicings in every part of London. In the two little churches of Fulham and Putney, nearly all the villagers, on their knees, must have thanked God for his mercy. Catholics and Protestants were almost equally delighted with the new and kind-hearted queen.

In Putney Elizabeth was loved from the first. She was seen quite frequently by the villagers for she paid at least a dozen visits to a Putney merchant, a cloth maker, who lived in a riverside mansion, known then as 'The Palace', which must have been close to the spot where the Star and Garter stands today.

On these occasions, arriving by river in her gilded barge, the queen most probably walked from the Putney landing stage, passing close to St Mary the Virgin (perhaps entering to see the beautiful chapel) followed by her procession of dazzling courtiers, to meet her host, John Lucy, in a chosen place, somewhere near the Star and Garter.

John Lucy was honoured and flattered by the queen's friendship. At each visit she was his guest in Putney for two or three nights of happy entertainment.

Another Putney friend was Sir Francis Walsingham, who entertained Elizabeth, by this time a middle-aged woman but dressed like a girl, at the mansion of Barn Elms. Once again she arrived with her courtiers by water, and was driven by Sir Francis to Barnes. Or was it a fine day, and did she decide to mount one of his horses and ride to Barnes by his side?

In Putney the villagers knew that of all her suitors and lovers Elizabeth had a special favourite, and this was the Earl of Leicester, who remained so in spite of his second marriage (when Elizabeth thought of sending him to the Tower, but changed her mind) until his death in 1588.

The villagers also knew that Leicester had a good looking step-son whose name was Robert Devereux, the Earl of Essex (nothing to do with Thomas Cromwell, of Putney), for Elizabeth now fell in love with him. Elizabeth was aged fifty-five. Essex was twenty-two. This made no difference to the feelings of the queen—nor to the affection of her subjects.

In Putney, where Essex later built a house in the High Street, calling it Essex House, all these proceedings were common gossip.

Essex was popular in the village. In 1590, greatly daring, he married the widow of Sir Philip Sidney, but kept his marriage secret out of fear of the queen. When Elizabeth found out she was excessively angry. In the end Essex agreed that his wife should "live retired in his mother's house", and Elizabeth was pacified.

Most of his time was spent at Court, with occasional permission to join an expedition against Spain. There were many quarrels. On one occasion they were discussing the appointment of a Lord Deputy to Ireland and Essex, greatly annoyed, on account of some taunting words from Elizabeth, actually turned his back on the queen. For this she slapped his face. Essex left her, swearing that such an insult could not be endured even from Henry VIII.

In 1599, after an unsuccessful campaign in Ireland, poor Essex was deprived of his freedom and ordered to live like a prisoner in his own house during the queen's displeasure. The villagers of Putney must have felt sorry for the unfortunate young man as they passed his closed door on their way to church. This was a serious quarrel. When he was even refused the renewal of his patent for sweet wines the infuriated Essex, making a demonstration, just as we do today, was followed through the streets by 300 retainers, shouting to the world at large: "For the Queen! A plot is laid for my life!"

It was a silly demonstration. Essex returned to Essex House in the Putney High Street, where the neighbours must have smiled at his air of confusion. We are told that the royal arms with the initials "E.R." were engraved in his drawing room, and also in one of his bedrooms. Tradition has it that the rooms were wainscotted with wood taken from a ship belonging to the Armada. After this episode poor Essex was finished. There was a dramatic trial in which Francis Bacon, his one-time friend, delivered a speech against him that ended his life at the age of thirty-five. He was condemned to death on 25th February 1601.

There seems to be no doubt that Elizabeth, at the end, suffered agonies of regret, and his tragic fate deepened her love for the wilful Essex. She was desolate in old age. Her work was done. With the defeat of the English Armada and the loss of her favourites, Leicester, Walsingham, Burghley, and Essex, there was nothing to keep her alive. She died on 24th March 1603—surviving her young lover by two years.

Elizabeth had brought a strong sense of unity and patriotism to Britain. In the villages of Putney and Fulham, where so much history had taken place, there was plenty of sympathy for Elizabeth, and later for the Stuart kings, especially for Charles I, in the war with Oliver Cromwell.

One of the king's strongest supporters was a lady who lived in the hamlet of Roehampton, not far from a public house called the King's Head, which still exists, and must have been used by her visitors and servants. This was a very fine lady called Christiana, Countess of Devonshire—as lovely as Georgiana, the Duchess of Devonshire, who later lived at Chiswick. Her house stood where the Froebel Institute for Teachers stands today.

The King's Head, so near her home, is still a charming little tavern, crowded in summer, and as we drink and laugh and eat our sandwiches it is pleasing to think of Christiana. She was a beautiful Scot. She was the daughter of Edward Bruce of Kinloss, who was once the special favourite of King James I. Her marriage to William Cavendish, second Earl of Devonshire, was magnificent. It was arranged by the king himself, and he was present at the ceremony. His gift was a grant of £10,000.

After the death of her husband in 1628, Christiana had the care of all the estates for her eldest son was still quite young. We are told that she managed to double their value.

Her second son was killed while fighting on the side of King Charles I against Oliver Cromwell. The beautiful Christiana, now settled at Roehampton, took charge of the king's possessions after the battle of Worcester. She seems to have been at the centre of the plotting and planning of this unhappy but gentlemanly war. She entertained the king's friends at her home. She suffered for him, and mourned his death. Later she received a private message from

General Monck, who wished her to know that the king's son would soon be restored to the throne.

We are told that King Charles II visited her house in Roehampton on many occasions, and the Queen Mother was a close friend until the end of her life. She is described by a contemporary writer as a lady "of that affability and sweet address, with so great wit and judgement, as captivated all who conversed with her".

Charles, who seems to have treated her with great affection, jokingly said: "Madam, you have all my judges at your disposal!" This was because Christiana had no less than thirty law suits while she managed her son's estates and freed him from a vast debt. She was old enough to be the king's mother, but Charles admired her greatly.

This brave and beautiful lady seems to have had a very strong will. For example, she annoyed her son by keeping Hobbes, the free-thinker, in her house as a tutor. Her son detested the religious and political opinions of Hobbes but put up with him, for his mother's sake, even when Christiana was dead and buried. They continued to live in the same house at Roehampton, the earl, his tutor, and his friend, Sir Stephen Fox—also a member of Christiana's household. Did they visit the King's Head, one wonders, or did they stay at home, still obedient to the old lady's wishes?

In the village of Putney there were many who sympathized with the Stuart kings and some who admired Oliver Cromwell. We know that he and his officers, plotting and planning for the death of Charles I, held meetings in the little church by the river. Poor St Mary the Virgin, where the villagers still gathered on Sunday mornings, was now used by soldiers who sat round the altar. This was resented by some. On the other hand, solemn doctrines did certainly emerge from their church. To give an example: "The poorest he that is in England hath a life to live as the greatest he." Here is another example: "A man is not bound to a system of government which he hath not had any hand in setting over him." As Winston Churchill expressed it, in our own day, this was "a brew of hot Gospel and cold steel".

It is certain that Oliver Cromwell had followers in Putney, also in Fulham, even though 3,000 men of Surrey gathered on Putney Heath, and actually marched to Westminster, demanding that Charles be restored to his throne. (He was then being held in captivity on the Isle of Wight.)

We are told that Oliver Cromwell planted the mulberry tree which still grows in a Putney garden and belongs to a beautiful Jacobean house (the only one left) near the Star and Garter, overlooking the river. Today this lovely house is the Putney Constitutional Club for Men, and the mulberry tree still bears delicious fruit.

Nobody knows why Oliver Cromwell should bother to plant a mulberry tree, but perhaps he admired Old Winchester House. It belonged later to James Baudoin, a Huguenot, who fled from Nimes in 1685 to avoid religious persecution. Much later, in 1885, it was occupied by Walter Rye, whose son is still a member of the club at the time of writing. Today, incidentally, a female visitor may not enter this delightful house but a male visitor is acceptable.

The village people soon forgot about Oliver Cromwell when Charles II was restored to the throne. They waited to see him, galloping or trotting down the King's Road, dismounting at the village of Fulham, crossing by ferry to Putney, on his way to the Countess of Devonshire. Sometimes the king would take a boat or barge, waving to the villagers, and travelling by water to Hampton Court—just as the tourists do today.

The villagers who pleasantly watched him were able to recall his narrow escape from Oliver Cromwell. Like everyone else they loved to remember the day when the king hid in the upper branches of an oak tree after the Battle of Worcester in 1651. That is why we still have public houses in England which are proudly called The Royal Oak.

Today we are reminded of Charles and his narrow escape when we enter the Fulham church on a Sunday morning. The floor is thickly covered with ancient tombstones. One of these is in memory of Thomas Carlos, who hid in the oak tree with Charles and was consequently allowed to change his name from Careless to Carlos (a great honour!) and to bear upon his arms a branching oak tree. The coat of arms is very distinct and the date is 1665.

Although, on several occasions, he prevented Englishmen from going to war, Charles could not prevent them from fighting duels. Putney was considered an ideal meeting place, and apparently they enjoyed a bit of duelling on Putney Heath as tennis at Wimbledon is enjoyed today. It was the proper place to go if a gentleman of London wished to injure or kill another gentleman. It was done with style. A famous duel was fought at Barn Elms when the wicked Duke of Buckingham killed the Earl of Shrewsbury after seducing the Countess of Shrewsbury. Not only was the poor earl killed by his rival, losing both his wife and his life, but the countess encouraged the killer. Dressed as a boy, she watched and enjoyed the duel.

But when Lord Chandos and Colonel Compton fought on Putney Heath, in May 1652, the colonel was killed. The Heath seems to have been more popular than Barn Elms.

More than 100 years later, on a Sunday afternoon, William Pitt, the Prime Minister, who then lived close by in Bowling Green House, fought a bloodless battle with William Tierney, M.P. In September 1809 a fight took place between Lord Castlereagh and George Canning. The latter was wounded in the thigh.

This final duel was fought near the Admiralty semaphore station, erected in 1796—where the Telegraph Inn stands today, and the locals gather for a peaceful meal, or a drink.

There are countless stories about the highwaymen on Putney Heath. They seem to have flourished in this wild part of Putney, especially a villain called Jerry Abershaw, who hung here in chains in 1785 after the execution on Kingston Common.

The spot where Jerry did his wicked work, at the top of Putney Hill, is today plainly marked by the roundabout which so many motorists go swirling round on their way from Putney to Wimbledon or Guildford. How many motorists have ever heard of Jerry?

If any motorist wishes to find the exact place where Jerry hung, and has the courage (which the author has not) to stop his or her car in mid-traffic, he will find, at the centre of the roundabout, planted in the grass like a lonely flower, almost unnoticed, a small metal memorial, lovingly carved in silhouette, to remind us of Jerry's undignified death.

They still talk about him at a small public house called the Green Man (not much changed apart from the modern patio outside) which was frequently used by Jerry and his friends. It is not far away from the place of the gallows. Inside a game is still played by the locals which was played by Jerry, or so we are told. There is a tale about Jerry's mother, who said he was a bad boy and would probably die with his boots on. So annoyed was Jerry with his mother that he pulled off his boots before he was hanged!

During all these turbulent times of religious persecution and civil war, followed by fights and duels and hangings on Putney Heath, the villagers, at the bottom of the hill, continued to seek refuge in the little church where they gathered on Sunday mornings, and St Mary the Virgin, undisturbed, was still seen as a place of beauty and peace and friendship.

It was charmingly described by Samuel Pepys who wrote:

... After dinner by water, the day being mighty pleasant, and the tide serving finely ... as high as Barn Elms and then took one turn alone and then back to Putney Church where I saw the girls of the school, few of which pretty; and then I came into a pew and met with little James Pierce which I was much pleased at, the little rogue being very pleased to see me; his master reader to the church. There was a good sermon and much company. But I sleepy and a little out of order at my hat falling down through a hole beneath the pulpit, which however after the sermon I got up by help of the clerk and my stick.

The church was familiar to William Pitt, the second Prime Minister of England, who lived on Putney Heath 100 years later—at the time of the wars with Napoleon. Alas, Bowling Green House, where he lived and died, has been pulled down. It was close to the Green Man. It was removed as recently as 1933, just before World War II, like so many other buildings, for at that time they enjoyed pulling down beautiful houses even more than the planners and improvers of today.

William Pitt was a bachelor Prime Minister, and for this he was sometimes criticized. "That man", the villagers probably said, "would be better with a wife to tell him what's what!"

Although Pitt never married he was said to have a deep admiration for the daughter of Lord Auckland. The embarrassment of his debts prevented marriage. In 1800 he owed more than £45,000, not to mention £600 for hats. But it was said about him that his real passion was for his work, and to that he gave his life.

In Putney some of us like to think of England's great Prime Minister (the man who hated Napoleon as Churchill hated Hitler) entertaining his distinguished visitors, including Lord Wellesley and perhaps Wellington, living with dignity in his large white house, a graceful building, said to have been as pretty and charming as if kept by a woman, pleased to walk in his garden, picking his roses, chatting to his friends, and all of this happening within a stone's throw of Jerry's body as it hung from the gallows on Putney Heath.

Mr Pitt may well have seen the highwayman's body. Did he and his friends walk on the heath in the opposite direction from the gallows, or did they deliberately take an interest in the awful sight— as some people nowadays hurry to see a car crash, or a plane accident.

Mr Pitt rented his house and lived in it for many years because he so much enjoyed the wildness of Putney Heath. In January 1806 he went to Bath to try to cure his gout. Canning brought him the sad news of the French victory at Austerlitz, and this, it seems, was the last straw.

On 9th January he left Bath with his personal physician, Sir Walter Farquhar, and arrived back at Putney two days later. He was received by his friend, Lady Hester Stanhope, and as he passed a map of Europe on the way to his room he said: "Roll up that map, it will not be wanted these ten years!"

Poor William Pitt, grieving for his country, died only twelve days later (23rd January 1806). Apparently, like William the Conqueror, this great man was deserted by all his circle and his servants. Where was Lady Hester Stanhope when he died? It seems that a messenger arrived at Bowling Green House to enquire after Mr Pitt's health. Unable to find any servants or members of the household he entered the front door, walked through a deserted building, and at last found the Prime Minister's lifeless body in his bedroom.

Pitt was only forty-seven. He had been a Member of Parliament for twenty-five years to the day. The famous Bowling Green House, as we know, was heartlessly demolished (in spite of great protest) in 1933. On the site was erected the present group of houses belonging to Bowling Green Close.

Putney Bridge, as we know it today, was built, or rebuilt, by the Victorians in the years 1884–6. In the time of William Pitt the villagers were still using an ancient wooden bridge.

It was this wooden bridge, close to the boats and barges, on which stood a sad young woman who tried to commit suicide by throwing herself in the river below. She was fished out by a passing boat— much to her annoyance.

The young woman's name was Mary Wollstonecraft. She was the first woman to publish her views on women's rights and nowadays, without a doubt, Mary would be hailed as the leader and inspiration of Women's Lib. Mary formed a close friendship with the philosopher, William Godwin. This was the literary man who most influenced Shelley, the poet. As Mary and Godwin both disapproved of marriage they decided to live in sin, which they both much preferred.

It was only when Mary found that another child was on the way that she married Godwin. The birth of a baby daughter (who later became Shelley's wife) was fatal to her and she died on 10th September 1797.

On her death bed Mary exclaimed in dramatic tones that she was "in heaven". Godwin, the philosopher, replied in a patient voice: "You mean, my dear, that your physical sensations are somewhat easier." Nevertheless Godwin lovingly compiled a memoir of his wife which appeared in the following year.

In the Victorian period the village of Putney became much more important and began to hold a special interest for many more people from other parts of London. There was, for example, the great excitement of the Oxford and Cambridge Boat Race. For others, even more unexpected, there was the astonishing appearance of Swinburne, known to the Victorians as "that decadent poet", who came to live in a respectable house called 'The Pines'. He remained in the same house, with his gentleman friend, Theodore Watts-Dunton, for twenty-eight years.

Then, as today, a walk by the river on a sunlit morning, looking across the water through the trees at Fulham Palace, the gentle freedom of feeding the gulls, admiring the boats, observing the boat houses, the boat builders, the men who create almost perfect oars and sculls, inspired by the Oxford and Cambridge Boat Race, at least one of them patronized by royalty, was and still is a most pleasant thing to do.

The boats built in Putney are said to be the best river racing boats in the country. The Oxford and Cambridge Boat Race ran for the first time from Putney to Mortlake in 1845. Today it is an annual sporting event and arouses the keenest interest all over the world.

Swinburne was among the eminent Victorians who took pride and pleasure in watching the boat race from Putney. Although he seldom walked by the river, preferring Putney Heath, he was a first-class swimmer, loving the sea, and must have enjoyed this beautiful new Victorian sight of boats and men and glittering water to be admired from Putney Bridge.

Swinburne, as we know, was thought to be a genius. He was educated at Eton and Oxford where he was said to have acquired his decadent ideas. In 1861 he formed an innocent friendship with Rossetti, who developed and guided with marvellous skill the genius of "my little Northumbrian friend" as he used to call him. Rossetti painted a portrait of Swinburne, attracted by his beautiful hair. The portrait was being painted when Rossetti's wife died so tragically through an overdose of laudanum, and Swinburne, deeply distressed, gave evidence at the inquest.

In 1866, when his *Poems and Ballads* were published, the name of Swinburne became as well known as the name of Byron. There had been no such literary scandal since Byron's *Don Juan*. And yet Ruskin, the most powerful critic of the time, indignantly said: "He is infinitely above me in all knowledge and power, and I should no more think of advising or criticizing him than of venturing to do it to Turner if he were alive again."

Swinburne now found himself in the position of Lord Byron before him, and Oscar Wilde after him. Suddenly he became the most talked of man in England. Portraits of him filled the shop windows, while London newspapers used every story, true or imaginary, about Swinburne's eccentric behaviour.

Lady Trevelyan, some time before, had written to him with a mixture of reproof and affection: "Now do, if only for the sake of living down evil reports, do be wise in which of your lyrics you publish. Do let it be a book that can be really loved and read and learned by heart, and become part and parcel of the English language, and be on everyone's breakfast table without being received under protest by timid people. There are no doubt people who would be glad to be able to say that it is not fit to be read. It is not worth while for the sake of two or three poems to risk the widest circulation of the whole."

To us his poems are innocent enough, almost adolescent, and yet the instinct of those who dared to call Swinburne 'decadent' without any real reason, turned out to be near the truth.

We now know that Swinburne, so much loved by his friends, was tormented by his admiration for the works of the Marquis de Sade. He became a regular visitor to an establishment in St John's Wood where he paid professional young ladies to flog him with a whip. He read and wrote about flagellation. He had at least one sexual relationship with a man, never with a woman as far as we know, but his weakness for the whip, apparently engendered at Eton, that home of licensed flagellation, was the central point in his neurotic life which drove him finally to drink and despair.

At the time when he published the famous *Poems and Ballads* the Victorians had no notion of Swinburne's pathetic weakness. In 1879, thirteen years later, he was found in his bedroom drunk and insensible by his friend, Theodore Watts-Dunton, who removed him to the family home in Putney. After this he transferred his family, and Swinburne with it, to 'The Pines', an ugly little house where they all lived happily and respectably for thirty years.

We are told that Swinburne promised his friend never to take a drink in a Putney public house. For this reason he walked every morning all the way from Putney to Wimbledon, and back (four miles), lunching each day at the Rose and Crown, in Wimbledon, but never, they say, drinking too much. Occasionally he stopped at the Green Man on his way home. It seems that his health, and sanity, and self-respect, were all completely restored by the dull and peaceful life with a bourgeois family in Putney.

In appearance Swinburne was a little gnome-like being. In height he was only five feet four inches. His large head was far too big and heavy for his narrow sloping shoulders and slender girlish body. He adored children. He peered into perambulators and wrote senti-mental poems to a special child called 'Bertie'.

In April 1909 he developed pneumonia and died at the age of seventy-two, a respected citizen of Putney, no more a 'decadent' than the respectable Mr Watts-Dunton, who protected him as a mother protects a child. The villagers were sad when he died, and 'Bertie', aged thirty-five, went to his funeral.

Today, in Putney, the beautiful houses have gone (except for Winchester House, which is now the Constitutional Club) but 'The Pines' is still standing. As a motorist, driving through to Guildford or Brighton, there is just time to notice it as you drive up the hill. It is now converted into flatlets. It has a blue plaque on its ugly grey face.

Even today the two little churches still dominate the village life of Putney and Fulham. Have lunch at the Star and Garter, in Putney, overlooking the river, and across the water, painted on the summer sky, you can see the grey tower of the Fulham church. In winter, through bare branches, you can partly see an ancient red brick building which is Fulham Palace.

At the time of writing Fulham Palace is deserted. The present Bishop of London has moved out because the building is too big by modern standards, and too cold. It is to be used, they say, as a museum. The peaceful garden is now filled with starlings and blackbirds and thrushes who seem to possess the old palace, haunted by Bishop Bonner, and they cackle with rage when a stranger dares to enter the courtyard. It is a place of beauty. Let us hope the planners and improvers will never be tempted to take Fulham Palace from the village of Fulham. There is nothing quite like it in London.

Fulham has another precious possession and this is the Hurling-

Putney Church with Fulham Church in the background. These two little churches have been facing one another across the river Thames for more than 700 years

In the time of William Pitt, who died at Putney in 1806, the villagers of Putney and Fulham were still using an ancient wooden bridge

The Grand Walk, Marylebone Gardens, became a place of fashion in the eighteenth century. Today we have in its place the London Clinic

Skating in Regents Park, 1838. It was 'Prinny', or George IV, who gave Marylebone the white graceful houses which stand round the lake

ham Club where polo used to be played in Edwardian times. It is a Georgian building overlooking the river, unspoilt, unchanged, expensive, delightful. In the gardens we can still watch the best tennis players in the world, or play croquet, as did King Edward VII, or practise golf, or swim in the swimming pool, or walk peacefully by the river, as did Edward and Queen Alexandra.

On the Putney side of the river, close to the spot where Queen Elizabeth used to land in her gilded barge, a stone's throw from the little Putney church, is the landing stage for tourists and visitors who wish, like King Charles II, to travel by river to Hampton Court.

This lovely place for racing boats, and boat builders, and barges, and scullers, and small white sails, tacking up and down the silvery river, is still the heart of the boat world, and of the village of Putney. The boat-loving King Charles would have enjoyed it as we do today.

PUTNEY AND FULHAM LOCAL HISTORY
Recommended Books

Hammersmith, Fulham, and Putney, Ed. Sir Walter Besant by G. E. Mitton & J. G. Geikie (Adam & Charles Black, 1903)

Twixt Heath and River, Ed. Catherine Purley Smith (Putney Press Ltd, 1908)

The Story of Wandsworth and Putney, G. W. C. Green (Sampson, Low, Marston & Co, 1926)

Fulham Old and New, C. J. Fèret (Leadenhall Press Ltd, 1900)

An Historical and Topographical Account of Fulham, Thomas Faulkner (1813)

6

Marylebone

When Londoners walk across Regent's Park on their way to the Rose Garden, or the lake, or the Zoo, how many realize it was Henry VIII who created and first used this beautiful place as a royal hunting ground as long ago as 1538? It was three years after the execution of Sir Thomas More, and two years after the execution of Anne Boleyn, Henry's second wife. England's wicked old king, who enjoyed sport as much as Elizabeth, his daughter, and was loved everywhere in spite of his faults, decided to make the manor of Tyburn (now called Marylebone) his hunting lodge, a kind of holiday palace, and to surround fifty-five acres of forest and fields with a wooden fence, creating a hunting ground for himself, his children, and his distinguished visitors from France.

Elizabeth entertained an embassy from Russia in the Manor House, and they hunted in Henry's Park in the year 1601. So did her sister Mary (Bloody Mary) and her brother Edward, on a number of occasions. They must have galloped their beautiful and glamorous horses, gaudy with gold and scarlet, like royal barges rising and falling roughly on the River Thames, jumping fences and fallen trees on the rough forest land which is now a football ground.

King James I frequently hunted in the park. The village of Marylebone, like the riverside village of Chelsea, was for many years the playground of kings and queens and their following of friends and enemies, mistresses and lovers and admirers. The hunting and entertaining continued until the time of Oliver Cromwell. Henry's playground became known as Marylebone Park but during the Civil Wars in the seventeenth century the land was mortgaged by King Charles I to pay for the battles with Cromwell. After that fields and farms appeared and London was supplied with milk and eggs and meat by the new farmers.

When the wars ended Marylebone remained for 100 years a country village, one hour's walk from London, with a church, a manor house, and a winding lane beside the River Tyburn. A farmhouse stood where Bedford College now stands and fields with cattle and sheep were prettily framed with thick hedges and small friendly woods extending to Hampstead as far as the eye could see. Its only distinction was a pleasure ground with bowling greens and this was called Marylebone Gardens—east of the High Street, and entered by a public house called the Rose of Normandy.

But a change could be seen in the eighteenth century. The isolated village was transformed as though by magic into a residential estate on the outskirts of the City. The development was started about 1760 by the Lord of the Manor of Tyburn, Edward Harley, second Earl of Oxford and Mortimer. Others followed his example. Although the church and the manor house remained as before, and also the bowling greens, the villagers were amazed to see a number of large houses, built in squares, looking down upon well-designed gardens with flowers and trees and noble statues. The first of these became known as Cavendish Square, and later Portman Square appeared. The new squares delighted the folk who worked in the fields and entirely altered the open country between Tyburn Road (now Oxford Street) and the village.

The development of Marylebone continued. When the farming leases ran out in 1811 it was time for Marylebone Park to be transformed by John Nash, the architect employed by the Prince Regent, or 'Prinny' as everyone called him. It became known as Regent's Park, London's new West End. Luckily for Marylebone most of the Nash terraces are still dreamily standing, like a gathering of white and well-bred brides, collected in a graceful semicircle round the green land, the lake, the rose garden, the lovely place which was chosen long ago by King Henry VIII and stocked by him with deer.

Strange to say the village church, a tiny but romantic building where Francis Bacon was married and Lord Byron baptized, was still peacefully standing at the top of the High Street during the years of World War II. It was demolished in 1949. Sadly it was pulled down owing to bomb damage and dilapidation. A garage now stands on the site of the old Manor House on the other side of the High Street.

The village church was built probably in 1400, on the edge of the Tyburn River (now one of London's underground rivers) at the heart of the Tyburn village. It was rebuilt in 1740. The church was at first called St Mary-a-le-bourne, or St Mary-by-Tyburn, and this became the name we know today—St Marylebone.

The long winding lane, still called Marylebone Lane, followed the course of the river and was the village's link with Tyburn Road (Oxford Street) leading to the Tyburn gallows. The famous gallows, known as Tyburn Tree, or Deadly Never Green, were a place of entertainment for the villagers. Among the victims we read about the Holy Maid of Kent, in the reign of Henry VIII. Elizabeth disliked executions, but she caused the hanging of a famous and brilliant Jesuit, Robert Southwell, believed by the Catholics to be a saint, because he was plotting (she believed) against her government.

Most incredible of all is the story of Oliver Cromwell. When King Charles II was restored to the throne the body of Cromwell, his enemy, who murdered his father, was dragged from its grave in Westminster Abbey and hanged in its grave clothes on Tyburn Tree. The dead Cromwell was then beheaded, the body buried beneath the gallows, and the head stuck on a pole on the top of Westminster Hall.

Jack Sheppard, the celebrated highwayman, dangerous but charming to women, was hanged at Tyburn. No doubt his dramatic death was well attended. By this time Tyburn Tree was a meeting place for villagers and aristocrats, as good as a theatre. Rich and poor paid for their seats to watch an execution. The gallows (a wooden structure supported by three stilts) stood on the site of what is now Connaught Place, near Marble Arch. For this reason Park Lane was called Tyburn Lane as Oxford Street was called Tyburn Road. The last man to be hanged was John Austen in 1783, after which Tyburn Tree was pulled down and all criminals were executed at Newgate.

It is difficult to imagine the mood of brutality which would induce a society lady to spend a happy afternoon visiting the gallows with her friends in order to watch an execution, paying for her seat, and then passing a pleasant social evening at Marylebone Gardens, listening to loud music, sometimes watching a dog fight, or even a boxing match between two women.

Marylebone Gardens became as fashionable as Tyburn Tree. Today we have in its place the London Clinic. It used to be a centre of entertainment, noisy, gay, rowdy, amusing, where the great Dr Johnson disported himself, and even the prudish and gentle Fanny Burney, who surveyed the noise and vulgarity with a smile of distaste. The part known as the Bear Garden contained pits for cockfighting and raised platforms for prize fighting, both male and female. Gay alluded to the Marylebone Gardens in *The Beggar's Opera*. As long ago as 1668 Pepys wrote in his diary: "Then we went abroad to Marrow-bone and there walked in the garden; the first time I was ever there, and a pretty place it is."

Later the gardens deteriorated, and became in the end a rough-and-tumble for the *hoi polloi*. The grounds were surrounded on summer nights by thieves and vagabonds, footpads, highwaymen, characters like Dick Turpin, eighteenth-century 'muggers' who were capable of murder. For this reason ladies and gentlemen were provided by the management with a mounted escort to and from the City Road. It was called a "Horse Patrol".

In 1738 Mr Gough, the owner of the gardens, issued silver tickets at twelve shillings each for the season (each ticket admitting two people). Mr Gough made the nightly promenade more fashionable than ever. He created an Assembly Hall with a covered arcade so that ladies and gentlemen might promenade even in bad weather without fear of spoiling their satins and brocades, their fine wigs, their curled and powdered hair.

Elaborate fireworks became an added attraction, adding an extra shilling to the cost of cheap seats in the pit. The great Dr Johnson, philosopher and wit and intellectual clown, loved fireworks and caused a violent demonstration one night because the manager announced that the fireworks were damp and could not be used. After waiting for a long time in the drizzling rain, seated in the pit, noticing that the fashionable five-shilling seats were empty, Dr Johnson rose indignantly to his enormous feet and shouted: "It's a mere excuse to save their crackers for a more profitable company!"

Sensation followed. The doctor's loud bellow of rage and disappointment was picked up by many others seated wetly in the pit. The doctor suggested they should threaten to break the lamps. His suggestion was adopted, some lamps were quickly broken, and soon after that the management gave the doctor his fireworks.

In 1751, at the height of their fame, the gardens were taken over by John Trusler, as sole proprietor. In 1759, inspired by his daughter, he opened the gardens for breakfasting. This was a new idea and it caught the public. Now the gardens were open at 6 a.m., and soon it became the done thing, 'the mode' as they said then, for all 'persons of quality' to dress and paint and powder themselves for a simple country breakfast to the sound of bird song on a fine summer morning. What could be more delightful and Arcadian?

In this way their little village was changed, and the villagers of Marylebone found it hard to understand what had happened. They still went to church on Sunday mornings, and fished in the River

Tyburn, and played bowls on the bowling green, and walked or rode along Tyburn Road to see a good execution. In old days the Lord Mayor had made an annual inspection of the conduit heads, celebrating afterwards with a hunt in the royal park and a banquet. Now, for some reason, the gentry had taken a fancy to Marylebone and had decided to share the pleasures of the village, including bowls and bear fights and executions, and the villagers were flattered but surprised.

By this time Lord Harley had created Cavendish Square. Lady Mary Wortley Montagu, the most witty woman in London, moved there as early as 1731. She was close friends with Lord Harley's wife, Henrietta, and also with Sarah, Duchess of Marlborough.

Almost everyone in this distinguished circle must have visited the Marylebone Gardens. The villagers observed them with interest. Among the inhabitants and visitors and lovers of Marylebone were Richard Brinsley Sheridan (who lived at one time in Orchard Street) and Mrs Thrale (at another time in Welbeck Street). She was Dr Johnson's friend, and so was Fanny Burney, who mentioned the gardens in her novel *Evelina*. There was also Edward Gibbon, the great historian, who lived at 7 Bentinck Street, Manchester Square, and the great hostess, Mrs Elizabeth Montagu, whose house in Portman Square was close to Home House, the magnificent mansion which is now the Courtauld Institute.

When the Tyburn Tree was pulled down Mrs Montagu and her circle, especially those who lived in and around Portman Square, were delighted—not because they disliked the executions but because they objected to the crowds and the noise. Incidentally, the hangmen were paid thirteen and a half pennies per head as wages, and were considered 'persons of quality'. These things are brought to life in Hogarth's angry picture of Tyburn in the series called 'The Idle Apprentice'.

No wonder Fanny Burney was shocked and puzzled by the ways of London society. Beautiful ladies drank beer at breakfast and seldom washed their hair and swore like troopers and gambled with vast sums of money which they lost at a single throw—not to mention the scandals and immoralities to which Fanny so strongly objected. At the same time they were elegant and courageous and dashing and witty and stylish and extremely captivating.

Lord Harley's wife had been Lady Henrietta Cavendish, so now we have Cavendish Square and Harley Street. Her only daughter was Lady Margaret Cavendish Harley, who married in 1734 William, second Duke of Portland. So now we have Portland Place. Her great woman friend was the shocking and fascinating Lady Mary Wortley Montagu, who lived in Cavendish Square, and was loved and feared by all in the village.

The letters of Lady Mary, even now, are fascinating and witty and descriptive and stylish and in some cases concealed from the public eye because considered indecent. She had the pen of a malicious angel. The lovely Lady Mary was often at Court and was well known to the poet, Alexander Pope, who by turns adored her and lampooned her in print. She had numerous admirers but her husband neglected her. She lived with him for a time in Constantinople, and when she returned home, to Cavendish Square, she astonished the villagers, and made history for British medicine, by explaining that smallpox could be ended by inoculation.

It seems that her son had been treated for smallpox in Constantinople, and now her daughter in Cavendish Square was treated in the same way—in the presence of three physicians and the family apothecary. The lovely Lady Mary, in her own way, waged a publicity campaign to defeat smallpox in England. It was then as prevalent as measles today. We are told what she did by Steele, who wrote in 1725 about her "godlike delight" in saving "many thousand British lives" every year. The villagers soon heard that Lady Mary was able to teach the doctors about smallpox, even to cure this terrible disease. Some of them came to her house to seek help or advice.

Pope was betrayed into a declaration of love which Lady Mary received with a fit of laughter. There followed a long literary warfare. No one except Lady Mary could write more maliciously than Pope and each barbed utterance was rushed into print.

Lady Mary was now on friendly terms with Lord Hervey, and on hostile terms with his wife—a situation which continued for many years. Hervey was another malicious writer of memoirs, as good looking and charming as Lady Mary, who presently fell in love with a young Italian, Francesco Algarotti. She was by this time in her early forties, twenty-three years older than Algarotti, who seems to have been a difficult and capricious young man. After nine years in Cavendish Square, she left the village of Marylebone to pursue her hopeless passion round Italy, and discovered too late that her unsuspected and successful rival was no other than her old friend, Lord Hervey!

This time Lady Mary was punished for being so witty. She had often said that human beings were divided into three sexes—men, women, and Herveys. She found it was only too true. At least her unforgettable joke has provided one of our best stories about Lord Hervey and Lady Mary.

About fifty years later she was followed by another great hostess. This was Mrs Elizabeth Montagu, who lived in Portman Square. The buildings on the north side were started in 1773 by Robert Adam, who created the beautiful Home House (now the Courtauld Institute).

It was built for the Countess of Home, widow of the eighth earl, who happened to be an heiress from Jamaica, and was able to spend a vast fortune on her London house. Poor Lady Home did not realize that Mrs Elizabeth Montagu, another rich widow, could make her life in London so difficult. Mrs Montagu, an ambitious lady, built a huge and palatial residence across the corner of Portman Square and Gloucester Place, as close as possible to the unfortunate countess from Jamaica, whom she christened for some reason 'The Queen of Hell', and opened her new home with a breakfast for 700 people.

Mrs Montagu seems to have hated Lady Home. Everything which could be done to harrass and humiliate the countess from Jamaica was done by Mrs Montagu, and done well. She had created a room in her house called a 'Feather Room'. It was much more successful than anything created by the countess. We are told in an excellent book by Gordon Mackenzie how she collected feathers of every type from her celebrated friends and hung them all, like trophies, from peacocks to sparrows, in huge frames round the 'Feather Room'. Even Horace Walpole was impressed by this. Only Mrs Montagu could do such an unexpected thing. The emotional experience of receiving an invitation from Mrs Montagu is described light-heartedly by Fanny Burney:

> Chocolate being then brought, we adjourned to the drawing room. And here, Dr Johnson being taken from the books, entered freely and most cleverly into conversation; though it is remarkable he never speaks at all but when spoken to; nor does he ever *start*, though he admirably *supports* any subject. The whole party was engaged to dine at Mrs Montagu's. Dr Johnson said he had received the most flattering note he had ever read or that anybody else had ever read by way of invitation. "But, so have I too," cried Mrs Thrale; "so if a note from Mrs Montagu is to be boasted of, I beg mine may not be forgot." "*Your* note," cried

Dr Johnson, "can bear no comparison with *mine*; I am *at the head of the Philosophers*, she says." "And I", cried Mrs Thrale "have all the Muses in my train." "A fair battle", said my father. "Come compliment for compliment, and see who will hold out longest."

The eighteenth century was the age of elegance as the nineteenth century was the age of expansion and the twentieth century is the age of escapism.

Another character who belonged very much to the gay world of Marylebone in the eighteenth century was Richard Brinsley Sheridan. Here was a typical gallant. Like his friend, the Prince of Wales, always called 'Prinny', he became a heavy drinker and a ferocious gambler, but he was loved by the ladies until his death.

At the age of twenty-two, Sheridan was married in the little church in the village of Marylebone. His bride was Miss Elizabeth Linley, a professional singer, already well known for her beauty. Having fought two duels with a certain Major Mathews, who also fancied Miss Linley, the romantic Sheridan gave up his studies for the bar, and his work at the Middle Temple, in order to marry the lovely Miss Linley. His father was much annoyed. In the *Morning Chronicle* the following announcement appeared:

"Tuesday was married at Marylebone Church by the Rev. Dr Booth the celebrated Miss Linley to Mr Sheridan. After the ceremony they set out with her family and friends, and dined at the Star and Garter on Richmond Hill; in the evening they had a ball after which the family and friends returned to town, and left the young couple at a gentleman's house at Mitcham to consummate their nuptials."

In the spring of 1774 they decided to settle in fashionable Marylebone, taking a house in Orchard Street. Quite soon, almost immediately, the large reception rooms were filled with ladies and gentlemen who moved, as Sheridan had never done before, in high society. They all came, the dukes and duchesses, the earls and countesses, as well as the blue stockings, the Burneys, the Montagus, the Garricks, the Thrales and Johnsons. It was as though Noel Coward, at the age of twenty-two, unknown and almost penniless, had suddenly opened a mansion in Park Lane in order to rub shoulders with nobility and even royalty. Oddly enough, it worked.

In November 1774 Sheridan informed his father-in-law that his comedy, *The Rivals*, would be rehearsed in a few days time at Covent

Garden Theatre. Apparently the author had no misgivings. It was performed in January 1775 and from that date to this it has always been a popular comedy.

Sheridan was now twenty-four years of age. By the end of 1785 he was well known, and became manager of Drury Lane Theatre in 1776, in succession to Garrick. In 1777 he presented *The School for Scandal*, which is still the best and wittiest exposition of eighteenth-century society, and in October 1779 a farce called *The Critic* was presented—as successful as the others.

In Marylebone the young Sheridans were watched with wonder and received with splendour. Fanny Burney met Sheridan at a 'blue party', and wrote afterwards: "His appearance and address are at once manly and fashionable, without the smallest tincture of foppery or modish graces. In short, I like him vastly, and think him every way worthy his beautiful companion. . . . By all I could observe in the course of the evening, and we stayed very late, they are extremely happy in each other; he evidently adores her, and she as evidently idolizes him. The world has by no means done him justice."

His wife was painted by Gainsborough and Hoppner, and by Sir Joshua Reynolds as Saint Cecilia. Sheridan himself had meanwhile become as great a favourite in society and parliament as in the theatre. He became a member of the Literary Club (by Dr Johnson's motion), a Member of Parliament for Stafford (in 1780) and soon afterwards, perhaps his happiest moment, a Member of Brook's Club, where he gambled and lost many thousands of pounds. It was Georgiana, the famous Duchess of Devonshire, who first introduced him to her friend 'Prinny', and now as adviser to the Prince of Wales his greatest ambition was achieved. He was still under thirty years of age.

While his wife lived he earned as much as £10,000 a year from the Drury Lane Theatre. Like 'Prinny', he managed always to be deeply in debt and continually tempted by wine and women, an inveterate gambler, yet so much in love with his badly treated wife that his heart was broken when she died. His friends were shocked when the Drury Lane Theatre was burnt to the ground. His second marriage with a young girl was not a success. He was arrested for debt. Poor Sheridan was found in a garret, a sick and humiliated man, half drunk, penniless, filthy. His friends rescued him too late.

Sheridan was buried in 1816 at Westminster Abbey, in Poets Corner (which he was said to detest) and if given any choice in the matter he would probably have preferred the little churchyard in the village of Marylebone, outside the old grey building where he married Miss Linley.

It was Lord Byron (baptized in the same little church) who summed him up, and gave us the shortest epitaph on Richard Brinsley Sheridan. Lord Byron simply wrote: "Alas, poor human nature."

There must have been a great deal of gossip in the village. It was so close to the fashionable squares where the great folk now lived. Lady Mary Wortley Montagu had once been the prettiest and wittiest, but later there was George Romney, the portrait painter, at 32 Cavendish Square. His rival, Sir Joshua Reynolds, referred to him scornfully as "the man in Cavendish Square", refusing to give him his rightful name. Why was this? It may have been because Romney had painted so many portraits of Nelson's Lady Hamilton, at one time Romney's mistress, or so it was said in the village. At any rate, she was a constant visitor to Romney's studio, and everyone knew it.

But few people knew that Lady Hamilton's daughter, by Nelson, was brought to the Marylebone church and baptized there on 3rd May 1803. The birth took place in Sir William Hamilton's own house, and somehow it was kept a secret, even from Sir William. One wonders how? The baby, concealed in a large muff, was taken by her mother in the family carriage to a person living in Little Titchfield Street, and a fortnight later was taken back to Sir William Hamilton's house to be shown to Lord Nelson. Two years afterwards the child was quietly and discreetly baptized and given the grand name of Horatia Nelson. For obvious reasons her parents were not mentioned and the secret was kept from the villagers.

In and around Cavendish Square there was much entertaining and gambling for high stakes and many stories of the glamorous goings on, especially at Chandos House (at the junction of Chandos Street and Queen Anne Street) built by Robert Adam for the third Duke of Buckingham and Chandos. In the duke's time there was stabling for twelve horses and four coaches. Chandos House remained in the duke's family for more than a hundred years. Today we still have Chandos House, which was bought in 1927 by Viscount Kemsley, the newspaper millionaire, for £40,000. It was sold by his family in 1963 and sub-leased to the Royal Society of Medicine in 1964. What would this beautiful building be worth today—perhaps £500,000?

Another great development was Portland Place, a 'street of

palaces', designed by the Adam brothers in 1773. The only entrance to this wonderful street was then a gateway facing Marylebone Road and the peaceful meadows by Marylebone Park. It was like a collection of country mansions on the edge of London.

The village people must have been amazed at the things they saw and heard. Close to all this wonder and wealth was the world of prostitution, Marylebone's underworld, between Oxford Street and Euston Road, lying east of Portland Place. In a book by a Prussian author called *A Picture of England*, published in 1789, we are told with authority that 50,000 prostitutes practised in London, and 13,000 of these were living in Marylebone. The best and most successful ladies of pleasure owned or rented their own houses for the entertainment of friends and admirers. About 1,700 Marylebone houses were used in this way.

One lady in particular, Kitty Fisher, was painted many times by Sir Joshua Reynolds, and remembered for her wit and beauty many years after her death. She died at the age of twenty-six unfortunately, but our author tells us with relish:

This priestess knew her value, and she exacted an hundred guineas for every night spent in her arms. The late Duke of York, brother of the present king, made one offering at her shrine. When he left her in the morning, he gave her a bank note for fifty pounds, which was all he had about him. This present offended Miss Fisher, who ordered her servants, before he was out of hearing, to tell him when he called again that she was not at home; to show the contempt she had for his present, she ate the note on her bread and butter for breakfast.

No doubt all these happenings in Marylebone were watched with disapproval by the Wesley brothers, John and Charles, the preachers and do-gooders who tried so hard to bring about reforms in the eighteenth century.

Charles, the most lovable of the two, lived with his pretty wife and family at 1 Chesterfield Street, and frequently rode his horse through the village, writing hymns in his head as he trotted down the High Street, leaping from the saddle to demand paper and pen from surprised villagers. He wrote hymns quickly, like a pop music writer today. His best and most popular hymns are known to most of us very well. It is pleasing to remember, as we sing or listen to "Hark, the Herald Angels Sing" or "Jesu, Lover of my Soul", that these hymns by Charles were most likely composed on his horse, in

Marylebone, where he lived and died. He was buried, as we know, in the graveyard of the village church.

At the time when Charles was writing his unforgettable hymns, and trotting his horse up and down the village High Street, not a week went by without a hanging at Tyburn. All could see the love and kindness which led the two Methodist preachers again and again to ride on a dirty cart, intended for criminals, with their arms round the men and women to be publicly hanged. They prayed and sang with them until the moment of death. Charles, the gentle composer of hymns, found the strength to do this for many terrified human beings until at last the gallows were removed in 1783.

In that same year, 1783, the much discussed 'Prinny' came of age, and the villagers of Marylebone, astonished by so many changes all around them, were now to see the greatest change of all. 'Prinny' was a handsome young man with an eye for the ladies. His tutor, Bishop Richard Hurd, said of the Prince of Wales that he would be "either the most polished gentleman or the most accomplished blackguard in Europe—possibly both".

His father, King George III, disliked him intensely, resenting his wit and charm almost as much as his extravagance, and was understandably annoyed when 'Prinny' made friends with Sheridan and associated himself with the Whig party. When he came of age he secured an income of £50,000 a year. Better still, £10,000 was voted by Parliament to pay his debts and start a separate establishment at Carlton House.

His first adventure was a love affair with an actress. Then the romantic 'Prinny' fell seriously and deeply in love with Mrs Fitzherbert, a Roman Catholic lady of impeccable character, a wealthy widow older than himself. 'Prinny' was then twenty-two, extremely attractive, and the lady was twenty-seven. Mrs Fitzherbert had nothing to gain from the Prince of Wales and at first resisted him, but she was tempted to marry him secretly for the simple reason that she loved him. He went to live with her in Brighton and the nine years which followed were the happiest in 'Prinny's' life.

'Prinny's' story was well known in Marylebone. In June 1794 he left Mrs Fitzherbert, the greatest mistake he ever made, it was said afterwards. Partly he did it to pay his debts, and partly to please Lady Jersey, who wished him to make an official marriage with a Protestant princess from Germany. This was, of course, Princess Caroline of Brunswick. She was far from attractive by 'Prinny's' standards, coarse and not very clean, yet in 1795 the marriage took place. It had to take place because 'Prinny's' father would not pay his debts unless it took place. After the birth of Princess Charlotte, their only child, 'Prinny' insisted on a formal separation.

In 1800 he returned to his true love, Mrs Fitzherbert. Ten years later his relations with Lady Hertford brought a final separation from Mrs Fitzherbert, and now there was little sympathy for 'Prinny'. Like Sheridan, he was never faithful, and yet always dominated by one woman.

In the village of Marylebone he was probably better understood than anywhere else. His yellow carriage was a common sight for the villagers. He was both admired and criticized. It was known that 'Prinny' was planning to give Marylebone the white graceful houses which stand in a semicircle round the lake in Regent's Park, and inspiring John Nash to build Regent Street, and hoping to drive his magnificent horses on a fine wide highway leading from Carlton House to a fabulous summer palace in the park. At the same time, he was visiting Hertford House, in Manchester Square, almost every day, wet or fine, in order to make love to Lady Hertford.

Nowadays, when we visit the Wallace Collection, we forget the story of Hertford House. It is filled with valuables, priceless mirrors and paintings, exquisite furniture, china, glass, and beautiful clocks. The rooms are so laden with riches and silence that the noise of London is forgotten. It is difficult to realize that here, in this peaceful house, now a museum, sleepily patrolled by grey-headed commissionaires, guarding their treasures like elderly spaniels, 'Prinny' used to breakfast, lunch and dine with Lady Hertford, leaving his yellow carriage at the door, so that everyone knew what was happening.

Marylebone was shocked by his behaviour. What made it worse, apparently, was that 'Prinny' and his new lady were both, to put it mildly, rather substantial, not to say fat. Somehow this put the lid on it. The cartoonists got busy and poor 'Prinny' became the object of ridicule and dislike. Had they both been thin the lovers might perhaps have been forgiven on grounds of romance, but a couple of middle-aged heavyweights—this was too much, even for Marylebone!

True, he was still called the "First Gentleman of Europe", but the charming 'Prinny' became very unpopular. There was a contemporary print satirizing the fat lovers entitled "Manchester Square Cattle Show". There was also a verse by Tom Moore, which was read by 'Prinny's' critics in Marylebone with malicious pleasure.

Through Manchester Square took a canter just now—
  Met the *old yellow chariot*, and made a low bow.
This I did, of course, thinking 'twas loyal and civil
  But got such a look, oh, 'twas black as the devil!
How unlucky!—incog: he was travelling about,
  And I, like a noodle, must go find him out!
Mem: When next by the *old yellow chariot* I ride
  To remember there *is* nothing princely inside.

The villagers of Marylebone were fond of 'Prinny', but they had
no love for Queen Caroline, his rejected queen. She was admired in
the village of Hammersmith but not in Marylebone. For many
years this uncouth woman had rampaged round Europe with
Bergami, the Italian servant who became her lover, and now she
wished to be crowned in the abbey and take her place as the reigning
queen of England. The villagers were thankful when Caroline was
turned away from the abbey. Can such a happening be imagined
today? Even in the permissive age?

'Prinny's' life ended in June 1830. His last love was Lady
Conyngham, an Irish beauty, older than himself like most of his
mistresses, and fatter! It was still said that his greatest love had been
Mrs Fitzherbert, and this he confirmed in his will. Knowing the story
of 'Prinny', it is impossible to pass Hertford House, in Manchester
Square, without thinking of him. He detested thin women and ugly
buildings. He left his royal mark upon Marylebone as King Charles
II left his upon Chelsea.

In the dull Victorian period which followed, Charles Dickens lived
for eleven years at 1 Devonshire Terrace, a charming house at the
north corner of the High Street (1839–50). He was twenty-seven years
old when the house was obtained. He lived with his wife, Kate, and
her teenager sister, Georgina, with a manservant and four maids. He
entertained a great deal. He was already famous as the author of
The Pickwick Papers, *Oliver Twist*, and *Nicholas Nickleby*, and he
seems to have enjoyed his social success.

Mrs Gaskell describes an evening with Dickens at 1 Devonshire
Terrace. (recently demolished):

In the evening quantities of other people came in. We were by
this time up in the drawing room, which is not nearly so pretty or
so home-like as the study. Frank Stone the artist, Leech and his
wife, Benedict the great piano-forte player, Sim Reeves the singer,
Thackery, Lord Dudley Stuart, Lord Headfort, Lady Yonge,
Lady Lovelace. . . . We heard some beautiful music. . . . There

were some nice little Dickens' children in the room—who were so polite and well trained.

Dickens wrote his most famous novels in the village of Marylebone, including *The Old Curiosity Shop, Barnaby Rudge, Martin Chuzzlewit, Dombey and Son,* and *David Copperfield.* He entertained his friends with private readings from his own books. He loved his sixteen-year-old sister-in-law who tragically died. He quarrelled with his wife and finally shocked his friends by leaving her. Late in life he fell in love with a young actress. All these traumatic happenings took place in Marylebone, a village which Dickens appears to have loved and hated.

Here is his description, for example, of Harley Street in *Little Dorrit*—or is it just another attack on the black respectability of the Victorian age? Dickens writes, as though with his lip curled: "Like unexceptional Society the opposing rows of houses in Harley Street were very grim with one another. Indeed the mansions and their inhabitants were so much alike in that respect that the people were often to be found drawn up on opposite sides of dinner tables, in the shade of their own loftiness, staring at the other side of the way with the dullness of the houses."

Today most of us love the solemn serenity of those simple, dignified, well-designed houses, like a line of brown-faced soldiers, undismayed by bombs, unimpressed by skyscrapers, unmoved by change. We find it hard to understand what annoyed Dickens.

Oddly enough Disraeli had the same reaction to the gentle brown brick houses in Harley Street. They have been taken over now, as everyone knows, by the medical profession. Londoners are proud of this well-preserved street in Marylebone. From Harley Street Swift dated some of his letters to Stella. From Harley Street William Pitt wrote his mother an account of his father's funeral. Later Lady Nelson died (4th May 1831) in Harley Street, not a stone's throw from Cavendish Square, where Nelson brought her as a happy bride. No. 7 (now 16) was for many years the home of Admiral Alexander Hood, Lord Bridport, who died in 1814.

It is interesting to find Disraeli writing like this:

Marylebone alone ought to have produced a revolution in our domestic architecture. It did nothing. It was built by Act of Parliament. Parliament even prescribed a facade. It is Parliament to whom we are indebted for your Harley Streets and Wimpole Streets and all those flat, dull spiritless streets, resembling each

Keats's House, Hampstead. In the garden, sitting beneath a plum tree, Keats wrote his famous *Ode to a Nightingale*

(left) John Keats. At one time the reviews were so bad that he seriously thought he would stop writing poetry, but his Hampstead friends encouraged him

(right) Fanny Brawne was born and bred in Hampstead. John Keats, who lived in the same house, loved her to distraction

(left) Nell Gwynne, favourite of Charles II, who spent much time
with him at Lauderdale House, in the village of Highgate
(right) Samuel Taylor Coleridge arrived in Highgate with the proofs
of Christabel in his bag and he lived there for eighteen years

Kenwood in 1781. This beautiful estate near the village of Highgate,
was once owned by Lord Mansfield

other like a large family of plain children with Portland Place and Portman Square for their respectable parents.

Dickens and Disraeli were both very critical. What would they have written about the huge and hideous modern buildings, like egg boxes, which spoil the London skyline, and where men and women are expected to live and work today?

The home of Dickens was very close to the large and fashionable church where Robert Browning and Elizabeth Barrett were secretly married. The little church has gone, but the big church is there still. Dickens must have been pleased when he heard the story of Robert and Elizabeth. They were deeply in love, and the elopement of two poets must have added spice to the boring tenor of existence, especially for Dickens, who had been living in the village for six years when it happened. One can imagine him talking it over with Wilkie Collins, who lived nearby at 17 Hanover Terrace.

Turner, the painter, made famous by Ruskin, who first described his remarkable work in *Modern Painters*, lived at 23 Queen Anne Street, near Cavendish Square. This was his official address for twenty-seven years.

Yet another Victorian celebrity was Anthony Trollope, who lived for eight years at 39 Montagu Square, settling there in 1872. An elderly man, he still rode to hounds, and exercised his horse in the park, driving about Marylebone in a brougham.

At about this time Marylebone gave way to Chelsea as the home of artists and writers. The great folk were turning to Belgravia, another fashionable development, perhaps not quite so beautiful as Marylebone but nearer to Buckingham Palace. There were further changes ahead. Society was now waiting for Edward, Prince of Wales, frustrated by his mother as 'Prinny' had been by his father. He came to London at the turn of the century (just as 'Prinny' had done).

Edward, like 'Prinny', was a lovable character. Alexandra, his lovely wife, bore him six children within seven years, then she became extremely ill, at the age of twenty-six, and the royal couple had no more children. Apart from a firm refusal to be faithful, he was a good husband and treated Alexandra with affection and consideration. The people adored her. Indeed each infidelity made Alexandra more lovable in the public eye—and there were many infidelities. The whole of London knew about the Countess of Warwick and Mrs

Keppel and Miss Keyser, not to mention the Princesse de Sagan and countless other ladies.

"But I was the one he loved best," said Alexandra, which was probably true.

During the 'naughty nineties' the gay prince, known as 'Bertie', seems to have been surprisingly popular. Even Charlotte Brontë unexpectedly said: "I like high life, I like its manners, its splendours, the beings which move in its enchanted sphere."

As for Princess Alexandra, her beauty and charm and purity, even her deafness when she grew older, endeared her to all. In the village of Marylebone she was very much loved. It was known that she had a platonic love affair which lasted for twenty-five years with Oliver Montagu (younger son of Lord Sandwich). Everyone understood, and respected her feelings, including her affectionate Bertie.

He was aged fifty-eight when he met Alice Keppel. He saw her first in the year 1898. In the same year he met Miss Agnes Keyser (until then a respectable middle-aged lady, the matron of a hospital) but when he became king his favourite mistress was still Mrs Keppel, and she remained his favourite for the last twelve years of his life. Her husband raised no objection, neither did Queen Alexandra, who accepted her as a friend. The Keppels (who lived in Portman Square at one time) were often invited to stay with the king and queen at Sandringham.

And so, when the king died in April 1910, in Buckingham Palace, it was not surprising that nearly everyone, young and old, rich and poor, went into black. Alexandra led Mrs Keppel into the king's room to say goodbye. The nation mourned for Edward. Town houses were closed and their owners, including Mrs Keppel, retired sadly to the country to rest and recover.

At the time of writing Alexandra is still remembered by at least one of the Marylebone villagers. This is Mooney, or Mrs Moone, for many years the owner of a public house called The Dover Castle, in Weymouth Mews, near Portland Place.

Mooney was born in The Dover Castle. It faced a row of cottages used as stables by the great houses in Portland Place and Mooney, from the bedroom window, could see the magnificent carriages and horses, the grooms and ostlers, the pot-bellied coachmen wearing their tall cockaded hats. They all came to The Dover Castle, where her father served them with rum. Her father had once been a proud butler to the Duke of Marlborough, and Mooney had a wonderful story about something which happened at Balmoral.

Mooney's father, because he had the honour to be the duke's butler, was standing at the foot of the great staircase. Near him stood King Edward. Guests were waiting in one of the drawing rooms and the queen, as usual, was much behind time.

At last Alexandra appeared at the top of the staircase, small and exquisite, a Dresden-china shepherdess. She descended slowly and gracefully to her fuming husband. The king said: "Madam, you are late."

Alexandra whipped out the most enormous fan which had ever been seen, and replied, with great dignity: "Do not forget, I am *ze queen*!"

Mooney had another good story about Alexandra. One afternoon, in Portland Place, when 'Mooney' was returning from school, she suddenly noticed the royal carriage approaching, on its way to Regent's Park, where the queen often went for an afternoon drive. Mooney was aged about eight. Like everyone else she worshipped Alexandra and in her excitement, because she was trying to see the queen's beautiful face, the little girl tripped, and fell off the pavement, tearing her long black stockings, and found herself lying in the gutter just when the royal carriage passed. Mooney began to cry. The queen noticed the little girl and ordered the carriage to stop. The groom descended and the little girl was picked up and comforted while the queen waited to know if all was well.

When it was over, Mooney ran all the way home to tell her father what a wonderful thing had just happened. She had torn her stockings but she had seen the queen's beautiful face, and the queen had stopped her carriage out of pity for Mooney.

This little story has been repeated many times in The Dover Castle. Many people can remember the bombing sessions and doodle-bugs in World War II, and Mooney serving us with drinks, making us laugh. She loved telling us about Queen Alexandra. We loved listening to her stories.

Mooney has now departed, but The Dover Castle (which must be the oldest and smallest public house in Marylebone) still provides a good cheap meal. Let us hope it will be spared to us by the planners and improvers and developers.

Marylebone is now an extremely respectable and expensive place in which to live, both rich and smart. Today the village has developed a style of its own which is not very easy to analyse—with its orderly houses round Harley Street, with its ambience of rolled umbrellas, white collars, consulting rooms, and stethoscopes. Marylebone is still London's most fashionable village. It has the charm and dignity of an elderly woman with a past—sedate, well preserved, inscrutable—an ageing courtesan, a forgotten *femme fatale*.

MARYLEBONE LOCAL HISTORY
Recommended Books

The Great Folk of Old Marylebone, Mrs Baillie Saunders (Henry J. Glaisher, 1904)

A Topographical and Historical Account of the Parish of St Maryle-Bone, Thomas Smith (1833)

Regent's Park, Ann Saunders (David & Charles, Newton Abbot, 1969)

Marylebone, Gordon Mackenzie (St Martin's Press, 1972)

Roundabout Harley Street, C. P. Bryan (John Bale, Sons, & Danielson Ltd, 1932)

7

Hampstead

The heart of Hampstead village is, of course, the parish church. It seems to belong in this peaceful place, to grow from the ground of Hampstead, like the silvery groups of soft crumbling tombstones and ancient small trees. A church has been standing here for at least 900 years. It began life in the time of William the Conqueror, as a small chapel, a meeting place for the villagers, but the years went by and at last, in the eighteenth century, they finally decided the parish church was falling to pieces. In 1745 the old building was demolished and a fine new building with a white and gold centre, rather like an exquisite drawing room, appeared as though by magic in the same position, on the same piece of ground.

It was approached then, as it is now, by a double row of eighteenth-century houses, prim and polite, where lived the most important people of the village. Beautiful trees, including a very old cedar, close to the church, gave a deep impression of peace and serenity. They still do. In spite of the ebb and flow of small cars and motor cycles the peace of Church Row can still be felt. In the High Street the traffic roars, the road drill screams, the teenagers yell, the babies shriek, but nothing from the noisy village seems to penetrate the calm and serenity which is here. It is still, and perhaps always will be, a little select place, a retreat from ugliness and uproar.

The present Church of St John is dignified and aristocratic and elegant. It has the style of the eighteenth century. It is difficult to remember that it took the place of a little humble chapel, in the Manor of Hamstede, which belonged to the monks of Westminster from the year 986 until the Dissolution of the Monasteries in 1539.

In the old days, the parish priest had always lived and entertained at the manor house (Hall Grange) and was visited there by the hale and hearty monks, the well-fed abbots, who directed and supervised this pretty village up in the hills. The manor house stood at the corner of what is now Frognal Lane (once West End Lane) facing the church on the opposite side of the road.

On the north side lay Windmill Hill, where the villagers took their corn to grind. The Frognal brook ran rapidly down the steep decline, into the cattle pond, which lay between the church and Hall Grange.

At that time Hall Grange served the village as police court, town hall, hospital and hotel. The monks looked after the villagers and controlled the farming of the land. Frognal was by far the most important part of the parish.

But the manor house, as we know, was taken from the monks by King Henry VIII, and was given by his son, Edward VI, to a favourite gentleman attendant. His name was Sir Thomas Wroth. He became Lord of the Manor of Hampstead about 1551.

The villagers continued to meet on Sunday mornings at the little Chapel of the Blessed Mary, now becoming very old and dilapidated. The manor passed to the third Earl of Gainsborough, and then to Sir William Langhorne, a wealthy gentleman who bought it from the earl. Sir William was an East-India merchant. When he became Lord of the Manor, the villagers appealed to him to build them a new church. They said the old one was dangerously rotten, the walls unsafe, the woodwork full of worm.

Sir William took no notice of this touching appeal and at first the villagers were greatly disappointed. However, he was not so hard hearted as he seemed, and at his death, in 1715, he bequeathed the village the sum of £1,000 for a new church. In 1744, when the old building was near to falling down, a subscription list made it possible for the villagers to get what they wanted, and the church we have today came into being. So did Church Row. In a few years time, to the surprise and delight of the villagers, Church Row became a meeting place for London society. The village of Hampstead became as fashionable in its way as the village of Marylebone.

It is strange how little we Londoners know about London. How many know, for example, that Hampstead in the eighteenth century was called Hampstead Wells? It was then, like Tunbridge Wells, a famous health resort, a fashionable spa, a meeting place for ladies and gentlemen who dosed themselves daily with chalybeate water from the famous well in Well Walk.

On Sunday mornings, after saying their prayers together, they paraded their silks and satins in Church Row, arm in arm, flirting and coquetting, exchanging witty remarks, to be repeated, they hoped in aristocratic drawing rooms and bedrooms for many weeks to come.

Today we still have a handsome fountain in Well Walk. It has no well water, and few people know why it is there, never having heard about Hampstead Wells. It is a memorial to the Earl of Gainsborough from his grateful village, and it reads like this:

> To the memory of the honourable Susanne Noel, who with her son Baptist, Third Earl of Gainsborough, gave this well with six acres of land to the use and benefit of the poor of Hampstead, Dec. 20th, 1698.

It was the earl and his mother who brought prosperity to the village of Hampstead, which now became known as Hampstead Wells. It happened suddenly, a quick change of fortune, and it never would have happened but for the Earl of Gainsborough, then a child, who was Lord of the Manor, and was instructed by his mother to help the poor people of Hampstead with a gift of land. Six acres of marshy land were offered to the villagers and gratefully accepted. At first no one in the village had a clear idea what should be done with the earl's unexpected gift, but they knew what to do when the famous chalybeate spring was discovered in Well Walk. The words carved on the fountain are filled with meaning. We know how it all happened and we still feel grateful to the Earl of Gainsborough, who rescued the village. In order to help the poor, as his mother wished, an advertisement was placed in the *Postman*, 18th April 1700. It started a new train of thought. Readers were informed about the wonderful chalybeate waters which were, they now discovered: "of the same nature and equal in virtue with Tunbridge Wells and highly approved by most of the eminent physicians of the college, as likewise by many of the gentry who formerly used to drink Tunbridge Waters".

Today we would call this a publicity stunt, which indeed it was. Newspaper stories, giving fascinating details, soon followed. Readers were told that the Hampstead water was easy to obtain. It had miraculous qualities and would cure almost anything.

Every day it was

> carefully bottled up in flasks and sent to Mr Phelps Apothocary at the Eagle and Child, Fleet Street, every morning at the rate of 3d. per flask, and if any person desires to have them brought to their own houses, they will be conveyed to them upon their leaving a note at Mr Phelps' aforesaid at 1d. more, and to

prevent any person being imposed upon the true waters are nowhere else to be procured unless they are sent to the Wells at Hampstead, and the said Mr Phelps to prevent Counterfeits hath ordered his servants to deliver to each person who comes for any of the waters aforesaid, a sealed ticket viz: a wolf rampant with 7 Crosslets. Note! the messengers that come for the waters must take care to return the flasks daily.

Today we still have the Flask Tavern, in Flask Walk, and this is the place where the mineral waters were bottled. The old original tavern has now been replaced but the new one keeps the name. At the time of writing it is a good public house, serving lunch, where writers and actors often meet for a drink.

When these things were happening to the old village the Earl of Gainsborough was much loved. It was a peaceful period. The villagers had recovered from the Civil Wars between King Charles I and Oliver Cromwell. They had lost Sir Harry Vane, who had lived in a fine house called Belmont. No one quite understood if the good Sir Harry had preferred the Cavaliers to the Roundheads, or the Roundheads to the Cavaliers, but at length he was taken away by the soldiers of the king and executed at the Tower of London.

Quite soon, in Well Walk, new buildings began to appear, a ballroom, called an Assembly Room, then a Pump Room, then a tavern. A clever gentleman called John Duffield took charge of the new developments.

Indeed John Duffield was Hampstead's first property developer. He leased the property for seven years with a new lease for twenty-one years by extension. It was Duffield who built the Assembly Room, at the north end of which was a large basin for the use of ladies and gentlemen taking the mineral waters. This part of the building seems to have been divided by a partition from the other, and was known as the Pump Room.

We are told that the Pump Room measured about 36 feet by 30 feet, leaving an Assembly Room of 60 feet by 36 feet. Not far from the tavern a new chapel appeared, known as Sion Chapel, and this was followed by some new shops. Gardens were laid out, and these included a large bowling green. Here is a typical advertisement which appeared in the *Postman*, dated 9th September 1701.

In the Great Room at Hampstead Wells on Monday next being the 15th inst. Exactly at 11 o'clock of the forenoon will be performed a Consort of vocal and instrumental Musick by the best Masters, and at the request of several gentlemen, Jemmy Bowen will perform several songs and particular performances on the violin by two several masters. Tickets to be had at the Wells and at St Stephen's Coffee House in King St, Bloomsbury at 1s. per ticket. There will be dancing in the afternoon as usual.

In another advertisement of slightly later date it is stated that: "1s. will be the price of the tickets by reason that the room will hold 500 persons."

The clever John Duffield continued for twenty years to provide whatever was wanted in Hampstead. Ladies and gentlemen arrived and took the waters in the early morning. The "consorts" of music began at 10 a.m. In the afternoon and evening there was always music, dancing and card playing for the ladies. If the gentlemen preferred outdoor amusements they went to the bowling green or strolled over the heath to Ken Wood, or to see Mother Hough, said to be a good fortune teller.

Meanwhile, sad to say, the poor people of Hampstead were receiving no benefit whatever from the gift of the Earl of Gainsborough. John Duffield was still making a great deal of money, but Hampstead was gaining a bad name, and Well Walk was becoming notorious.

Daniel Defoe wrote, in 1724: "But as there is (especially at the Wells) a Conflux of all Sorts of Company, even Hampstead itself has suffered in its good name; and you see sometimes more Gallentry than Modesty; so that the ladies who value their Reputation, have of late more avoided the Wells and Walks at Hampstead, than they formerly had done."

In the end, the villagers were rescued from John Duffield. After several tedious law cases the reputation of Hampstead was saved and Well Walk was reformed. New Assembly Rooms were built. Prices were raised. A guinea subscription admitted a gentleman and two ladies to the ballroom every other Monday. Admittance to non-subscribers was half-a-crown each night.

Hampstead Wells became even more amusing than Marylebone Gardens, and as fashionable as Ranelagh Gardens in Chelsea. The village was now more prosperous than ever before. It was patronized until his death by the great Alexander Pope, who brought his friend Mr Gay, author of *The Beggar's Opera*, not to mention Jonathan Swift, Fanny Burney, Dr Johnson, and numerous lords and ladies from London.

The little crippled figure of Alexander Pope, frail and bent, hiding his thin legs with three pairs of stockings, soon became as well known in Hampstead as in Chiswick. In the village of Marylebone he was ridiculed by some, feared by others, after his battle of wits with Lady Mary Wortley Montagu. In Battersea he was at first loved and then detested owing to his treatment of Lord Bolingbroke.

In Hampstead we see him at his best. He was still a young man, aged thirty-four, when he decided to nurse his friend back to health by bringing him to Hampstead Wells. John Gay was the one person he seems to have trusted and deeply loved. He did as much as anybody to increase the standing of Hampstead which now became more select and stylish and social than ever before or since.

The friends arrived in the year 1722. Pope was visiting Hampstead for health reasons and brought John Gay with him by order of Dr Arbuthnot. The village was flattered by the visit of two such well-known literary men. Two years previously Gay had made the large sum of £1,000 by publication of his poems. Unfortunately he had lost the whole of his fortune by investment in the South Sea Bubble. Pope was full of sympathy. He managed to restore his friend's health, and Gay, while in Hampstead, managed to write a tragedy called *The Captive*. Later the play was produced at Drury Lane by request of Caroline, Princess of Wales.

John Gay was a man who made friends as easily as Alexander Pope made enemies. His expenses at Hampstead were paid by the Duchess of Queensberry, who seems to have loved him as Pope loved him. His age was thirty-seven, and the duchess, only twenty-two, was happily married but extremely generous and affectionate. Later, about 1727, Gay joined her household as a permanent guest and while there, to give her pleasure, he wrote his most famous work, *The Beggar's Opera*, in which Sir Robert Walpole was satirized. It was an immediate success.

Gay continued to live with the duchess, who persuaded him not to squander his money as before. In a private letter to Jonathan Swift he wrote: "To the lady I live with I owe my life and fortune, she has so much goodness, virtue and generosity I have pleasure in obeying her."

Ten years after Pope had nursed him back to life at Hampstead Wells, Pope wrote to Jonathan Swift in Dublin with the news of his friend's death. He said in his letter: "In every friend we lose a part of ourselves, and the best part."

The lovable John Gay was buried in Westminster Abbey, where a monument to his memory was created by his many patrons and

friends. The epitaph on his tomb is by Pope and is followed by Gay's
own mocking couplet:

> Life is a jest, and all things show it,
>   I thought so once, and now I know it.

Meanwhile, the village of Hampstead grew accustomed to the sad
little figure of Pope, by this time the most feared man in literary
London. After losing John Gay, he continued to visit Hampstead
until 1744, sometimes coming with William Murray, afterwards Lord
Mansfield, who became Chief Justice and finally bought the mansion
and fine estate of Kenwood Place. Today, of course, it is open to the
public.

As Pope died in 1744 he never saw the parish church as it is now.
(It was rebuilt in 1745–7.) Among his friends who visited the church,
and admired it as we do, were Sir Joshua Reynolds, Gainsborough,
Oliver Goldsmith, David Garrick, Jonathan Swift, and the dainty
little fop, Colley Cibber (bordering on eighty but still gallant to a
lady).

Fanny Burney, by the way, described Hampstead in *Evelina*, a
charming book which gave Fanny her position in English literature
as first woman novelist.

At the time of writing Hampstead is London's only village which
has been allowed to keep and cherish such a large number of
beautiful old houses, and most of them date back to the eighteenth
century. On Sunday mornings the ladies who lived in them might be
carried to church in sedan chairs. After the service, weather permitting, they might promenade in their rustling silks, up and down
Church Row, before returning by chair to their homes—sometimes
in other parts of London.

At night the illuminated houses in Church Row, lit and made
lovely by glowing link lights, were a pleasing sight for ladies and
gentlemen, returning by carriage, or lingering for a few moments of
love, when the Assembly Room had at last been closed. The night-
watchman, with his lantern, moving in the shadows, would be heard
to cry, in comforting tones, from the half darkness, beneath the
trees, like the cry of an owl: "All's Well! All's Well!"

The Hampstead church is different from most other churches for
the chancel was placed on the west side of the building, not on the
east. The change was made in 1745 owing to the crowds of visitors
who settled in the village to be near the Assembly Rooms in Well

Walk. For this reason the main doors were deliberately switched to the east wall of the church, opening into Church Row and leading into the village.

Then as now, Church Row was considered the most delightful place to live. At No. 8 Church Row, a house with a high iron gate, lived Mrs Anna Barbauld, from 1785 till the end of the century. This was an interesting lady, beautiful and gifted. Her volume of poems was published in 1779. It was admired, apparently, by Charles James Fox, Wordsworth, and Garrick. Later she wrote a biography of Samuel Richardson.

However, she seems to have annoyed the more amusing Fanny Burney, who speaks a little unkindly of her "set smile, her air of determined complacency and prepared acquiescence, also a sweetness which never risks being off its guard". There must have been a grain of truth in this feminine observation for Mrs Chapone said of her to Miss Burney: "She is a very good young woman, as well as replete with talent, but why must one always smile so?"

The permanently smiling Mrs Barbauld got on the nerves of both these ladies. On the other hand, she was a friend of Mrs Elizabeth Montagu (then living in Marylebone) and she trained the sons of several well-known families, including Lord Dunman, Lord Chief Justice. Evidently she had something to smile about!

Miss Lucy Aiken, niece to Mrs Barbauld, lived in No. 18 Church Row (just opposite) from 1830 till 1844. Lucy Aiken published a life of her father, one of her mother, and another of her aunt, Mrs Barbauld. She was the author of a mammoth work entitled *Memoirs of the Courts of Queen Elizabeth, of James I, and of Charles I*. It was published in six volumes and was warmly recommended by Lord Macauley. It occupied her for fifteen years and was mostly written at her house in Church Row. At her death she was buried in the churchyard.

The Church Row celebrities are numerous. They include Wilkie Collins, who lived at No. 25, and John James Park, Hampstead's first historian. (Notice the plaque at No. 18.) We are told about two sisters called Gillies. Miss Margaret was a painter who once painted a portrait of Wordsworth. (Her sister was a writer.) Then there was Bishop Selwyn, remembered for his work in New Zealand as a missionary, who lived in No. 21 from 1813 till 1817.

Better still, we know that Austen Dobson lived in Church Row. His biography of Hogarth was published in 1891, that of Richardson in 1902, that of Fanny Burney in 1903. George Du Maurier (afterwards in New Grove House) lived in Church Row in the late 1860s, and while there he developed his skill as a 'black-and-white' artist. Last but not least, H. G. Wells lived at No. 17 Church Row. One wonders what the neighbours thought of him?

Perhaps the most fascinating and 'villagey' bit of Hampstead is behind and above the church, those steep and winding lanes and narrow walks leading to Holly Hill and Windmill Hill, an undisturbed circle, protected by trees and gardens and walls, where every house and every cottage seems to speak of the eighteenth century.

The house of the famous painter, George Romney, is still there at the top of Holly Hill. Opposite is Bolton House, once lived in by Joanna Baillie, the writer friend of Walter Scott and Wordsworth.

Higher up, in Hampstead Grove, stands the magnificent Fenton House (open to visitors) with its beautiful enclosed garden, and its two engaging little statues, a pretty shepherdess, still being courted by a slightly indecent young shepherd, whose flies are still undone.

The cottages on the other side are equally charming. Right at the top, leaving behind the admiral's house (once lived in by the architect, Sir George Gilbert Scott, and painted by Constable) and also Grove Lodge, the house of John Galsworthy, we find a mysterious house on the edge of the heath, at the summit of Windmill Hill. It seems to have a different personality, an indefinable feminine air, a perfume from the past. It is Capo Di Monte, home of the great Sarah Siddons in 1803. There is no plaque here, but the date is given, with a large ornamental letter "S", above the door. A very nice house indeed, but not like any other. It must have been loved by Sarah Siddons.

Hampstead has always been an ideal village for artists. When the great George Romney came to Holly Hill, at the end of the eighteenth century, he was about sixty-six years old, a tired and discontented man, at that time suffering from depression and declining health. Artists and writers were now becoming much more important in the village than lords and ladies.

Romney, of course, was a man of fashion. The villagers knew that the painter had lived for twenty years in princely luxury in Cavendish Square in Marylebone. Emma Hamilton had long been his model as well as his mistress. As an artist he was a rival to Gainsborough, and also to his enemy, Joshua Reynolds.

In the village, they soon heard his story, and enjoyed repeating it. It was known to every gossip that Romney had left a wife and two children in a village in the Lake District. He seems to have repented while in Hampstead. After thinking it over for two more years he decided to return to his wife as though nothing at all had happened. He returned home after thirty-seven years. Incredibly enough his wife forgave him, and nursed him until he died.

Not far from Romney's beautiful house there lived another world famous painter, in style the most English of them all. This was John Constable, who stayed for about six years at No. 2 Lower Terrace. In 1827 he and his family moved into Well Walk, a house they retained until his death. It is now rebuilt, and numbered 44, and honoured with a blue plaque.

In the village John Constable soon became popular. The villagers understood the cheerful Mr Constable better than the sad Mr Romney.

Three of Constable's best pictures are Hampstead subjects and they hang in the Tate Gallery. They are "Hampstead Heath", "The Grove, Admiral's House", and "Hampstead Heath with Rainbow".

He once said: "I came to live in Hampstead that the beauties of nature be ever before me. I love every stile and stump and lane in the village, and, as long as I am able to hold a brush, I shall never cease to paint them."

He felt the spirit of the village as we feel it now in some of his pictures. No wonder he was liked by the villagers. It is difficult to believe but the truth is that Constable, in England, was not appreciated until after his death. He was almost forty years of age when he sold his first picture in England and he lived, we are told, by copying the works of other painters. His own work was considered too life-like!

At the age of fifty-two, when his wife inherited £50,000, he was able to hold his first important exhibition in London. In 1835 and 1836 he gave lectures in the Assembly Room at the back of Holly Bush Inn. In the end, Constable was brought from his London house and buried beside his wife in the much loved churchyard by the Hampstead Parish Church.

Joanna Baillie was a very different character. To most of us her name is unknown, but Joanna Baillie, in her time, was as famous as Jane Austen. She arrived with her mother and her sister Agnes from Bothwell, Lanarkshire, in 1802, and stayed in Hampstead for the rest of her life. It is easy to picture the Baillie family living in Bolton House (facing Mr Romney's house), a solid red brick building of extreme respectability. Joanna stayed there for forty-five years, and was buried, needless to say, in the churchyard.

As a writer she became known to Wordsworth, who walked to Windmill Hill across the fields from London to see the author of *Basil* and *De Montfort*—produced in 1800 by the Kembles at Drury Lane.

Sir Walter Scott said: "If you wish to speak of a real poet, Joanna Baillie, of Bothwell, is now the greatest genius of our country."

Walter Scott often visited Bolton House for the pleasure of a talk with Joanna. She was then a spinster lady of forty-four, living with Miss Agnes, her elder sister. She met Walter Scott through a third poet, Southey, and the friendship continued for the rest of her long life. They exchanged many letters. They visited one another in Scotland as well as Hampstead.

Another admirer was Lord Byron, who remarked: "Joanna Baillie is the only woman who can write a tragedy."

The gifted Joanna died at the age of eighty-nine after one day of illness. Miss Agnes died at the age of one hundred and one. Both sisters were buried beside their mother in the family grave, not far from the church they all knew so well.

It was now becoming a village of poets. While Wordsworth and Walter Scott were visiting Joanna at Bolton House, another celebrity, no less than the poet John Keats, was visiting Leigh Hunt's cottage in the Vale of Health. Indeed the villagers were surrounded by notable people who came to Hampstead to be near one another and to walk on the heath. At one time Byron lived next door to Leigh Hunt's cottage, and Shelley was said to be lodging in Pond Street, while Coleridge was driving over from the village of Highgate.

This was a wonderful period for lovers of English poetry. Inspiration was in the air. In Hampstead, for some reason, Leigh Hunt was the centre of a dazzling collection of poets.

Leigh Hunt was one of the first to see a great poet in Keats. He was himself an essayist and poet, but despised by the critics, and in 1808 he became editor of a journal called *The Examiner*. He was then sent to prison for two years following a cruel editorial attack on the Prince Regent. In fact he had annoyed 'Prinny' by calling him "a fat Adonis of fifty".

His imprisonment, luckily, seems to have brought Leigh Hunt a great deal of pleasure, for it gave him the friendship of Byron, Moore,

Brougham, and many others who came to see him in gaol. It seems that he never had a dull moment. Among his friends and visitors was Charles Cowden Clarke, who called at his home on the day of Hunt's release. Outside the house, looking nervous, Charles Cowden Clarke found Keats, an old schoolfellow, who put in his hand a sonnet entitled "On The Day Mr Hunt Left Prison".

On that day Keats was born, we might say, as a rising poet. Of course the sonnet was given to Leigh Hunt, who discovered him to be a medical student, aged twenty, and immediately became his friend.

Leigh Hunt had a profound influence on the young Keats. They seem to have understood one another, not at all disturbed by the difference in age and style. They both wished, like Wordsworth, to overthrow the 'classical' school of Alexander Pope. The central point was to write in a more free form than the heroic couplet. But Leigh Hunt and his devoted little circle in Hampstead became known as the 'Cockney School', and Keats was condemned in the eyes of the critics by his friendship with Hunt.

In 1817 Hunt and his friends arranged publication of the first book of poems by Keats. Later, when living in Well Walk, he began to compose *Endymion*. It was finished and published in 1818, and bitterly criticized in *Blackwood's Magazine* by Lockhart, the editor (son-in-law to Walter Scott) who despised Leigh Hunt and all his followers, including poor Keats.

The villagers of Hampstead were not judges of poetry. At this time they only knew that Keats and Shelley were new writers who belonged to the so-called 'Cockney School' which had gathered round the cottage of Leigh Hunt in the Vale of Health. Hunt's cottage, always crowded with visitors, was near the pond where Shelley used to sail his paper boats. Hunt's companions included William Hazlitt, Charles Lamb, Benjamin Haydon, C. W. Dilke, and John Hamilton Reynolds, but his favourite seems to have been the medical student, John Keats, so young, so small, so gifted.

When Keats was still living at Well Walk (to be near Hunt) he became friendly with Charles Wentworth Dilke and Charles Armitage Brown. These two enterprising young men had built themselves a pair of semi-detached houses, with a communal garden, calling it Wentworth Place.

It is now called Keats House, and is better known than any building in Hampstead. It is used as a small museum, a memorial to Keats, and is visited by tourists from every part of the world. Keats lived here, and worked in these small rooms. Some of us can

feel his presence as in Chelsea, in another sad house, we feel the
personality of Thomas Carlyle.

Here, in the main sitting room, he met Fanny Brawne for the first
time, and loved her, and later shared the house with Fanny, loving
her, separated from her, at first by the walls of their double home,
then by illness, and poverty, and finally by death. Poor Keats. Poor
Fanny. In these rooms so much youthful suffering came to them both.

When his brother died, Keats went to live with his new friend,
Charles Armitage Brown, who has given us a very good description
of what happened.

> Early next morning, [he writes] I was awakened in bed by a
> pressure on my hand. It was Keats who had come to tell me that
> his brother was no more. . . . I said nothing . . . at last, my
> thoughts returning from the dead to the living, I said, "Have
> nothing more to do with those lodgings, and alone too! Had you
> not better live with me?" He paused, pressed my hand warmly,
> and replied, "I think it would be better". From that moment he
> was my inmate.

So Keats went to live with his kind and sympathetic friend in
December 1818. He was twenty-three years old. He started work on
Hyperion. Fanny Brawne became known to him as a highly
conventional young lady who lived nearby. In 1819, between
February and June, all but one of the great "Odes" were written.
"On Indolence" was completed about 19th March, "On A Grecian
Urn" about 15th April and "To A Nightingale" a week or two later.

According to Brown it was this same nightingale "who built her
nest in our garden", and he gives us the following picture of his
friend and companion.

> Keats felt a tranquillity and continual joy in her song: and one
> morning he took his chair from the breakfast table to the grass-
> plot, where he sat for two or three hours. When he came into the
> house, I perceived that he had some scraps of paper in his hand,
> and these he was quietly thrusting behind the books. On enquiring,
> I found these scraps—four or five in number—contained his poetic
> feeling about our nightingale. The writing was not well legible:
> and it was difficult to arrange the stanzas . . . immediately
> afterwards I searched for more of his fugitive pieces. From that day
> he gave me permission to copy any verses he might write, and I
> fully availed myself of it. He cared so little for them himself when
> once his imagination was released from their influence.

The spring and summer of 1819 must have been the happiest time
in the poet's short life. At that time the ode which he decided to call

"To A Nightingale" was carelessly written, as Brown tells us, in the Hampstead garden, beneath a plum tree, where Keats often used to sit. By now Fanny Brawne was living with joy, and much laughter, in the other part of the house, occupied by her mother, sharing the garden with Keats and his friend. Today we can still see the mulberry tree, more than 300 years old, known so well to the young lovers, and a plum tree—not the original one—to mark the place where the nightingale poem was composed. Inside the house we can still see the actual bookcases where the poem was hidden by Keats and triumphantly discovered by Brown.

Keats loved to sit in the garden. He shaded himself from the hot summer sun beneath the thick dark leaves of the mulberry tree. During that golden summer, inspired by sunlight and love, surrounded by trees and flowers, he was able to write four of the five great odes, also "La Belle Dame Sans Merci", "Lamia", and several sonnets as well. "Ode to Autumn", the last of his great poems, was written during a visit with Brown to Winchester, after which his happiness ended.

The winter which followed, still in Hampstead, living so close to the laughter loving Fanny, aged nineteen, and yet hopelessly separated from her, was a time of bitter disappointment for Keats. For one thing, the reviews were so bad that he seriously thought he would give up writing poetry. Then his health became a problem. On 3rd February 1820 he had to endure the first attack of tuberculosis. Brown could see that he was unwell and sent him upstairs to his bed. Here is Brown's vivid description.

Before his head was on the pillow he slightly coughed, and I heard him say, "That is blood from my mouth". I went towards him: he was examining a single drop upon the sheet. "Bring me a candle, Brown, and let me see this blood." After regarding it steadfastly, he looked up in my face with a calmness of countenance I can never forget and said, "I know the colour of that blood—it is arterial blood—I cannot be deceived in that colour—that drop of blood is my death-warrant—I must die." I ran for a surgeon; my friend was bled; and at five in the morning I left him after he had been for some time in a quiet sleep.

The little quiet bedroom where all this happened seems peaceful enough when visited today. Downstairs, in the sitting room used by Brown, there is a chaise-longue, placed before the window. It is a copy of the original "sopha-bed" where Keats lay, writing notes and love letters to Fanny in the room behind the wall, so close to his own, not allowed the excitement of speaking to the girl he loved, hoping to catch sight of her, through the window, when she crossed the garden, or came with outstretched hand for his letters. They lived in one house but to Keats it seemed they were living in two different worlds.

His good friend Brown, who nursed him through illness and loved him as a brother, was unconsciously the cause of further suffering. Keats was twenty-four years of age. Brown, too, was young and virile, and was now spending happy nights with Abigail O'Donoghue, the Irish maid-of-all-work, while Keats, poor Keats, across the passage, was burning with love in his lonely bedroom, and Fanny, in another part of the house, was longing for Keats. She was puzzled by his despair. Even Brown, who seems to have been a happy-go-lucky character, blissfully giving his housemaid a child, was puzzled also.

In this little house of passion and frustration, where Keats wrote his best poems, the letters were written to Fanny Brawne which tell us of his agonizing loneliness and jealousy. He went so far as to offer Fanny her freedom, but Fanny refused. "I must impose chains upon myself," he wrote to her once.

At another time he left off eating meat, and explained this jokingly to his sister. "My brains," he told her, "may never henceforth be in a greater mist than is theirs by nature." To us it seems likely that Keats put himself on a low diet in the hope of lessening physical desire. He knew in his heart that marriage with Fanny was impossible. Neither Fanny nor his sister were able to understand.

When Brown went to Scotland in the month of May his unhappy friend took lodgings near Leigh Hunt at No. 2 Wesleyan Place, Kentish Town. Again he fell ill. Hunt moved him to his own house, and nursed him. On 12th August, after quarrelling with Hunt because one of Fanny's precious letters had been opened and read by mistake, he returned in a mood of misery to the little house in Hampstead.

Brown was still away, and Brown's rooms had been let, so Mrs Brawne, Fanny's mother, took pity on the tragic young man who was now so close to death. For a time he was nursed by his beloved Fanny, no longer separated from her, yet unable to consummate his love, existing from day to day, between sunlight and sadness. At last he was ordered by the doctors to leave Hampstead and live in Italy.

In the village of Hampstead it was soon realized by everyone who knew him that this was the end of poor Keats. On 13th September 1820 he left England forever. He died, as we know, in Rome, on 23rd February 1821. His last words to Joseph Severn, the friend who painted his portraits, and stayed beside his bed, holding his hand, were full of courage. "Severn—Severn—lift me up—I am dying—I shall die easy, don't be frightened—be firm and thank God it has come."

He was twenty-five years old when he died.

In the village, naturally, there was afterwards much gossip about Keats and Fanny Brawne. There were some who thought Keats a wicked young man because he was never seen on Sunday mornings in the Hampstead church. Fanny Brawne on the other hand, was said to be unfit for the love of so great a poet. She might even be to blame in some ways for the loneliness of his tragic death so far from his home in Hampstead. Today we see things differently. No doubt Fanny was too young and inexperienced, and much too conventional, and could not be expected to understand the intensity of her lover's passion, either physical or spiritual. It was not her fault. In her own way, she suffered as much as he did.

Fanny Brawne was born in Hampstead, christened in the Hampstead Parish Church, a young lady of the well behaved middle-class, not in the least intellectual, or gifted, or unusual, only pretty and light-hearted, and perhaps rather coy. For this she has been criticized. Nevertheless she inspired a great love in a great man.

When Keats died she surprisingly changed from a laughing young woman to a faded and frail young girl, her prettiness almost concealed by heavy black veils and black dresses, worn by Fanny for three years, a long period of mourning and grieving. The villagers now felt sorry for Fanny. They hoped she would recover from her loss, and eventually she did. Ten years later she married one of her admirers and became known to her new friends as Mrs Louis Lindon. In Hampstead, where the story of her love affair was repeated many times by mothers to their daughters, she would always be remembered as Fanny Brawne.

Ironically enough, there is a bust of Keats which occupies an important position in the Hampstead church. This was considered a wrong decision by Canon Ainger, who remarked: "Keats could not, indeed, be said so much as to have forgotten what the inside of a church was like as never to have made the discovery."

However, to mark his centenary, in July 1895, British and American authors and lovers of poetry, met there to unveil the Keats Memorial. First they gathered at Sir Walter Besant's home, Frognal End, and then the whole company trooped to the church. Among the celebrities who loved Keats and enjoyed this rather strange ceremony were Algernon Swinburne, William Morris, Alfred Austin, Henry Irving, and Ellen Terry.

He may not have been a Christian, but Keats appears to have held a strong belief in reincarnation. His doctrines about soul-building seem to have been related in many ways to some of the Indian teachings, and he clearly believed in life after death.

Today, in Hampstead, adjoining the modest house where he lived with Charles Brown and the Brawne family, we have a Keats Memorial Library. There are more than 5,000 volumes, a unique collection, including almost every book ever written about Keats, his family, his friends. Keats House was rescued from destruction by the planners and improvers. This was done by public subscription in 1921. The money came largely from Americans living in the United States. It was vested in the borough council which undertook to maintain the house forever as a memorial to Keats.

To the casual visitor Hampstead is spoiled a little by the stream of heavy traffic which always appears to be pounding up the long steep hill to the Heath. Even the peaceful old church is not protected, as it should be, from this pest of noise.

Here is a quick impression, not quite the truth. Hampstead may still be seen as an old London village of beautiful red-brick buildings, and somehow it has managed to retain the dignity and charm of the eighteenth century.

So much elegance remains in Hampstead, so many old houses, peaceful, hidden away, at the end of leafy lanes, approached by tall hills, unchanged by traffic or teenagers or time. No one can resist their appeal, and certainly the villagers love them, as did Constable, the artist, and Keats, the poet.

Some people know the history of Hampstead, and happen to possess an old house, or a beautiful cottage, or just a room with a view, above or below the High Street. They are the lucky ones. They could not bear to leave the village, or to live anywhere else.

HAMPSTEAD LOCAL HISTORY
Recommended Books

Hampstead Wells, George W. Potter (George Bell, 1904)
Hampstead, Anna Maxwell (James Clarke & Co, 1912)
The Annals of Hampstead, T. J. Barratt (Lionel Leventhal, 1912)
Hampstead, Ian Norrie (High Hill Press, 1966)
Keats House, A Guide (London Borough of Camden, 1971)
Hampstead, Building A Borough, F. M. L. Thompson (Routledge & Kegan Paul, 1974)

8

Highgate

Four hundred years ago the good and sometimes capricious Queen Elizabeth was very much loved in the village of Highgate. Indeed she was idolized. She paid many visits to the village, before she became queen, and afterwards.

Today we still have the Highgate Grammar School, standing proudly on the crest of a high hill, above the old village, to remind us of Elizabeth. She encouraged the founder, Sir Roger Cholmeley, and gave her royal permission—"for the education, institution and instruction of boys and youths in grammar and the best learning, at all times for ever to endure".

Not far from the Elizabethan school, close to the place where the Highgate Literary and Scientific Institution stands today, there used to be a fine Tudor building, a house where Elizabeth was entertained by the Cornwallis family. Later it belonged to the Earls of Arundel and became extremely well known as Arundel House. It was a large black and white building with gables and oak beams, typically English in style, flanked by two wings fronting on a large courtyard. (The last wing was taken down in 1824.)

Sir Thomas Cornwallis had once been comptroller of the household of Queen Mary. In 1554 Princess Elizabeth, at the age of twenty-one, spent a night in his house. The villagers were excited by her visit. They were still more excited, on her accession to the throne, four years later, for Elizabeth not only came back to Highgate but actually received the lord mayor and sheriffs and bishops in this same house, meeting them as the new Queen of England.

For the rest of her life she paid repeated visits to the house. On 11th June 1589 we are told that the bell-ringers of St Margaret's, Westminster, were "paid sixpence when the Queen's Majesty came from Highgate".

Elizabeth's friendship with Sir Roger Cholmeley began when she was a girl. Sir Roger was a remarkable man, greatly respected in

Highgate and everywhere else as the Lord Chief Justice of England. In the time of Bloody Queen Mary, Sir Roger was sent as a prisoner to the Tower of London. Although he had done nothing wrong he had witnessed the will of Edward VI, in which the late king had tried to exclude Mary from the throne. This was considered unforgivable. Bloody Queen Mary set him free on the payment of a heavy fine but he was never restored to the office of Lord Chief Justice.

He was a retired gentleman, living in Highgate, when Elizabeth first knew him. She was then spending most of her time at Hatfield House, and used to pass through Highgate on her way to Court, calling on Sir Roger, spending the night at least once.

Elizabeth ascended the throne at Mary's death on 17th November 1558 amid universal rejoicings. She boasted of being "mere English" and no sovereign since Harold had been so purely English in blood. She continued to visit her friends in Highgate. To the great happiness of the villagers the grammar school made its appearance in 1565 and the young queen, we are told, did grant and ordain to Sir Roger Cholmeley that there should be a Free School in Highgate, to be called The School of Sir Roger Cholmeley, Knight. Seven years later, encouraged by Elizabeth, the Chapel of Highgate was built by Sir Roger close to the school, on the site of the former one, a humble building which had stood from the earliest times of the Highgate hermits.

In 1866 both school and chapel were rebuilt in grander style (Victorian Gothic) but there they still stand, dignified, untouchable, perhaps the most distinguished group of buildings in Highgate today.

The villagers' love for the queen was understandable. They owed Elizabeth almost as much as they owed Sir Roger. They saw her frequently, admiring her courage, forgiving her faults, as if the queen belonged to their village as they and their families did.

Elizabeth was known to be a jealous character, so jealous that she could not bear her courtiers to look at another woman, but most of her people were at all times ready to follow, obey, and worship her. Men called her "Gloriana".

In Highgate the queen's jealousy was taken for granted. There was a young girl of great beauty and intelligence, Lady Arabella Stuart, of whom the queen was extremely jealous. Most people knew that Lady Arabella was next in succession to James VI of Scotland to the thrones of England and Scotland, after Queen Elizabeth. She was descended from Henry VII (through Margaret, Henry's daughter, who married twice). If James should produce no children Arabella would be the next heir to the throne. In fact she was much too royal to be popular either with Elizabeth or James.

To make matters worse, the queen was forty-two years older than the lovely Arabella. Not only this, the queen had been declared illegitimate, because her father had married Anne Boleyn before the divorce from his first wife, Catherine of Aragon.

It seems that Arabella had no desire to be Queen of England but she certainly had many suitors. Elizabeth did everything possible to prevent her marriage. Some were in sympathy with Arabella, but not in the village of Highgate. In 1590 a scheme was formed to marry Arabella, at the age of fifteen, to Renuccio, eldest son of the Duke of Parma (descended from John of Gaunt) and of raising her with Spanish support to the throne.

Elizabeth discovered the plot and was furious. Arabella, this chit of a girl, had now to be closely guarded at Harwick by the dowager Duchess of Shrewsbury.

In 1602 the queen was greatly annoyed by another plot to marry Arabella to Edward, eldest son of Lord Beauchamp. Elizabeth knew that here was an attractive young man, grandson of Edward Seymour, Earl of Hertford, who was heir to the throne after herself, according to her own father's will. Of course Elizabeth was angry. Naturally she hated Arabella. The village of Highgate watched and understood, and sympathized.

When Elizabeth died in 1603 the village grieved. King James I, who also came frequently to Arundel House, was not popular. Most people now felt a sudden sympathy for Lady Arabella. Although James received her at court, and treated her with favour, he too made every effort to prevent her marriage. She was granted a pension of £1,000 a year by the not very generous king. Another plot failed—this time involving Sir Walter Raleigh, who was punished by a stretch of twelve years in the Tower of London.

Arabella became known to the villagers when she stayed at Arundel House, which seems to have been at the heart of all these intrigues and jealousies. To the indignation of James she now had the impertinence to fall in love. Against the king's wishes, after promising not to do so without permission, she secretly married William Seymour, younger brother of Edward, and grandson of Lord Hertford. In fact her lover was as royal as herself. He was descended from Henry VII, and there were some who thought his claim to the throne was better than the new king's. Arabella had been his love since early youth, and now she married him.

At the time of her marriage there must have been a great deal of gossip about Arabella in the village of Highgate. James was almost as angry and jealous as Elizabeth had been in the past. In 1610 the married couple were both imprisoned, Arabella at Lambeth, her husband in the Tower. Finally James decided to send Arabella to Durham, in charge of the Bishop of Durham (who was probably not very pleased) and so she was dragged from her bed, in the middle of the night, shrieking and resisting, carried to a boat, and then rowed up the River Thames.

It seems that she arrived by carriage at Barnet. By this time Arabella was hysterical and beginning to have what today might be called a nervous breakdown. A physician was called. He declared that Arabella's life was in danger and she must not be carried any further.

After that James relented. Arabella was returned to Arundel House in Highgate, and the villagers now felt sorry for the poor unfortunate bride. To please James, she was shut up, like a prisoner, in the very same house where Elizabeth had so often spent happy times with her courtiers and friends.

She was held as prisoner for two months in Arundel House, only seen by the villagers when allowed to walk in the fields under escort. The gossips wondered what would happen to the beautiful woman, now thirty-five years old, who had managed to anger both Elizabeth and James. Quite soon there was further excitement in the village. After two months in captivity Arabella escaped from Arundel House. On 3rd June 1611 she boarded a ship bound for Calais. Her husband (having escaped from the Tower) was expected to travel with her to France, but unfortunately things went wrong.

We are told that Arabella, disguised as a man, left Highgate in a man's doublet, a man-like peruke, with long locks over her hair, a black hat, black cloak, russet boots with red tops, and a rapier by her side. She was accompanied by a gentleman called Mr Markham and together they walked to what was described as a "sorry Inn". Hired horses were ready for them, they mounted, and rode to Blackwall. The courageous Arabella, still dressed as a man, found boats and attendants who rowed her down the river to Gravesend, and there she found a French boat to take her to France. She was hoping to find her husband already on board, but Seymour, although he had managed to escape from the Tower (disguised as a physician) had not yet arrived. The French captain refused to wait any longer, and put to sea.

What happened then was very sad indeed. Seymour arrived at Gravesend according to plan, but too late. Finding Arabella had departed, he engaged the captain of a collier to carry him over to Flanders for the sum of £40. This was successfully done. But the unlucky Arabella was captured. Her escape had soon been discovered at Arundel House, her boat was followed, and she was carried back to London by her enemies. Worse still, she was carried as a prisoner to the Tower of London, where she was to spend the rest of her unhappy life.

The touching story of Arabella was not easily forgotten in the village of Highgate. In France, as we know, the bridegroom was safe and sound, but it seems that no one bothered to tell the heart-broken bride. King James was still angry with her. She sank into melancholy, perhaps insanity, and died four years later, about 25th December 1615. She was buried in the tomb of Queen Mary of Scots, in Henry VII's Chapel in Westminster Abbey.

Arundel House, where she had suffered so much, was still the scene of many excitements and festivities. King James and his queen had visited the house in 1604, and we are told that he was much entertained by a charming masque produced in his honour. This was *Penates* by Ben Jonson. Was Ben Jonson present, and if so, was his friend, Mr Shakespeare, with him? Why not? Here is a pleasing thought, for King James was a man of culture and would have welcomed them both.

Lord Arundel, who bought the house in 1610, was also a man of culture. He had a decidedly chequered career under King James and King Charles, sometimes in favour, sometimes not, more than once punished, spending much time in the Tower of London. In spite of these hazards, he loved both James and Charles, and contributed about £34,000 to the king's cause.

Lord Arundel (or Thomas Howard) was now the man who dominated the village of Highgate. He was the first man to form a considerable collection of art in Great Britain. His marbles, statues, pictures, gems, coins, books and manuscripts were all deposited in Highgate at Arundel House. His library was later given by his grandson to the Royal Society.

He happened to be in prison (in the Tower of London of course) when his friend, Lord Bacon, lay dying in Arundel House. It occurred at a time when he was out of favour, in the March and April of 1626. His friend was out of favour too.

Francis Bacon (Viscount St Albans) was often seen at Highgate. He was known to everyone as philosopher, statesman, essayist, at one time Lord Chancellor of England. At the close of 1591 Bacon was acting as adviser to the Earl of Essex, Elizabeth's favourite. Somehow he offended Elizabeth and was excluded from Court. A few years later (in June 1600) the same thing happened to the foolish and impulsive young Essex—after a plot to seize the queen's person and compel her to dismiss his enemies (Raleigh, Cobham, and Cecil).

Essex was executed, as we know, and this was hastened by the brilliant speeches delivered by Francis Bacon. Hoping to please the queen he drew up a "Declaration of The Practices and Treasons Attempted and Committed by Robert, Late Earl of Essex". We are told that his first draft was altered and corrected by Elizabeth, who still loved her bold bad Essex.

However this may be, he kept himself in favour at Court. When Elizabeth died in 1603 his services to King James brought him a knighthood and he managed to acquire favour with the king's favourite, Sir George Villiers. In the end his downfall was the charge of receiving bribes. He tells us with pride that he was never swayed by a bribe but admits that he received many—like numerous men of his time.

Today many people think that the last five years of his life, spent as an author, and ending in Highgate, were the most important. As a philosopher he claimed that he "rang the bell which called the wits together". We are told that Bacon's writings and philosophy gave birth to fresh ideas and new thought forms and finally to the foundation of the famous and much admired Royal Society, which exists to this day.

At any rate, his life ended tragically at Arundel House, and the villagers felt sorry for him, as they had done for Lady Arabella. One day he was out driving in the country near Highgate. It was very cold, the fields were white with snow, and Francis Bacon, whose restless mind was searching for new problems, suddenly decided to make an experiment. Could snow be used in some way to help preserve the body after death?

The great philosopher stopped his carriage, purchased a fowl, and with his own hands assisted to stuff it with snow. The result of this experiment was his own death. He was taken with a sudden chill and was driven to Lord Arundel's house nearby. He died about a month later, still in his friend's house, suffering from bronchitis. Lord Arundel, as we know, was languishing in the Tower—where Lady Arabella had died only eleven years before.

If the following story is true, Lord Arundel must have been furious when his enemy, Oliver Cromwell, decided to build a house in Highgate. It is there now, although Arundel House has disappeared. There are those who tell us that Cromwell House was built by Oliver Cromwell about 1630 for the home of his daughter, Bridget, and her husband, General Ireton, who was one of the Commanders of his Army. Some tell us it was a Jacobean house of somewhat earlier date and was re-built by the Sprignell family, who were friendly with General Ireton. Unfortunately there are others who tell us that neither of these pleasing stories are true. However, in the village of Highgate we have firmly believed the Cromwell story for many years, and Prickett, in his *History of Highgate*, says: "Cromwell's house was evidentally built and internally ornamented in accordance with the taste of its military occupant."

Whether true, or untrue, most of us like to think that Cromwell House was visited by Cromwell when his daughter, Bridget, was living there. If so, it is easy to imagine the angry feelings of Lord Arundel when his new neighbours moved into their new house. He had always hated Cromwell, and had suffered severe losses during the Civil War. Cromwell House is a fine looking mansion to this day. It stands proudly on Highgate Hill, looking down with scorn at the stream of heavy traffic below. It has an air, like Cromwell, of stubborn dignity. It has seen many changes.

Inside Cromwell House the chief attraction today is a beautifully carved staircase. It is richly decorated with oak figures which are said to represent characters in the General's Army, and they stand on the posts of the staircase, each about one foot high.

These unusual figures really represent the different kinds of soldiers who fought for Cromwell—a piper, drummer, targeteer, officer of infantry, musketeer, pikeman, caliverman, targeteer carrying a pike, and another musketeer. Did Cromwell ever see the figures? If he did, he would certainly have loved them!

Highgate has never been a smart or fashionable London village like, for instance, Hampstead or Marylebone. On the other hand, it used to be considered a gathering place for the aristocracy. Perhaps they were drawn to Highgate by the Earl of Arundel. Certainly there were many aristocratic families in the neighbourhood, including such well known names as Cholmeley, Dorchester, Pemberton, St Albans, Lauderdale, Argyll, Bute, Cornwallis and others. The villagers took pride in their memories of Queen Elizabeth. They still repeated stories of the famous Dick Whittington.

Today, on Highgate Hill, near the hospital, we have a statue of a large and commanding black cat, with a memorial bearing this inscription.

WHITTINGTON STONE

Sir Richard Whittington, Lord Mayor of London

1397   Richard II
1409   Henry IV
1419   Henry V

Here Dick sat, we are still told, in a moment of despair, and listened to the ringing of Bow Bells, which called him back again to the City of London. He rose to be a man of immense fortune, three times Lord Mayor—followed by his cat, who seems to have assisted him more than anyone else. The original stone where Dick sat was the base of an ancient cross. The present stone, accompanied by the cat statue, was erected on the same spot. The villagers used to say that Dick, now Sir Richard Whittington, loved to ride up Highgate Hill, mounting and dismounting, always on the same stone, in order to save his horse. He frequently sat there to rest and think.

There are many tales of his generosity and today we have in Highgate the Whittington Hospital to remind us of him. At one time we had the Whittington Almshouses. They were built in the Victorian period (opposite the stone) for the benefit of twenty-four single women receiving a yearly income of less than £30. The buildings were said to be very pretty, of one storey, Gothic, forming three sides of a quadrangle. In the centre was a chapel with a shrubbery and sloping lawn.

Like Arundel House the almshouses have now disappeared. Only Cromwell House remains, and Lauderdale House, to remind us of the past.

Cromwell had his supporters, even in Highgate, but the villagers had always loved their kings and queens, and were loyal to the Earl of Arundel. No doubt many breathed a sigh of relief when Cromwell died, and King Charles II was restored to the throne, in

1660. By this time the old Lord Arundel was dead, but his grandson (Henry Howard) was soon befriended by the new king. It was like old times.

Charles did more than visit the house of his friend in Highgate. As patron for the famous Royal Society (the oldest scientific society in Great Britain today) the new king arranged meetings on Wednesday afternoons at 3 p.m. for discussions and experiments, and these meetings took place every week at Arundel House. The full title was The Royal Society of London for Improving Natural Knowledge by Experiments. Christopher Wren had been a member from the start. The meetings had once taken place at Gresham College in the City, but after the Great Fire of London in 1666 the College rooms were needed by City authorities, and so Charles eventually invited the philosophers and scientists to Arundel House—then occupied by Thomas Gardner.

It seems that the new earl and the new king were equally delighted with the members of the Royal Society. The earl gave them his grandfather's library, a most valuable collection of books and manuscripts, many of which are today in the British Museum.

Charles became a well-known figure in the village of Highgate. He was popular, although better loved in the village of Chelsea, where in spirit he still seems to belong. His grandfather, James, was well remembered by the elders in the village. We are told that James "went on Sunday, 2nd June 1624, towards evening, to Highgate, and lay at the Lord of Arundel's to hunt a stag early the next morning at St John's Wood". And now Charles, "who never said a foolish thing and never did a wise one", the gentleman king, who loved philosophy and science and beautiful women, became the centre of village gossip.

Half way up Highgate Hill, on the left hand side, stood Lauderdale House, where the king had many meetings with Nell Gwynne. For this reason he climbed the hill many times.

Lauderdale House is still standing, unpretentious and charming, with an air of past happiness, intended at one time for summer holidays and laughter, a simple house with beautiful gardens overlooking Waterlow Park. Today it is only used by the park attendants and has been fitted up with a refreshment room and sleeping quarters. Nell Gwynne's bath has been placed in a recess in the hall. All the old panelling has been preserved. Some of us think it ought to be used as a small museum, like the house where Keats lived in Hampstead.

This pleasing house was rebuilt about 1666 for the Duke of

Lauderdale, who seems to have been a bad character, though protected by Charles. He is described by Macauley like this: "Loud and coarse both in mirth and anger, was perhaps, under the outward show of boisterous frankness, the most dishonest man in the whole Cabal. He was accused of being deeply concerned in the sale of Charles I to the English Parliament."

When he was Lord Deputy in Scotland, we are told that he worked with racks, thumbscrews and iron boot, in which his minions used to crush the legs of their victims with wedges, so vividly described by Walter Scott in *Old Mortality* and in the *Tales of a Grandfather*.

Let us hope this is not true. We only know for certain that Charles remained his friend, and used his house when the owner was in Scotland for the purpose of entertaining Nell Gwynne.

According to Nell's account (given us by Pepys) she was "brought up in a brothel, to fill strong waters for the gentlemen". Her wit and extreme good nature seem to have endeared her to everyone, especially on the stage, as an actress. We are told that Dryden "had Nelly to appear in a hat as large as a coach wheel". The audience was delighted and the king who was present, was taken completely by her charm. As she was already the mistress of Lord Buckhurst, Charles decided to negotiate the transfer of Nelly for an earldom, making his rival the Earl of Middlesex.

Another story, frequently told, especially in the village of Highgate, took place at Lauderdale House. It seems that Nelly was annoyed because the king had so far refused a title for her child. The eldest sons of his other mistresses had all received titles, so why not Nelly's child? One day, in a fit of indignation, at Lauderdale House, she held the infant out of an upper window, and said: "Unless you do something for him, here he goes!" Charles quickly replied: "Save the Earl of Burford!"

In this witty way the child was lucky enough to gain his title as the Earl of Burford, and afterwards became the Duke of St Albans.

It is easy to see why Nelly became the people's idol. She had the double advantage of being a Protestant, and an English woman with a working-class background. She was ranged on the side of the people against France, the Roman Catholics, and the Duchess of Portsmouth (the king's French mistress, who was a Catholic).

That was why, in Oxford Street, when her coach was mistaken for that of the duchess, the mob collected and ran after it, hooting and shouting rude names. Nelly knew exactly what to do. She merely

Canonbury Tower is today one of the most interesting buildings in Islington. In 1530 it was owned by Thomas Cromwell, as Lord of the Manor

(left) Spencer Compton, Earl of Northampton. He inherited the Canonbury estate from Sir John Spencer who died in 1609. Part of it is still in the family

(right) Oliver Goldsmith. It is said that he wrote "The Deserted Village", "The Traveller" and part of *The Vicar of Wakefield* in Canonbury House

(left) Edward Alleyn was a contemporary of Shakespeare. He founded the College of God's Gift, commonly called Dulwich College
(right) John Ruskin, well known in the village of Dulwich, the friend of Turner, the enemy of Whistler, and influential art critic

Dulwich College in 1790. On Sunday mornings the villagers walk up the path, as did Edward Alleyn, to the little friendly chapel where he lies today

thrust her head through the window and smiled at the enraged crowd.

"Be silent, good people, I am the *Protestant* whore!" she said affably, and of course the hissing changed to cheers.

In Highgate most of the villagers loved her, but one man did not approve. This was Andrew Marvell, the reformer, whose cottage walls were uncomfortably close to the gaiety and laughter at Lauderdale House.

Andrew Marvell was just as hostile to King Charles II as Cromwell had been to Lord Arundel. Today, unfortunately, his cottage has vanished, but the stone step, which formed the entrance, has been lovingly built into the boundary wall of Waterlow Park, in order to mark the place.

This man who hated Charles was a close friend of the poet Milton. Indeed they both acted as Latin secretaries to Oliver Cromwell. Even the beautiful Nell Gwynne could not find a way to please him.

Marvell spent his life exposing corruption in Church and State. From the time of the Restoration he wrote his constituents in Hull a weekly letter about the evils and immorality of London life. He talked and wrote so much about Charles, attacking his way of life, his extravagance, his mistresses, that finally, when it was found that nothing would make him keep quiet, Charles lost patience. Out came a royal proclamation offering a high reward for the apprehension of Andrew Marvell. At this point he retired to Hull for safety. He died soon afterwards. Some said that he died by poison.

When Charles was dead and gone, the village life began to change. In the eighteenth century there were no more royal carriages to be seen rumbling up and down Highgate Hill, bringing kings and queens, followed by courtiers and mistresses, to dine or spend the night at Arundel House or Lauderdale House. There was less employment for villagers and less excitement for those who loved a bit of gossip and scandal.

To amuse themselves they now had to ride or drive across the heath to the village of Hampstead Wells, where much was always going on, and the gentry gathered for music and dancing and bowls. But Highgate was never boring. A new entertainment was on its way.

At the top of the hill, gathered round the Grammar School, many more cottages appeared, and more public houses. Today we still have Pond Square, the village centre, but the two ponds have now been covered by paving stones and comfortable seats, making a place for children and lovers. Beyond the square is the charming Flask Inn.

In Highgate there used to be no less than nineteen licensed taverns. What would Andrew Marvell have said about that? In 1780, upwards of eighty stage coaches stopped every day at the Red Lion Inn alone. What is more, Highgate became famous for a strange ceremony known as 'swearing on the horns'. It was a mock serious occasion when the innocent traveller, descending from the stage coach, was welcomed by his host with a set of horns, placed on a pole about five feet high. He was then required to take off his hat, all present doing the same, and the landlord, in a loud voice, proceeded to 'swear in' the guest, who was ordered at intervals to kiss the horns. He then made all kinds of merry and slightly scandalous promises. For example, the landlord would solemnly tell him:

> To kiss the fair maid when the mistress is kind,
> Remember that you must be loth, sir,
> But if the maid's fairest, your oath does not bind,
> Or you may, if you like, kiss them both, Sir.

After this the bewildered traveller would be forced to make further promises, kiss the horns several times again, and finally the landlord would say: "And now, my good son, I wish you a safe journey through Highgate and through this life. . . . If at any time you are going through Highgate, and want to rest yourself, and you see a pig lying in a ditch, you have the liberty to kick the animal out and take its place; but if you see three pigs lying together, you must only kick out the middle one and lie between the other two. God save the King!"

We are told that the 'swearer-in' usually performed this remarkable ceremony in a black gown, mask and wig, and was accompanied by a person who acted as his clerk and carried the horns. How it all started nobody seems to know. Probably it began at the Gate House Tavern, this being the oldest Inn at Highgate, forming part of the toll gate at one time.

An old landlord is quoted by Hone as saying: "No one came to Highgate in anything of a carriage without being 'sworn', and so much was doing in this way that at one time I was obliged to hire a 'swearer-in'. I have 'sworn' one hundred to one hundred and twenty persons a day! Parties of tailors used to come up on Mondays to initiate new shopmates; officers of the Guards; ladies and gentlemen arranged dinner parties for the fun of the initiation; and for admission to sundry convivial societies, the freedom of Highgate was indispensable." When the stage coaches ceased to pass through Highgate the custom gradually slipped away, though remembered by the villagers. (Today a pair of Highgate horns can still be seen at the Flask Inn).

The custom continued for about 300 years. The 'swearing' took place originally on stag's, bullock's, or ram's horns. At the Flask Inn ram's horns were kept for the ceremony. Some think the horns were used as a symbol of the cuckold. No doubt Byron thought so, for he alluded to the custom in his *Childe Harold's Pilgrimage*. It was Byron who wrote:

> Some o'er thy Thamis row the ribbon's fair,
> Other along the safer turnpike fly;
> Some Richmond Hill ascend, some scud to Ware,
> And many to the steep of Highgate hie.
> Ask ye, Boeotian shades! the reason why?
> 'Tis to the worship of the solemn horn,
> Grasp'd in the holy hand of mystery,
> In whose dread name both men and maids are sworn,
> And consecrate the oath with draught, and dance till morn.

Hogarth was well known at the Flask Inn, bringing other celebrities, all of them much entertained by the amusement of 'swearing on the horns'. Some came over to observe and criticize from the fashionable village of Hampstead Wells, including such men as Alexander Pope.

It was Pope who introduced Lord Mansfield to Hampstead, and together they visited a beautiful Highgate estate called Caen Wood, which Lord Mansfield bought. Kenwood, as it is now called, is open to the public and the park is as popular today as Hampstead Heath.

There is one story which really must be told before returning to the village proper. Lord Mansfield (who came from a poverty stricken Scottish family) was now the most distinguished advocate in England. He was denounced as a Papist, some said a Jesuit. This was because he directed a jury to find a verdict of 'not guilty' in the case of a Roman Catholic priest for celebrating Mass. (The law still forbade it and Catholics, naturally, still did it.)

Lord Mansfield became extremely unpopular, and soon afterwards came the Gordon Riots, when his house in Bloomsbury Square was burnt to the ground, his books and pictures all destroyed. When the infuriated mob had done this wicked thing they set out to destroy his house at Kenwood.

Fortunately the landlord at The Spaniards (the famous public house at the end of Hampstead Heath) stood at his door and invited them to drink whatever they wanted. He threw open his cellars to these thugs, come straight from Bloomsbury, and sent a messenger to the barracks for a detachment of the Horse Guards. He also sent word to Kenwood, and more drink came back by return. By the time the soldiers arrived the mob was hopelessly drunk, unable to fight, and fled.

In this way Kenwood House was saved from destruction. The man who saved it, the brave landlord of The Spaniards, was Giles Thomas.

Lord Mansfield continued to live at Kenwood until his death on 20th March 1793. Some of the cedars opposite the house were planted by him.

In 1816 the most interesting and remarkable character ever seen by the villagers came to live in Highgate village. He was a genius. He was also a drug addict. He entered the family of James Gillman, a Highgate surgeon, who lived at that time in a charming house which still exists, at the Grove, not far from the Flask Inn.

Samuel Taylor Coleridge became the great man of Highgate, as John Keats became the great man of Hampstead. Both men were friends of Leigh Hunt. Both were romantic poets, influenced by Wordsworth, but in every other way as different as chalk from cheese.

Here is a description of Coleridge, as a young man, by Hazlitt.

His complexion was at that time clear and even bright. . . . His forehead was broad and high, light as if built of ivory, with large projecting eyebrows, and his eyes rolled beneath them like a sea with darkening lustre. . . . His mouth was gross, voluptuous, open, eloquent; his chin good-humoured and round; but his nose, the rudder of the face, the index of the will, was small, feeble, nothing—like what he has done. . . . Coleridge in his person was rather above the common size, inclining to be corpulent. . . . His hair (now, alas! grey) was then black and glossy as the raven's, and fell in smooth masses over his forehead.

Dorothy Wordsworth, who was in love with him, wrote another vivid description. She saw him as: "thin and pale, the lower part of the face not good, wide mouth, thick lips, not very good teeth, longish, loose, half-curling, rough black hair—but all was forgotten in the magic charm of his utterance".

Coleridge was educated for the Church, like his father before him.

There is no doubt that Dorothy Wordsworth loved him, and the force of her love kept him within the circle—a magic circle of three frustrated people, in love with love—so that he was able to write "The Ancient Mariner", followed by "Christabel".

He wrote in a letter to a friend: "Wordsworth and his exquisite sister are with me. She is a woman indeed! in mind, I mean, and heart; for her person is such, that if you expected to see a pretty woman, you would find her rather ordinary; if you expected to see an ordinary woman, you would think her pretty! but her manners are simple, ardent, impressive."

What would have happened, one wonders, if Dorothy had become either his mistress or his wife? Their love was unfinished, like some of his poems, for Dorothy was tied by her brother's love and Coleridge by his wife's love. In the end, driven by frustration perhaps, he transferred his affections to Sarah Hutchinson, a young woman he met with the inseparable Dorothy and William.

After numerous quarrels with his wife, who dutifully bore him four children, and was understandably jealous of his women friends, Coleridge wrote to the poet Southey (his brother-in-law) in an effort to explain his marital problem.

"Mrs Coleridge's mind", he wrote, "has very little that is bad in it; it is an innocent mind; but it is light and unimpressable, warm in anger, cold in sympathy, and in all disputes uniformly *projects itself forth* to recriminate, instead of turning itself inward in silent self questioning. . . ."

In September 1798, in company with Wordsworth and his sister, he left England for Hamburg. In 1800 he went to the Lakes where he wrote the second part of "Christabel".

William Wordsworth married Mary Hutchinson (sister to Sarah Hutchinson) in 1804, thus ending the strange relationship with Dorothy, who still loved her brother as much as Coleridge. They were no longer, as they said, "three persons with one soul". Later poor Dorothy had a serious nervous breakdown and the last twenty-six years of her life seem to have left her quite broken, in mind and body. Although she had loved two men so deeply, she had never been wife or mistress.

Coleridge arrived in Highgate in the year 1816. Deeply hurt by a misunderstanding with William, separated from Dorothy, he was now thought to be an almost hopeless drug addict. He was sent by a doctor to James Gillman, the surgeon, who described the meeting like this.

"I felt", he wrote, "indeed almost spell-bound, without the desire of release. My situation was new, and there was something affecting in the thought, that one of such amiable manners, and at the same time so highly gifted, should seek comfort and medical aid in our quiet home."

The following Monday Coleridge appeared in Highgate, the proofs of "Christabel" in his bag, and settled in the house of Ann and James Gillman, where he stayed for the last eighteen years of his life.

While Dorothy Wordsworth battled with her loneliness of heart, Coleridge battled with his addiction to opium. In the end it was Dorothy who lost the battle and Coleridge who won. His name became a legend in the village of Highgate. The villagers took pride and pleasure in him. Mr Gillman's coachman, in after life, used to boast of the proud distinction of having "driven Mr Coleridge about".

While he lived in Highgate village, increasingly loved and honoured, no longer taking opium, visiting the Leigh Hunt circle in Hampstead, he continued to fascinate his every audience with lectures on philosophy and brilliant conversation. He did much, it is now believed, to deepen and liberalize Christian thought. Highgate is still proud of him, even today.

What is it that makes Highgate different from other villages? There is, for one thing, the cemetery where Karl Marx was buried. Red flowers are dutifully placed on his grave. Beneath his enormous head, on the tombstone we read these alarming words: "The Philosophers have only interpreted the world in various ways. The point, however, is to change it."

In Highgate we are not quite happy about some of the changes. We have a second cemetery on the opposite side of the road which now, at the time of writing, has to be locked and chained and guarded, like a prison, because of the vandals who open the coffins and litter the ground with skeletons. In this spooky and mysterious place—forty acres of beautiful wilderness—lies the family grave of Rossetti, where his tragic wife was buried. As we know, he placed his unpublished poems in her coffin. Later he allowed the coffin to be opened and the famous book of poems to be removed. Ruskin said: "Just like Rossetti! Unfaithful to Lizzie, even in her grave!"

This enormous cemetery of catacombs and mausoleums and rich Victorian memorials has even been used at night for the practice of black magic. What *would* the Victorians say?

Those who live in Highgate today would not care to live anywhere else. As in Hampstead, there is still a strong sense of loyalty and identity. But in Highgate the beautiful houses are a mite less expensive, the way of life a touch less fashionable, and in spite of the thundering traffic up and down Highgate Hill, there is still a pleasant and rather unexpected feeling of villagey friendliness, the scent of fresh air blowing across Ken wood and Waterlow Park. Few Londoners have ever heard of Waterlow Park. It happens to be one of the most beautiful parks in London. The villagers love it, as they love Highgate, in a possessive way, because no one outside the village knows much about it.

HIGHGATE LOCAL HISTORY
Recommended Books

Northern Heights of London, William Howitt (Longmans, Green & Co, 1869)

History of Highgate, John H. Lloyd (Highgate Literary & Scientific Institution, 1888)

Highgate Village, Walter K. Jealous (Baines & Scarsbrook, 1919)

9

Islington

Thomas Cromwell is often remembered as the evil genius of the village of Putney. Trained by Cardinal Wolsey, he was employed as political agent by Henry VIII, for whom he happily organized and directed a reign of terror, killing and torturing Catholic priests, becoming hated by all, even by the villagers in Putney, gaining his title as the Earl of Essex, and finally, to the great relief of Henry's other friends and advisers, losing his head. This was the man who became Islington's Lord of the Manor in 1530—at the time when Henry was in love with Anne Boleyn.

In the fields between Islington and Finsbury, and between Islington and Newington Green, Henry and his courtiers frequently joined the archers and sportsmen who came there from London. The village became known as "Merrie Islington". Henry was a keen archer, using the long-bow with skill. The villagers admired him for this and enjoyed his visits to their peaceful green fields. The king compelled every man to furnish his son at the age of seven with a bow and two arrows, and in the sixth year of his reign (by Henry's well known Act) all men, "except clergy and judges", were obliged by the king to shoot at butts.

Soon the villagers became as skilled as the king, and learned to love the sport as he did. Later he granted a patent to Sir Christopher Morris so that he and certain others should direct what was called "the science of artillery, to wit long-bows, cross-bows, and hand gonnes". They were given liberty to organize shooting "at all manner of marks and butts, in the city and suburbs, as in all other places". This patent seems to be the origin of the Honourable Artillery Company, still flourishing in the City today.

There is no doubt that wicked old Henry, all his life, loved the village of Islington, and shared with Londoners their passion for sport and archery. He gave distinguished archers such titles as Duke of Shoreditch, and Marquis of Islington, and Earl of Pancras. The

Duke of Shoreditch was a title which descended for several generations and carried with it the captainship of the London Archers. Even now we have archery clubs in Islington.

In those days a skilful archer was expected to hit a mark at almost any distance within eyesight. For example, the distances between the marks in some of the fields round Islington were as long as 380 yards!

At the time of Henry's romance with Anne Boleyn, he stayed quite often at Newington Green, probably in the house later owned by Sir Henry Mildmay. It was close to Highbury and Islington. The walk on the south-east corner of the green, leading to Ball's Pond, still bears the name of King Henry's Walk.

A neighbour, hated by Henry, was the unfortunate Henry Algernon Percy, Earl of Northumberland, who happened to know and admire Anne Boleyn before the king ever saw her. The poor young fellow was in attendance on Cardinal Wolsey. Henry blamed Wolsey for permitting the attachment to Anne Boleyn. So then they were both given the fright of their lives by Henry's jealousy, and the young earl was made to write a letter (from Newington Green) to Thomas Cromwell (acting for Henry), in which he disclaimed, on pain of damnation, any previous promise of marriage between himself and Anne Boleyn.

Henry was still not satisfied. The king made Wolsey send for the young earl and force him into a marriage with Lady Mary Talbot, daughter of the Earl of Shrewsbury, a reluctant bride for whom the bridegroom had no feeling whatever.

We are told that Anne Boleyn never forgave Wolsey for his part in all this. She and her father worked incessantly for the downfall of Wolsey. In the end, Henry sent for him from his palace in Yorkshire and the messenger was the same young Earl of Northumberland, who was forced to say to his friend, by way of greeting: "My Lord, I arrest you of high treason!"

Worse was to follow. Henry had the great cruelty to appoint the Earl of Northumberland as one of Anne's judges before putting her to death. We are told that the trial was too much for the young earl's feelings. He was seized with such agitation and illness in the court that he was obliged to withdraw. He died a few months afterwards.

Today one of the most interesting buildings in Islington is Canonbury House, which was owned at this time by Thomas

Cromwell, Lord of the Manor. He was executed because Henry had turned against him. Cromwell had arranged his [the king's] unhappy marriage with Anne of Cleves and this was too much for the ruthless Henry. No one grieved when Cromwell died, not even in the village of Islington. He was friendless. Thomas Cromwell, until the end of his life, seems to have had no feeling for any man except his master, Henry, and Wolsey, at whose death he shed tears.

There are many stories about Canonbury House. The next owner was as famous as Thomas Cromwell, and he too lost his head. This was John Dudley, the Earl of Warwick. He aimed at securing the crown for his son, Lord Guildford Dudley by a marriage with Lady Jane Grey. Like Cromwell he was executed at the Tower of London.

The manor then reverted to the Crown and was granted by Bloody Queen Mary to Thomas, Lord Wentworth, who transferred it to a charming gentleman called Sir John Spencer, Sir John was a cloth worker and an alderman, greatly respected in the City of London, and later became the Lord Mayor. He was said to be a millionaire and the richest commoner of his time. His residence in the City was the beautiful Crosby Hall—so beautiful that in 1910 it was finally removed from Bishopsgate to the village of Chelsea, where it now stands.

Sir John loved Canonbury House. For him it was a perfect country home, so close to his place of work in the City, so peaceful and pleasant, surrounded by green fields and open country which was shared between farmers and gardeners and sportsmen and archers.

The house had been built for the Canons of St Bartholomew in 1532. Sir John altered, enlarged, and beautified his new property, and enjoyed the daily ride on horseback to and from the City.

He seems to have been an endearing character with a sense of humour. He had one child, a daughter, heiress to all his wealth, said to amount to at least £800,000. It was, of course, a stupendous sum in those days. His daughter, understandably, had many suitors. No one, except Sir John, was much surprised or shocked when Lord William Compton managed to win her love, and smuggled her away in a baker's basket. This was necessary, apparently, and successful, but the bread basket must have been a big one. The man who did it was the future Earl of Northampton. Anyway, the truth of the story has been proved by a painting of the elopement, basket and all, preserved for a long time at Castle Ashby, the seat of the Marquess of Northampton.

Of course Sir John was furious. He was so annoyed and insulted

by the audacity of this undignified elopement that he disowned his
daughter and vowed he would cut her off with a shilling.

At this point in the story Queen Elizabeth came to the rescue. One
day, meeting Sir John, she treated him most kindly and invited him
to stand sponsor with her to the first child of a young couple abandoned by their father. Sir John agreed. As he had renounced his own
daughter, he said, he would adopt this boy, Her Majesty's protégé.

The queen took him at his word. In a little while, upon meeting
the young parents, Sir John Spencer found he had adopted his own
grandson!

He seems to have taken the queen's joke very well, laughing about
it afterwards. He died in the year 1609, leaving his immense fortune
to his daughter and her fortunate husband.

The story, however, is not quite finished. Lord William Compton,
later the Earl of Northampton, was so overwhelmed by his sudden
wealth that he lost his reason. We are told that it was necessary to
keep him bound. The Lord Chamberlain took over the administra-
tion of his goods and lands. But he soon recovered, and his wife, not
long out of the bread basket and full of spirit, wrote him a long and
delightful letter, which really must be quoted, telling him just what
to do.

> My Sweet Life,
>   . . . Now I have declared to you my mind for the settling
> of your state, I suppose it were best for me to bethink or
> consider with myself, what allowance were meetest for me. [she
> wrote] For considering what care I have had of your estate, and
> how respectfully I dealt with those which, by the laws of God, of
> nature, and of civil polity, wit, religion, government, and honesty,
> you, my dear, are bound to, I pray and beseech you to grant
> me £1,600 per annum, quarterly to be paid.
>   Also, I would, besides that allowance for my apparel, have
> £600 added yearly, quarterly to be paid, for the performance of
> charitable works; and for these things I would not, neither will be,
> accountable for.
>   Also, I will have three horses for my own saddle, that none shall
> dare to lend or borrow; none lend but I, none borrow but you.
>   Also, I will have two gentlewomen, lest one should be sick, or
> have some other lett; also believe that it is an undecent thing for a
> gentlewoman to stand mumping alone, when God hath blessed
> their lord and lady with a great estate.
>   Also, when I will a hunting, or hawking, or travel from one
> house to another, I will have them attending me; so, for either of
> those said women, I must and will have for either of them a horse.

Also, I will have six or eight gentlemen. And I will have my two coaches, one lined with velvet to myself, with four very fair horses; and a coach for my women, lined with sweet cloth; one laced with gold, the other with scarlet, and laced with watchet lace and silver, with four good horses.

Also, I will have two coachmen, one for my own coach, the other for my women.

Also, at any time when I travel, I will be allowed not only carroches and spare horses for me and my women, but I will have such carriages as shall be fitting for all, orderly, not pestering my things with my women's, nor theirs with chambermaids, nor theirs with wash-maids.

Also for laundresses, when I travel, I will have them sent away before with the carriages, to see all safe; and the chambermaids I will have to go before with the greens, [she meant green rushes for the floors] that the chambers may be ready, sweet and clean.

Also, for that it is indecent to crowd up myself with my gentleman-usher in my coach; I will have him to have a decent horse to attend me either in city or country; and I must have two footmen; and my desire is, that you defray all the charges for me.

And for myself, besides my yearly allowance, I would have twenty gowns of apparel, six of them excellent good ones, eight of them for the country, and six other of them very excellent good ones.

Also, I would have to put in my purse £2,000 and £200; and so for you to pay my debts.

Also, I would have £6,000 to buy me jewels, and £4,000 to buy me a pearl chain.

Now, seeing I am so *reasonable* unto you, I pray you to find my children apparel, and their schooling, and also my servants—men and women—their wages.

Also, I will have my houses furnished, and all my lodging-chambers to be suited with all such furniture as is fit, as beds, stools, chairs, suitable cushions, carpets, silver warming-pans, cupboards of plate, fair hangings and such like: so for my drawing-chambers in all houses, I will have them delicately furnished, both with hangings, couch, canopy, glass, carpet, chair-cushions, and all things thereunto belonging.

Also, my desire is, that you shall pay all my debts, build Ashley-house, and purchase lands; and lend no money—as you love God—to the Lord Chamberlain, who would have all, perhaps your life, from you. Remember his son, my Lord Warden, what entertainment he gave me when you were at Tiltyard. If you were dead, he said, he would be a husband, a father, a brother; and he said he would marry me. I protest, I grieve to see the poor man have so little wit and honesty to use his friend so vilely. Also he fed me with untruths concerning the Charter-house; but that is the least; he wished me much harm. You know him. God keep you and me from such as he is!

So now that I have declared to you what I would have, and what that is that I would not have, when you be an earl, I pray you to allow £1,000 more than I now desire, and double attendance.

Your loving wife,

Eliza Compton.

Her husband became an earl, as she intended, being created Earl of Northampton in 1618, and a little of Canonbury is still owned by the Northampton family to this day. It would be nice to know if Eliza Compton got her extra £1,000 *per annum*, and double attendance, when she became a countess. Probably she did!

The house was leased in 1616 to Sir Francis Bacon, then Attorney General, who used it until 1625. For him it was an easy drive, or ride, to the village of Highgate, when he visited his friend the Earl of Arundel.

Meanwhile, great things were being done for the village of Islington by another character, whose statue now stands before Islington Green. This was, of course, Sir Hugh Myddleton.

Sir Hugh was a wealthy goldsmith. It was his dream to help the people of London, and especially his own village, by finding a way to improve the water supply. The population of London was then about 300,000. In the reign of King James I the water came from the Northern Heights—that is to say, it came by conduit from the hills round Hampstead and Highgate. The villagers complained there was not enough water. Some of it was laboriously drawn from wells and delivered by water-carriers. Quite often it was contaminated.

Sir Hugh's dream was to find a way to bring water from the springs at Amwell and Chadwell, in Hertfordshire, partly by means of an open channel and partly through underground pipes, to a reservoir near his own house—a distance of thirty-eight miles. Sir Hugh was a rich man but the mayor and corporation refused to help him. The project was too expensive. He decided to invest the whole of his personal fortune in the New River Company. He then spent four years fighting to carry out his dream.

He was watched with sympathy by the villagers. When at last he had cut the river bed as far as Enfield he came to the end of his financial resources. Finally he went to the king himself, and James, making a good bargain, agreed to bear half the expense if Sir Hugh would divide the property with him. Sir Hugh accepted. On 29th September 1613, to the joy of the villagers, the water flowed for the first time into the New River Head at Clerkenwell.

It is pleasing to know that the New River Company still has offices near the place where Sir Hugh used to live more than 350 years ago. The address is now 30 Myddleton Square, and the New River Company can be found in the telephone book.

In 1622 Sir Hugh was created a baronet by the grateful King James. He died about nine years later. Today we have streets and squares and at least one public house named after him, not to mention the Hugh Myddleton Schools of Clerkenwell, and the statue at Islington Green.

We still have the New River, which still appears and disappears, like a smile, between the houses and under the streets. Not far from Canonbury House, for example, we come upon New River Walk— a delightful brown stream, winding between trees and flowers, where ducks are resting on green banks, or being fed by children. Suddenly the stream disappears beneath a street.

It is a pity that so much of the river has now been covered over. Near the Angel, for example, we have Duncan Terrace, where Charles Lamb and his sister passed four of the happiest years of their lives. They lived in Colebrook Cottage (afterwards it became 64 Duncan Terrace) and in those days the New River flowed prettily in front of their doorstep. In fact one of their friends, walking out of the gate, being perhaps a little drunk at the time, fell into the river. This was George Dyer, who never recovered from the shock to his pride.

Here is a description of 'Merrie Islington', in 1657, by Howell, speaking of the outdoor life of Londoners in the time of King Charles II.

For healthful corporeal recreations, and harmless pastimes, London may go in the van to any place that I ever saw yet. Go and walk in the fields, you shall see some shooting at long marks, some at butts; some bowling upon pleasant dainty greens; some upon bares; some wrestling, some throwing the barre, some the stone; some jumping, some running; some with dogs at ducking ponds. [These were favourite ponds where the Londoners went with dogs and hunted down the unfortunate ducks procured for the purpose.]

Unfortunately the fields of Islington, in 1666, were crowded by the thousands of men and women who had fled from the burning city. John Evelyn, describing the Fire of London, writes like this:

The poore inhabitants were dispersed about St George's Fields and More Fields, as far as Highgate, and several miles in circle, some under tents, some under miserable huts and hovells, many without a rag, or any necessary utensils, bed or board, who from delicatenesse, riches, and early accommodations in stately and well furnished houses, were now reduced to extremist misery and poverty.

The villagers were horrified by what they saw, and yet 'Merrie Islington' recovered quickly from the Great Fire. Since Henry's day the sport of archery had declined. It was neglected during the Rebellion, but later, as might be expected, King Charles II revived it, and it continued throughout the eighteenth century.

Charles loved sport. In 1682 there was a grand meeting of the Finsbury archers, at which Charles was present, and the old titles of Duke of Shoreditch, Marquess of Islington, etc., were again handed out by the king to his happy and skilful Londoners. Islington was soon the most important centre of sport, as it had been in Henry's time. So jealous and possessive were the Chartered Company of Archers (which formed a division of the Honourable Artillery Company), that they never failed to knock down and destroy every fence, bank, or mound, raised by the farmers on or near their practising grounds.

In the end archery died out, but the reputation of 'Merrie Islington' continued for many years to come. No one loved it more than Oliver Goldsmith, in the eighteenth century, who came there to escape his creditors.

The village of Islington, then as now, lay north of the Angel—a public house of such great fame that the place where it stood for hundreds of years is still a landmark to Londoners. Today we have Upper Street, leading past Islington Green and the statue of Sir Hugh Myddleton. We have the solid looking parish church, called St Mary's, which was being rebuilt in 1751 when Goldsmith, aged twenty-six was a gay young man about town. On the right, farther north, is Canonbury Lane, taking us quickly to the famous Canonbury Tower.

It is a red brick tower, sixty-six feet high, and the chief relic of the sixteenth-century house once used by the priors of St Bartholomew's. On the west side are two delightful buildings, in the first of which are the beautiful oak panelled rooms called the Spencer Room and the Compton Room. Since 1952 Canonbury House, including the Tower, has been occupied by the Tower Theatre (used by the Tavistock

Repertory Company), but visitors are admitted by appointment to the panelled rooms where so much history took place.

Oliver Goldsmith moved to Canonbury House at the close of 1762. No longer the country home of a city millionaire it was left to the care of a steward, and the chambers were let as lodgings to gentlemen from London who wished for peace and quiet.

Such a gentleman was Oliver Goldsmith. It is said that he wrote "The Deserted Village", "The Traveller", and part of *The Vicar of Wakefield* in Canonbury House. He was certainly a lovable character, a clown, a buffoon, an inspired idiot, a genius. He was also a rather ugly young man, painted for us by Reynolds, one of his devoted friends. He came to London from Ireland. What makes him so lovable is that Goldsmith, although he happened to be a genius, behaved very much like a fool.

"Noll", said Garrick, "wrote like an angel, and talked like poor Poll".

Dr Johnson made a delightful remark when told that Goldsmith was writing a natural history. "Goldsmith, sir, will give us a very fine book upon the subject; but if he can distinguish a cow from a horse, that, I believe, may be the extent of his knowledge of natural history." Dr Johnson was perfectly right. Goldsmith solemnly stated in his book that cows lose their horns at the end of three years and then grow new ones!

Perhaps the best story is the one about Goldsmith and his Islington landlady, which was told by Dr Johnson, and repeated by Boswell and Mrs Thrale. It happened, probably, in 1782, when his rent had been owing for such a long time that his landlady called in a sheriff's officer.

Goldsmith sent a messenger to Johnson, who sent back a guinea, and promised to follow as soon as possible. When Johnson arrived on the scene, prepared for trouble, he found that Goldsmith had changed the guinea and was busy explaining matters to the indignant landlady over a bottle of Madeira. Johnson was careful to put back the cork in the bottle, then he made enquiries. Goldsmith, he discovered, had a novel ready for the press. He glanced at the manuscript, saw that parts of it were extremely readable, decided to take it without delay to a publisher, sold it for £60, and returned a little later to Canonbury House with the money in his pocket. In this way the rent was paid for Goldsmith. The indignant landlady was soothed and settled, and the sheriff's officer was persuaded to depart. Meanwhile, Goldsmith finished the bottle of Madeira.

Greenwich Hospital with the Queen's House in the background.
This little white cottage with a flag on top is the artist's idea of a
masterpiece by Inigo Jones!

(left) Emma Hamilton, the love of Nelson's life, who clearly
returned his love, was allowed by an ungrateful nation to die in
poverty
(right) Horatio Nelson. After the Battle of Trafalgar his body was
brought home to Greenwich for a magnificent state funeral

(left) Anne Boleyn, executed by Henry VIII, gave him a daughter, the future Queen Elizabeth, who was born in the royal village of Greenwich

(right) Elizabeth I. Like her father, Henry VIII, she loved entertainments and gave them, as he did, in Greenwich Park

(left) King Charles II is still much loved in Chelsea, because he founded the Chelsea Royal Hospital

(right) George IV. His yellow carriage was a common sight for the villagers of Marylebone—visiting Lady Hertford in Manchester Square

The novel sold for £60 was, of course, *The Vicar of Wakefield*. Today it is known to every student of English literature. As Thackeray wrote in *The English Humourists*, it was a novel which "found entry into every castle and every hamlet in Europe". It was translated into French seven times and into all the major European languages, as well as Hungarian, Bohemian, Rumanian, Hebrew and Icelandic. "We read it in youth and age," wrote Walter Scott, "we return to it again and again, and bless the memory of an author who contrives so well to reconcile us to human nature."

The man who wrote this wonderful book (which was not appreciated at the time), came to Canonbury House because John Newbury, his publisher's father, lived there too. Newbury had undertaken to act as his guardian. The landlady's accounts show that Newbury paid her £50 a year in quarterly instalments, plus extras, such as port wine, or tea, or paper and pens, ordered by Goldsmith for himself and his many friends.

The life in 'Merrie Islington' suited Goldsmith very well. It permitted him to drink and forced him to write. In May 1770 appeared "The Deserted Village", which followed "The Traveller", and a not very successful drama called *Good Natur'd Man*. In 1773 his second play was an immediate and brilliant success. Today the name of it is well known to most of us. It was called *She Stoops to Conquer*.

No one who knew him at the time he was living in Islington could quite understand the genius of Goldsmith. Boswell was inclined to be patronizing. "I like very well," he said, "to hear honest Goldsmith talk away carelessly."

"Why, yes, Sir," Johnson retorted, "but he should not like to hear himself."

Goldsmith seems to have stimulated Johnson into some of his best and wittiest remarks. On one occasion Boswell wrote: "Mr Johnson was exceeding good company all this evening," and added that Goldsmith was "in his usual style, too eager to be bright." The friends were discussing Scotland. " 'No, no,' said Goldsmith, with a sneering laugh, 'it is not a rich country'." At this a Scottish poet, John Ogilvie, told him indignantly that Scotland had a "great many noble wild prospects".

Then came Johnson's famous line, repeated with enjoyment to this day: "I believe," he said, "the noblest prospect a Scotsman ever sees is the road which leads him to England."

In Islington, where he moved in 1762, Goldsmith spent some of his happiest times, drinking and talking with his celebrated friends, walking through the fields, visiting other villages and public houses. His publisher continued to give him work, taking charge of his earnings, paying his debts, giving him pocket money when needed. For him it was an ideal life in an ideal village.

In 1767, when his permanent home was in the Temple, he still kept apartments in Canonbury Tower for use in the summer. He still dined with his friends at the Crown in the Lower Road. He still did much of his best writing in the room he loved, high up in the tower, overlooking green meadows and distant hills and nearby cottages, beautiful country which was spread like a carpet round the village of Islington.

At this time Goldsmith often walked with his friends to Highbury Barn, a tavern with tea gardens, a bowling green and trap-ball grounds. The numerous farms, and the pretty dairy maids, the cream and cheese, sweet cakes, tarts, pies, and fresh fruit, were clearly a great attraction. Many Londoners came to Highbury Barn. The *hoi polloi* were known then as the "cream and cake boys". The gentry were known as the "toffs". Another great attraction was the Sadler's Wells Theatre, with its acrobats, jugglers, tight rope dancers, and musical performers.

It seemed to the villagers that Goldsmith was part of the Islington scene. He belonged in Canonbury House, where he lived and worked, producing his best and most popular books. When he died at the age of forty-six, the villagers were grieved, feeling they had lost a good friend, one of themselves. The date was 4th April 1774.

Fifty years later, when Charles Lamb was living with his sister in Colebrook Cottage (afterwards known as 64 Duncan Terrace) Islington was still a small and beautiful village. There were still some ancient and famous public houses. The most delightful of these was probably the old Queen's Head, in Lower Street, built in 1558. It was said to have been at one time the summer home of Elizabeth's favourite lover, the young Earl of Essex (meaning the good earl, not the bad earl, although both lost their heads).

Nelson, in his *History of Islington* (1811) describes this house as "one of the most perfect specimens of ancient domestic architecture remaining in the neighbourhood of London, or perhaps in the whole kingdom".

Lovers of Islington were horrified when this lovely old building was pulled down in 1829. Less beautiful, but fascinating in its own way, was the Angel, at the corner of High Street and Pentonville Hill. Dickens used it, and other houses like it, in describing the hustle and bustle when a stage coach arrived from the North of England, or Scotland.

Charles Lamb came to Islington in 1823, partly because the village was peaceful and partly because he had always admired Oliver Goldsmith. On a summer evening, when his work was done, Charles Lamb loved to walk across the fields to watch the sunset from the top of Canonbury Tower, once the home of Goldsmith. His daily trips by stage coach to India House, in the City, gave him no trouble at all. He enjoyed these journeys. He lived with his sister, Mary, in a state of mental and emotional bliss—as Wordsworth lived with his sister, Dorothy—in spite of the well known fact that Mary was what we would now call a manic depressive. She spent much of her time in a mental home, then just called a 'mad-house'.

In Islington much sympathy was felt for Charles and Mary Lamb, for by now their problem was common knowledge. Most people knew of the tragedy which had happened when Charles was only twenty-one years of age, and Mary was thirty-one. At that time he wrote to Coleridge, his dearest friend, to break the news.

White, or some of my friends, or the public papers [he wrote] by this time may have informed you of the terrible calamities that have fallen on our family. I will only give you the outlines. My poor dear, dearest sister, in a fit of insanity, has been the death of her own mother. I was at hand only time enough to snatch the knife out of her grasp. She is at present in a mad house, from whence I fear she must be moved into a hospital. God has preserved to me my senses—I eat and drink and sleep, and have my judgement, I believe, very sound. . . . Write—as religious a letter as possible—but no mention of what is gone and done with— With me "the former things are passed away", and I have something more to do than to feel—God almighty have us all in his keeping.

C. Lamb.

We are told that Mary, his beloved sister, "worn down to a state of extreme misery by attention to needlework by day and to her mother at night", was suddenly seized with acute mania, in which she stabbed her mother to the heart.

It seemed to his friends that such a tragedy would be the end of gentle Charles Lamb as poet, essayist, or human being. With their help, however, he succeeded in obtaining his sister's release from the life-long restraint in a 'mad-house' which at first was threatened. He promised that he himself would be responsible for Mary for the rest of his life. He kept his promise.

It is true that Mary Lamb, another genius, who loved Charles in the way that Dorothy Wordsworth loved her brother, perhaps even more, was forced to retire to a 'mad-house' many times, leaving poor Charles each year, sometimes for three weeks, or six weeks, or longer. He was miserable, as all could see, without his sister. And yet, as soon as she returned home, they managed to live as happily as possible, writing together, holding long conversations, entertaining their friends.

In 1807 appeared *Tales Founded on the Plays of Shakespeare* by Charles and Mary Lamb. (Charles wrote the tragedies and Mary wrote the comedies.) In 1808 Mary Lamb published *Poetry for Children* and *Mrs Leicester's School*. Charles contributed humorous articles to the *Morning Post*.

Before he came to Islington, Charles spent about ten years entertaining his celebrated friends on Wednesday or Thursday night, each week. In spite of his stammer he became a conversationalist, and inspired the work of William Hazlitt, who did much to make known Lamb's character and charm.

When he came to Islington he was still writing the *Essays of Elia*, assisted by Mary. He did not know that Benjamin Disraeli, a small Jewish boy, had been sent to school not many doors from his new country cottage. It was a whitish, detached house, at the end of Colebrook Row, overlooking the New River, which is now, unfortunately, covered over.

He loved Islington as Goldsmith had loved it. He was visited there by Southey, Coleridge, Hazlitt, and many other well known men of his time. Like Goldsmith, he probably spent the happiest period of his strange, sad, successful life, in this pretty village.

The truth is that Islington, at the turn of the twentieth century, was on its way down, sinking slowly downwards on the social scale. The Crufts dog show (until 1939) and the motor show (until 1908) were still held at the Agricultural Hall, which is now derelict, but nobody living in or near London would have dreamed of moving into Islington for pleasure.

The new sad Islington had an appeal for the painter, Walter Sickert (1860–1942). Sickert said he lived in Islington because its people were "too busy wrestling with realities to bother about social status". He loved to paint the seedy streets of brown brick houses with balconies and fan lights.

"We begin to live," said Sickert, "when we conceive life as tragedy."

The seedy sadness of pre-war Islington appealed to a modern writer of two brilliantly humorous novels. This was Evelyn Waugh, who lived in 17a Canonbury Square in 1928—during his brief and disappointing first marriage.

"He had discovered a temporary paradise," we are now told (by Harold Acton) "in Canonbury Square, Islington, a shabby genteel square such as Sickert loved to depict, no longer a fashionable quarter, but agreeably symmetrical and soothing to the eye."

Waugh wrote *Decline and Fall* and part of *Vile Bodies* to finance his unfortunate first marriage, but his bride fell in love with someone else, and sadness overcame him.

George Orwell, another well known modern author, settled at 27b Canonbury Square in 1944–5. To the villagers he became a familiar figure for about twelve months, peacefully pushing a pram, perhaps remembering his famous line: "All animals are born equal, but some are more equal than others."

Somehow this line by Orwell describes it, for the people of Islington seem to be a good deal less equal than others.

We have in Islington, sad though it quite often looks and feels, both in winter and summer, a number of actors and actresses and budding writers and young architects. They seem to love it, giving reasons which are difficult to explain to an ignorant outsider. Islington has a nostalgic past. It has an air of endearing sadness which is somehow part of its personality. It has an air of shabby distinction and down-at-heel arrogance which some people find irresistible. That is why it is now becoming more expensive and more fashionable.

To some it may seem depressing. For those who love it, the village has a pleasing sense of reality, like an aristocrat in a dirty coat, no longer distinguished, not at all grand. This is what makes a lively village of hard working people so unusual and friendly.

ISLINGTON LOCAL HISTORY
Recommended Books

Northern Heights of London, William Howitt (Longman's Green & Co, 1869)

The Story of Islington and Finsbury, W. Vere Mingard (T. Werner Laurie, 1915)

Islington, Charles Harris (Hamish Hamilton, 1974)

Islington, Pieter Zwart (Sidgwick & Jackson, 1973)

10

Dulwich

Dulwich village has still the air of a quiet little country village. It can still be approached by Croxted Road—until a hundred years ago no more than a leafy lane, known to everyone as Croxted Lane. Indeed Ruskin, our great Victorian critic, writes:

"In Croxted Lane my mother and I used to gather the first buds of the hawthorne, and there, in after years, I used to walk in the summer shadows . . . to think over any passage I wanted to make better than normal in *Modern Painters*."

Even today it is easy to imagine Dulwich village, this little peaceful place, when it belonged to the Cluniac monks of Bermondsey and the manor house was their summer residence. It stood in the angle of Park Hall Road and the west side of South Croxted Road. At the corner near the existing old burial ground stood the Stocks and Cage, for village villains, bearing the righteous inscription, short and sweet, which pleased everyone except the villains: "It is a sport to a fool to do mischief—Thine own wickedness shall correct thee."

The manor house came into the hands of King Henry VIII when the monasteries were dissolved. It was offered willingly by the sensible abbot and he was rewarded in 1539 by a substantial pension of £333 *per annum*. Afterwards the manor passed through various hands to Edward Alleyn, a contemporary of Shakespeare, in 1606. It was Alleyn (pronounced A-lane) who founded the College of God's Gift, commonly called Dulwich College, and opened it with great state on 13th September 1619, in the presence of the Lord Chancellor, Sir Francis Bacon, and the architect, Inigo Jones, and others.

The villagers were flattered and delighted. They enjoyed having visitors. Croxted Road had once been used by the pilgrims, on their way to the shrine of Thomas à Becket at Canterbury. It was known then as the Pilgrim Way. Strangers came by the Thames ferries through Lambeth, across Dulwich Common, over Sydenham Hill, then down to Penge and onward to the Cathedral. The peaceful villagers had turned their heads to see many pilgrims—lawyers, doctors, monks, common yeomen, begging friars, vagrants (rather like hippies today) dressed in the pilgrim uniform with hood and cape, staff and scrip, water bottle and low crowned hat.

And now, still more wonderful, a well-known actor from London had decided to live in Dulwich Manor, to build a college, to brighten this little contented village with his rich and successful and glamorous friends. At first the surprised villagers could hardly believe the tales they were told about Edward Alleyn, the actor from London.

Alleyn's rise to fame was no less startling in his day than the sudden importance in our own society of gifted young men like the Beatles. It must be remembered that no theatres existed in London until 1576. Alleyn was then ten years old. Plays were performed in the courtyards of public houses and as Alleyn's father was a London 'pub holder', the little boy must have watched and listened with interest.

In the next few years no less than seventeen theatres were constructed in London on either side of the Thames. The Corporation of London prohibited playhouses but this was no problem. Fortunately for Alleyn and Shakespeare and Burbage and Henslowe it was possible to make a great deal of money in spite of the angry corporation. By good luck the monasteries, dissolved by Henry VIII, had all passed to the Crown and their lands, therefore, were outside the City's control.

Actors and managers saw their chance. For example, the First Blackfriars Theatre was created in what had once been the Buttery of the Blackfriars Monastery on the City side of the river. The Second Blackfriars Theatre (on the site of the modern building which was until recently *The Times* printing office) appeared as though by magic in place of the parlour and hall of the *frater* of the same Monastery. The Rose, the Globe, and the Hope, were three theatres on the Bishop of Winchester's estate on the Bankside, Southwark.

At the age of twenty we find Alleyn enrolled among the Earl of Worcester's players and he rose to fame very quickly and cleverly. At the age of twenty-six we hear of him again—a glowing description, in 1592, when Nashe published his *Pierce Pennyless* and alluded to Alleyn like this: "Not Roscius nor Aesope, those tragedians admyred before Christ was borne, could ever perform more in action than famous Ned Allen."

In those days his name was spelt in many different ways. His own spelling left much to be desired. Nevertheless Alleyn was already among the most famous actors and managers, a wealthy young man, a close friend of Philip Henslowe—whose step-daughter he married, and greatly loved, in 1592.

He was now manager of Lord Strange's company, playing at The Rose Theatre. The Rose, built on the Bankside about 1587, was the first theatre to be erected on the Surrey side of the River Thames. It was situated quite close to the bear garden and Paris Garden Manor, a place of ill repute, which later was acquired by the wealthy Alleyn and greatly increased his fortune.

In 1593 (the year after his marriage) the plague broke out in London and the theatres were closed by royal edict. Alleyn was persuaded to go on tour, through the provinces, when he wrote those tender and charming letters to his young wife, waiting for him at home—letters which are still preserved at Dulwich College.

Here is an example of Alleyn's love letters to his wife, Joan:

> My good sweete harte and loving mouse, [he writes], I send thee a thousand commendations, wishing thee as well as well may be; but, mouse, I littall thought to hear that which I now hear by you, for it is well known they say that you wear by my lorde maior's offices mad to rid in a cart, you and all your fellowes, which I am sorry to hear; but you thank your two supporters, your stronge leges I mean, that would nott carry you away, butt let you fall into the hands of such tarmagants. But, mouse, when I com hom, I'll be revenged on 'em; till when, mouse, I bed thee fayerwell. Farewell mecho mousin, and mouse, and farewell bess dodipoll.

The nickname for his wife comes from a play called *Dr Dodipoll* (selections from which may be found in Charles Lamb's *Elizabethan Dramatists*).

He was at this time only twenty-seven years old and yet Alleyn, a kind of Elizabethan pop star, was already at the peak of his profession. In 1594 Henslowe and Alleyn became joint managers of the Paris Bear Garden. This was a truly revolting entertainment, in those days new and popular, even patronized by good Queen Elizabeth, not to mention King James, and most of his blood-thirsty favourites, the men and women who enjoyed the brutality of bear-baiting and apparently revelled in the latest forms of violence and death.

Today we have strip-tease clubs in London as a special type of underground amusement—not patronized, however, by kings and queens, and much less harmful than bear-baiting. Shakespeare's London was more barbaric in some ways than London today.

Paul Hentzner, the German writer, gives us a detailed description of bear-baiting:

There is still another place, built in the form of a theatre, [he writes] which serves for the baiting of bulls and bears; they are fastened behind, and then worried by great English bull-dogs, but not without great risk to the dogs from the horns of the one and the teeth of the other, and it sometimes happens that they are killed upon the spot; fresh ones are immediately supplied in the places of those that are wounded or tired.

To this entertainment there often follows that of whipping a blinded bear, which is performed by five or six men standing circularly with whips, which they exercise upon him without mercy, as he cannot escape from them because of his chains; he defends himself with all his force and skill, throwing down all who come within his reach and are not active enough to get out of it, and tearing the whips out of their hands and breaking them.

The writer adds, with a final touch of German disgust: "At these spectacles, and everywhere else, the English are constantly smoking tobacco."

As Paul Hentzner visited England in 1597 we know that the managers of the Paris Bear Garden, responsible for so much brutality and butchery, were Philip Henslowe and the young Edward Alleyn—the idealist who gave us Dulwich College.

Indeed we can see one of Alleyn's advertisements, a hair-raising document, which has been lovingly preserved at Dulwich to this day. It reads like this:

Tomorrow, being Thursdae, shal be seen at the bear garden, on the bank side, a great match plaied by the gamesters of Essex, who hath challenged all comers whatsoever, to plaie five dogges at the single beare for five pounds, and also to wearie a bull dead at the stake, and for their better content shall have pleasant sport with the horse and ape, and whipping of the blinded bear. *Vivat Rex.*

Alleyn soon became known to King James. In Stowe's *Chronicles* we learn that the king and queen, not long after Elizabeth's death in 1603, heard about Alleyn and his way with dogs and lions. The king sent for Alleyn and ordered him secretly to fetch "three of the fellest dogs in the garden".

Apparently the battle took place at the Tower of London. We are told that the dogs were sent in to face the lion, one by one. The first two were terribly mangled but the third survived.

We learn thankfully that "the last dog was well recovered of all his hurts and the young prince commanded his servant, E. Allen, to bring the dog with him to St James's where the prince charged the said Allen to keep him and make much of him, saying he that had fought with the king of beasts should never after fight with any inferior creature".

Fortunately for Alleyn, and Henslowe, and for the Burbages, also for Shakespeare, Marlowe, Ben Jonson, Beaumont and Fletcher, and many other public favourites, King James was a friend to the theatre. Indeed it was James who kept it alive.

We know that the city authorities were constantly attempting to hoax and harass the managers. When there was no other way to prohibit a good comedy or tragedy, they tried the influence of the Privy Council. For example, the Blackfriars Theatre was nearly closed because there were "such multitudes of coaches that sometimes all the streets cannot contain them, but they clog up Ludgate Hill also".

As usual King James came to the rescue. James had his own theatre at Whitehall Palace. It was known as The Cockpit in Court, and was designed by Inigo Jones.

By this time the theatre trade was booming, and everyone knew it was aided by the king. In Dulwich the villagers were as interested as everyone else by the exciting changes in London life.

Most people knew the names of the famous theatres on the Bankside. These were the Rose (at the corner of what is now Southwark Bridge Road and Park Street) the Swan (at the corner of Hopton Street and the passage under the railway) and the Globe (on part of the brewery premises in Park Street adjoining the Cannon Street Viaduct).

John Taylor, a contemporary writer, known as the "Water Poet", because he worked on the River Thames as a waterman, brings the Shakespeare scene to life. There were no less than 40,000 watermen who gained a living, he tells us, by ferrying passengers across the river to the Surrey side—taking them to the new theatres clustered round the popular bear garden. "The cause," he writes, "of the greater half of which multitude hath been the players playing on the Bankside."

As owner of the bear garden, Alleyn was much respected, an extremely rich man by the time he came to Dulwich. In 1605 we find him beginning to buy land in Dulwich from Sir Francis Calton, eventually owning nearly 1,200 acres. The manor and neighbouring lands must have cost him over £10,000.

At this time he was still under forty years of age, happily married, religious, kind hearted, a man of high principles and high ambitions, not only a celebrated actor but master to the king's bears. He gave us Dulwich College, today one of our important public schools, mainly from the proceeds of bear-baiting—a strange thought!

In 1613 this astonishing man signed an indenture for the building of what was then called a hospital. Inigo Jones may or may not have been the architect chiefly responsible for the pretty little chapel, and afterwards the small but charming college buildings. At any rate, he was present at the banquet in Dulwich when the college was finally opened.

If one of our famous Beatles came to live in a country village today, and decided to spend his fortune on building a house of charity, it would cause no more surprise and wonder than was felt by the residents and villagers at the sight of Edward Alleyn and his remarkable college.

The new Lord of the Manor seems to have been a lovable and friendly person. The villagers seized their opportunity to gain employment and perhaps tickets to the bear garden in London. There were some who disapproved of theatrical stars and considered all of them a bit lower class and *nouveau riche*, an immoral lot. In the village, however, everyone wished to make the acquaintance of Edward Alleyn, a man who was admired by the king, on friendly terms with the Earl of Arundel, whose house was visited by nobles, as well as by actors and poets.

We know that Shakespeare was acquainted with Alleyn. It may even be that Shakespeare visited Dulwich to see Alleyn, or to see the new college. Certainly John Donne did so.

On 20th August 1620, by which time the college was built, Alleyn wrote in his diary: "I had doc Donne at Camberwell." Next year, on 22nd May, he "baited before the king at Greenwich". On 14th July 1622 he heard the celebrated John Donne preach at Camberwell. On 1st September he wrote, in his charming way: "Wee took the Communion, feasted the poor and gave the 12 the new gownes, and this being my birthday I am full 56 years old; blessed be the Lord God the giver of Lyffe. Amen."

It seems that the kind hearted Alleyn spent much time in his college with his twelve poor scholars, entertaining and living there, with Joan, his wife, his "dear sweet harte and loving mouse". Anyone who gave a helping hand, or brought a turkey, or a pig, or a cake, might be invited to dinner with the Lord of the Manor. On Sunday mornings, he and the almspeople said their prayers in his beloved little chapel, looking much as it does today.

His school was divided by Alleyn into three distinct classes: first 12 poor scholars, then children of inhabitants of Dulwich, to be taught free of charge, and lastly a group called by Alleyn "towne or foreign scholars".

The almspeople consisted of six "poor brethren" and six "poor sisters". Alleyn announced that the headmaster and warden were always to be unmarried men, having the same surname as himself—a decision which caused trouble.

Probably for this reason the school was mismanaged after his death. The foundation was entirely reconstructed in 1857, and again in 1882. At any rate, during his life time, the college created much interest, and Alleyn, with his charming character, made many important friends. Unfortunately he lost his affectionate wife, his dearest Joan, in the year 1623.

The Lord of the Manor then did a most unexpected and unwise thing. Instead of mourning his good little wife, he quickly married again. The woman he chose was a young girl, nearly forty years younger than himself, the daughter of the great John Donne, the Dean of St Paul's Cathedral.

The villagers were surprised and shocked by this second marriage, and there seems to be no doubt that Alleyn was socially ambitious. He was by now a remarkably rich man, holding property at Dulwich, Bankside, Lewisham, Lambeth, Blackfriars, and Cripplegate, even in Yorkshire. He was still good looking, with a fine beard, an air of consequence. The villagers knew that he wished to be knighted, and so perhaps, by marrying Constance Donne, he thought he would gain more importance. Or was he an old man, taken by a pretty young girl, a man who ought to know better?

There must have been much gossip in the village. Constance had met Alleyn at the home of her aunt, Lady Grymes, of Peckham. Soon after this meeting the unsuitable marriage was discussed by Alleyn and John Donne (who was four years younger than his future son-in-law), in the parlour of the Deanery. It was quickly arranged. The marriage settlement was adjusted between Sir Thomas

Grymes and Alleyn—who seems to have held a poor opinion of Donne as a business man.

And so Constance, a girl of eighteen, was married from her aunt's house in Peckham to a man of fifty-eight, and then lived with him for three years at Dulwich. The villagers found it hard to understand. Why did John Donne, the romantic, the metaphysical poet, the preacher of inspired sermons, the man who believed all his life in the power of love, agree to his daughter's loveless marriage? He was not satisfied with Alleyn as a husband for Constance. There were many recriminations and much bitterness on both sides. Constance seems to have done her best. Among the Alleyn papers there is a prayer in her handwriting that she may prove a faithful wife. Did she find fidelity so difficult?

We know that Constance was a motherless girl when she married Alleyn, and that when he died, three years afterwards at the age of sixty-one, she soon found another husband. Alleyn only left her £1,600, which does not seem very much, and the bulk of his property passed to his beloved college.

The marriage is still a mystery. We shall never know what made John Donne permit such a strange union, but there is nothing to show that Alleyn treated his young wife unkindly. Indeed he seems to have been incapable of unkindness to women, or men—only to the king's bears! Nevertheless Donne disliked him intensely. Could it be that Constance, being so young and foolish, annoyed her parent by falling in love with her good natured husband?

He died on 25th November 1626, and was buried in his little chapel beside his first wife. He must have stirred in his grave, poor man, for most of his dearest wishes were firmly disregarded by those who now controlled his college. It is said that members of his family and college staff lived there in luxury for more than 200 years, and yet nothing was done to improve the college or help the unfortunate scholars.

In 1675 Evelyn paid a visit to Dulwich. On 2nd September he wrote in his diary: "I went to see Dulwich College, being the pious foundation of one Allen, a famous comedian in King James' time. The Chapell is pretty, the rest of the Hospital was very ill contrived, yet it maintains divers poore of both sexes. 'Tis in a melancholy part of Camerwell parish."

Years later, writing to his two young ladies, the Misses Berry, Horace Walpole describes the state of things in June 1791.

This morning, [he writes] I went with Lysons the Reverend to see Dulwich College, founded in 1619, by Alleyn, a player, which I had never seen in my many days. We were received by a smart divine (*très bien poudré*) and with black satin breeches, but they were giving new wings, and new satin breeches, to the good old hostel too, and destroying a gallery with a very rich ceiling, and nothing will remain of ancient, but the front and a hundred mouldy portraits among apostles, sybils, and Kings of England.

But better things were to come.

The villagers now spent their evenings in The Greyhound, on the west of the Hamlet High Street, or sometimes in a public house called The Green Man, which stood at the corner of Lordship Lane, where The Grove Tavern now stands. They remembered the happy days when Edward Alleyn was Lord of the Manor, and wondered what would happen to Dulwich College, now so neglected.

Lord Thurlow, the Lord Chancellor, lived in a building on the site of The Grove Tavern (about 1780). After he left Dulwich Grove, as it was then called, it became Dr Glennie's Academy. Lord Byron was a pupil there for two years before he went to Harrow.

A matter of great interest to the villagers was the first meeting of the Dulwich Club, which was held on 26th March 1791. Today the club is still flourishing though very much changed. It is now called the Dulwich Working Men's Club with a mixed membership of 484 men, 693 women. When it started, the idea was to find an excuse for an annual dinner when the gentlemen of Dulwich could escape from the ladies of Dulwich and drink themselves under the table.

Strangely enough the gentlemen changed their minds. At the very first meeting it was solemnly resolved that the members of the club should "entertain the ladies of the Hamlet of Dulwich to a ball and supper". This was a most unexpected decision. It must have been made by nervous club members, uncertain of their wives and daughters, fearing they might be displeased if left at home while the gentlemen enjoyed themselves.

After that the principal toast at every meeting was: "The Hamlet of Dulwich and the ladies thereof." For many years "the ladies thereof" were invited to the summer banquets. In 1886 the club became known as the Dulwich Liberal Club. Today, as the Dulwich Working Men's Club (started about 1934) it is still dominated by "the ladies thereof".

Those of us who love Dulwich are extremely proud of the Dulwich Picture Gallery, which came into being at the beginning of the nineteenth century. It was the first public picture gallery in London. It was opened twenty-four years before the National Gallery in Trafalgar Square. The architect of the new building was Sir John Soane, and in 1814 it was ready to receive the pictures.

No doubt the villagers were astonished at this new sign of good fortune. It was totally unexpected. When the rumour went round the village and was first discussed over a glass of beer in The Greyhound, or The Green Man, nobody quite believed it. Why should the little hamlet of Dulwich be chosen for this honour by an unknown lady and gentleman of great wealth? Who were these generous strangers? Where did they come from?

To the villagers it was all very strange and exciting, an unlikely story, almost as strange as the gift of Dulwich College from Edward Alleyn.

The man responsible for the picture gallery was a good looking Frenchman. We now know that he was born at Douai in 1745 and educated at the University of Paris. Later he came to London as a teacher of languages, and Margaret Morris, one of his pupils, fell in love with him and married him. This part of the story is easy to believe. His portrait as a young man is now in the gallery, and it certainly explains his charm for women. (There is a strong resemblance to the actor, Derek Nimmo.)

Margaret, who fell in love with him, was the sister of Sir John Morris, of Glamorganshire, and brought her delightful French husband a considerable fortune. He now began collecting and dealing in pictures. He seems to have been a sympathetic character, loved by many, and his favourite companion was an artist, who later became known as Sir Peter Francis Bourgeois. The three lived together, apparently in perfect harmony.

Noel Desenfans was a gifted young man, a writer, and among his works (much discussed at the time) was a vindication of Fénelon's memory from an attack by Lord Chesterfield. There is a picture in the gallery showing Lord Chesterfield in the guise of a serpent. He is winding himself wickedly around the pedestal on which stands a bust of the virtuous Fénelon. The hero, of course, is our dear Monsieur Desenfans, who is guarding Fénelon from the attack of Chesterfield, the serpent.

After his romantic marriage, Monsieur Desenfans was appointed as the Polish Consul General in London, and King Stanislaus employed him to collect pictures for the formation of a National Gallery in Warsaw. Poland, however, ceased to be a kingdom. When the king abdicated, leaving Desenfans unpaid, the pictures were left to him as a kind of unwanted legacy. Margaret, his loving wife, encouraged him to keep them, and so he continued to collect pictures (paid for by his wealthy wife) and his friend, the artist, continued to assist him.

In 1799 Monsieur Desenfans proposed to the British government the formation of a National Gallery—offering to contribute both pictures and money. The offer was not accepted! Meanwhile his friend, Sir Peter Francis Bourgeois (known now as Sir Francis), was urging him to buy more and more pictures, and helping him in matters of selection and restoration. Sir Francis, by the way, was a pupil of De Loutherbourg, R.A. (whose portrait by Gainsborough is in the Gallery). In 1791 he was appointed Painter to the King of Poland, and knighted by him—a knighthood accepted by George III.

By this time the two friends, aided by the loving Margaret, had acquired a great number of valuable pictures in London. They seem to have been very happy and successful. When Monsieur Desenfans died, in 1807, he left the whole collection to Sir Francis Bourgeois, who bequeathed them to Dulwich three years later. It was done, we now believe, at the suggestion of an actor, John Philip Kemble— brother to Mrs Siddons—probably as a tribute to Alleyn.

Knowing all these stories about them, it is a fascinating experience to enter the gallery and find immediately the pictures of Edward Alleyn, handsome and solid and bearded, not far from Joan, his "sweete-harte and loving mouse", and Monsieur Desenfans, two pictures of him, romantically good looking when young, and, to tell the truth, slightly bloated but still attractive at the end of his life. Margaret, his loving wife, is there, and also the good looking Sir Francis. It is like a family reunion. You feel, as the villagers do, a personal affection for each of these charming and friendly characters.

A number of pictures were left when he died by Edward Alleyn, and some of these are now in the gallery. Among them is a picture of the Queen of Bohemia, daughter of James I. (Through her daughter, Sophia, who was the mother of George I, the English people gained a king who could not speak English.) There is also an interesting picture of James himself.

The Cartwright Collection was given to Dulwich in 1686 by William Cartwright, a bookseller and actor. As a result we have portraits of many famous actors who played principal parts in the

original productions of Shakespeare and Beaumont and Fletcher—
among them Burbage, who was Shakespeare's intimate friend.

At Dulwich we also have pictures given by the Linley family in
Bath. As we know, Sheridan's wife was the beautiful Miss Linley,
who married him in the village of Marylebone. Her brother, the
Reverend Ozias Linley, became organist for Dulwich College in 1816.
For this reason the Gainsborough and Lawrence portraits of the
family can now be seen in the gallery.

This valuable collection includes works by Velasquez, Cuyp, Van
Dyck, Murillo, Rubens, Rembrandt, Watteau, and Reynolds. The
cost of the gallery was about £14,000, most of which was paid by Sir
Francis Bourgeois and Margaret Desenfans. As the Dulwich
collection was then much larger than the one which appeared later
in Trafalgar Square, it became the favourite haunt of Victorian
painters. Among the artists who loved it and used it were Turner and
Holman Hunt, and afterwards John Ruskin, the great Victorian
critic—who spent much of his time making studies and water colours
of his favourite pictures.

All this we owe to the charming Monsieur Desenfans, and
Margaret, his loving wife. Margaret seems to have been devoted to
her husband's friend until the last. She mentioned in her will that
Sir Francis wished the President of the Royal Academy to visit the
Dulwich Gallery once a year, with his colleagues, to give their
opinion on the state and preservation of the pictures. It was
Margaret who decided that an annual dinner should be given for
them in the gallery.

In her will, to make sure of this, Margaret left £500, the interest
to be spent on entertainment. In those days it seemed more than
enough! She also left a large and complete service of silver plates,
spoons, a bread basket, and cutlery, a dinner and dessert service, a
table, decanters, etc., for the benefit of the guests from the Royal
Academy.

Margaret's dinner is usually followed by a garden party with
several hundred visitors. These garden parties are nearly always an
annual event, in Dulwich, even when there is no dinner. In this way
Margaret continues to entertain her guests, and the past is
remembered.

As we know, Alleyn intended to establish a great public school,
and this he did. The present Dulwich College, a showy red-brick
Victorian building, erected in 1870, was officially opened by the

Prince of Wales, the future King Edward VII—known as 'Bertie'. In place of the "twelve poor scholars" we now have about 1,360 public schoolboys. We also have Alleyn's School and James Allen's Girls' school, both extremely successful.

Unfortunately the Manor House is gone but we have managed to keep Belair, an Adam house built in 1785. On Dulwich Common we still have the Blew House, a lovely old building used by the college as a boarding house. Oddly enough it does not belong to the college. It was given by Alleyn in 1626 to the Parish of St Botolph, Bishopsgate (where he was born) so that the rent could be distributed on his birthday to the poor. In addition to the original chapel the villagers of Dulwich now have the church of St Barnabas in Calton Avenue, built about 1894—but many are still faithful to the old chapel on Sunday mornings. At the end of every service they still remember Edward Alleyn. They always give "humble and hearty thanks for the memory in this place of Edward Alleyn, our Founder and Benefactor, by whose benefit this whole College is brought up to godliness and good learning".

Lovers of Dickens will know that Mr Pickwick lived for several happy years in Dulwich, and was a constant visitor to the picture gallery. Dickens himself spent much time at The Greyhound, one of his favourite public houses. It was pulled down in 1898.

John Ruskin used to take his classes of working men to sketch in Dulwich, and in his own words: "The outing would finish with tea at The Greyhound."

The villagers knew that John Ruskin spent more than fifty years of his life at Herne Hill and Denmark Hill nearby. Sometimes, in Dulwich, one can still feel the presence of this sad and dignified Victorian gentleman, this brilliant and powerful critic, the man who could make or break a struggling artist, the friend of Turner, the enemy of Whistler, the man who wrote *Modern Painters*, delighting his enormous public, the unhappy husband whose pretty wife left him.

At one time the villagers knew him well. He was loved, and feared, sometimes pitied, another fascinating character, part of the Dulwich scene at the time of Queen Victoria.

Everyone in the village knew that Mr Ruskin was rich and important. His parents were Scottish. His father came from Edinburgh to London, where he made an enormous fortune in the wine trade. His mother was often seen, walking with Mr Ruskin, her arm through his, on a summer evening.

When he was four the family removed to 28 Herne Hill, then a country village close to Dulwich village. His mother trained him in reading the Bible, and he read through every chapter of every book, year by year.

At the age of seventeen the romantic Ruskin first saw Adèle, the French daughter of Monsieur Domerq, his father's partner, and fell rapturously in love. His unspoken passion lasted about three years and was ended by Adèle, who married a French baron. This led to Ruskin's illness, a kind of melancholia, which interrupted his studies and caused him to wander sadly about Europe for another two years. For this reason he did not become a graduate of Oxford until 1842, in his twenty-fourth year—five years after his entrance at the university.

His famous first book was written at Herne Hill when Ruskin was little more than twenty-four years old. *Modern Painters, Vol. I*, was published in May 1843. It was an elaborate defence of Turner, his favourite painter, and was attacked by the critics. Even Turner, Ruskin's hero, seems to have been a trifle disconcerted, until the Ruskin family put things right by hastily buying his pictures.

In 1845 the author of *Modern Painters* was working on *Vol. II*, which was published in 1846. By this time the villagers of Dulwich were beginning to feel proud of him. Three years later he published *The Seven Lamps of Architecture*. It was illustrated with his own exquisite etchings.

At the age of thirty-one, John Ruskin was already considered a remarkable man. The Victorians loved and flattered him. Then, in 1848, he married a beautiful girl, Euphemia Chalmers Gray, known to all her friends as "Effie". The marriage seems to have been arranged by his parents. It lasted about seven years, and then Effie, who could bear it no longer, complained annoyingly that the marriage had never been consummated, and obtained an anullment under Scottish law. Ruskin was hurt. To make matters worse, she immediately became the happy wife of John Everett Millais, the most successful young painter of the day.

Sadly John Ruskin returned to his parents, with whom he lived at Herne Hill until their death. Neither his marriage, nor the whispers of scandal when Effie left him for John Everett Millais, seem to have affected his work. He preferred cathedrals to pretty girls!

The first volume of *The Stones of Venice* appeared in 1851. In 1860 the fifth and final volume of *Modern Painters* was published, a symphony in words, as musical as a long and elaborate poem.

He spent the last forty years of his life expounding his views on industrial problems, education, morals, and religion—always showing that art becomes a means to a higher and more spiritual life. The Victorian intellectuals seem to have honoured him more than any other critic, or preacher, or reformer. In the village of Dulwich he was probably considered a genius. How would the modern intellectuals have treated him if Ruskin had lived today?

Dulwich village, at the time of writing, would probably still be chosen by the fastidious Mr Ruskin as a dignified London village where a gentleman of taste might agree to live. It is not spoilt by the continuous revving and rattling of passing lorries. Small cars are sometimes driven politely, and often slowly, up and down the High Street. There is even an old fashioned Toll Gate for motorists using the private road through fields and open country owned by the red brick Victorian stronghold which is now a famous public school.

Ruskin would admire the row of Georgian houses as much as we do. He would smile tenderly, as we do, at the Post Office, which is partly a draper's shop, and displays ladies' woollen underwear in the window. He would be pleased by the comfort and charm of the large Victorian public house, the *Crown and Greyhound*, patronized by respectable men and women, gleaming with polished copper and brass, as English as Mr Pickwick himself. Above all, he would enjoy the chapel, and the picture gallery, as we do today.

Dulwich village is dominated still by the name and personality of the man who first created the peaceful pretty chapel, and then the little pale-faced buildings which were added on either side, for the benefit of the poor scholars, and their teachers. It is now just called The Old College. It stands benevolently at the cross roads, where the High Street ends. It still gives the village an air of beauty and modest importance.

These, then, are the elegant buildings which were lived in for 200 years by a master, a warden, four fellows, and twelve poor scholars. Today the small rooms are still used as homes for almspeople and old age pensioners, though some are offices for college governors.

Dulwich is very much a village even today. The Dulwich Tollgate is the last tollgate in use in the London area. On Sundays the chapel is still used by students from Dulwich College, Alleyn's School, and James Allen's Girls' School, also by the pensioners and local residents. On Sunday mornings the villagers still enter by the beautiful iron gateway and walk, as Ned Alleyn did, on the long straight path between green lawns and flower beds to the little friendly chapel where his tomb may be seen.

Behind the chapel is the picture gallery, surrounded by a peaceful garden. On every side are the streets and gardens and parks and schools left for Dulwich by Edward Alleyn, some of them still bearing his name.

As King Charles II left his mark on Chelsea and 'Prinny' on Marylebone, this interesting actor left his mark on Dulwich. The villagers, who still love him, have managed to keep the spirit of his charming and dignified village.

DULWICH LOCAL HISTORY
Recommended Books

Norwood and Dulwich Past and Present, Allan Galer (Truslove & Shirley, 1890)

Dulwich History and Romance, Edwin T. Hall (Bickers & Sons, 1922)

Dulwich Discovered, William Darby (Heinemann Educational, 1966)

11

Greenwich

It is best to see Greenwich for the first time from a boat, in the summer sunlight, and to feel the magic of the Queen's House, attended by the stately white and grey buildings, courtiers in stone, like maids of honour, standing calmly there, on either side, leading with incredible beauty and grace to the water front. The wide steps running down to the river Thames have been used by many kings and queens. The magic is still there.

Greenwich is a royal village, and has been brilliantly described in a book of great detail called *Royal Greenwich* by Olive and Nigel Hamilton. It has seen more of English history than any other village in the land, with the exception of Windsor.

The life of the village has always centred round the royal family, as in Battersea, and certain other villages, it has centred round the Lord of the Manor.

King Henry VIII was born in Greenwich, and baptized in the little parish church of St Alphege. There was nothing surprising about this to the villagers. As there was no other church, and Greenwich was only a small fishing village, they were accustomed to the sight of the royal family, nodding and smiling, as they came to kneel, in the royal pew, on Sunday morning. It was felt that the village belonged to the royal family and the royal family belonged to the village.

Even in those days the church had a long history. Before the time of William the Conqueror, in the year 1012, Archbishop Alphege was captured by the Danes at the sacking of Canterbury. He was imprisoned at Greenwich. Because he refused to let his people pay the ransom demanded by the Danes he was slaughtered. In fact he was stoned to death—or so we are told—on the spot where the church now stands. The villagers remembered, the archbishop was canonized, and to honour his brave death the church of St Alphege bears his name to this day.

King Henry VIII was born and brought up in the palace near the church. His father loved it, and so did he. It had been built by his ancestor, Humphrey, Duke of Gloucester, who was brother to Henry V. Henry was known to the villagers from childhood. His love affairs, his bravery, his cruelty, his passion for sport—every side of his character was seen at close quarters, and for this reason he was better understood in Greenwich, perhaps, than anywhere else. At first they were proud of their charming and talented prince. He looked well on a horse. He loved archery. He tilted and rode and shot with unusual skill. It is pleasing to think of him in the riverside palace, lived in so happily by his parents and grandparents, visiting the village church with his mother, smiling down at the villagers from the royal pew, placed over the door, speaking to them in the church-yard, remembering their names and recalling their troubles. In spite of his faults he was loved by most of his people (though hated by the villagers in Chelsea) and in Greenwich, where he was born and bred, one can imagine the personal interest which was taken in Henry by those who knew him so well.

Before Anne Boleyn came on the scene, he managed to live here contentedly and graciously for twenty years, married to the dignified Katherine of Aragon.

He took little interest in politics. Katherine bore him seven children, including four sons, but none survived for more than a few weeks except Mary, who was born at Greenwich, and later became known as Bloody Queen Mary. The villagers, waiting for a son and heir to the throne, must have been almost as disappointed as Henry.

Meanwhile there were numerous entertainments in Greenwich Park. We are told in that excellent book by the Hamiltons how Henry ordered a stand to be carefully placed for the queen, and her ladies, to watch the fights and displays of skill and strength. A long day of sport usually ended in a banquet. The queen was expected to present the prizes. Sometimes Henry arranged a great feast for the common people, and then the villagers, who loved both food and sport as much as he did, enjoyed themselves with the gentry.

All this good feeling was suddenly ended in 1523 when the fatal Anne Boleyn appeared on the scene as maid-of-honour. The king fell in love. As much to the amazement of Katherine as to the villagers he began to talk quite openly of divorce. His argument was that if Katherine remained his wife there would never be a male heir to the throne. It was true they had a daughter, Mary, but no queen had yet ruled England. To this there was no answer, and the crafty Henry convinced himself that a curse had fallen upon Katherine. It was because she had once been his brother's wife. They had been living, said Henry, in mortal sin. As Henry desired Anne Boleyn to become his queen, not his mistress, it seems probable that he truly was worried about an heir to the throne.

Most people, especially in Greenwich, felt sorry for Katherine. Every Sunday Cardinal Wolsey came down by river from London to see Henry. At this time, we are told, Anne Boleyn was so hated that she dared not visit London. In 1531 the unfortunate Katherine left the palace where she had lived and entertained with Henry for more than twenty years—defeated by her youthful rival. One can imagine the gossip in the village. She died five years later at Kimbolton, a damp isolated mansion, longing on her deathbed for one kind word from the king, which never came.

It is safe to assume that the villagers, who had known Katherine for so many years, were not at all pleased when Henry married Anne Boleyn in 1533. He saw to it that the coronation procession from Greenwich to the Tower of London was the grandest pageant ever beheld. He was known to be very much in love. Arrangements were made for the mayor, in his scarlet robes, and all the sheriffs and City lordlings, also in scarlet robes, to embark in a special barge on which a band was loudly playing. They were escorted by fifty other barges, gaily decorated, gilded, gorgeous, on their way to Greenwich. Meanwhile Anne Boleyn was rowed in procession to the Tower of London, where the bridegroom "received her affectionately".

No doubt the villagers were hoping that Henry would soon have the happiness of presenting England with a son and heir. On 7th September 1533 the heir was born. Anne Boleyn gave Henry a daughter, the future Queen Elizabeth, and she was born in Greenwich. One imagines that everyone in the village must have been affected by Henry's disappointment, but no one, least of all Henry, was willing to admit that anything was wrong. Three days later the mayor and his colourful companions, once more in their scarlet robes, again entered their gilded barges, and went this time to the christening of Elizabeth.

By this time Henry was a changed man. The heartless Thomas Cromwell became Secretary in May 1534. The Dissolution of the Monasteries, and the reign of terror, had already begun.

On May Day 1536 a grand tournament took place at Greenwich Park, and the new queen, with her brother, Lord Rochford, was of course present. Some of the villagers were there to see her. We are told by the Hamiltons in *Royal Greenwich* that the sports were at their height when Henry, in a bad mood, took his departure and proceeded to London with six domestics. The same night Anne Boleyn's brother, and three friends, were arrested and carried up the river to the Tower, bound like criminals.

Next morning Anne Boleyn was herself arrested, and also carried to the Tower to be imprisoned. Her day of glory was over. On 26th April 1536 she was found guilty of unfaithfulness before the King's Council at Greenwich.

Cruel Henry signed her death warrant at Placentia, and arranged matters in his own most brutal way. On the third anniversary of the new queen's coronation, she was beheaded. More than that. He married Jane Seymour on the following day.

Henry was punished for this by the death of Jane Seymour, who lived only long enough to bear him a son—afterwards King Edward VI. Most of his people still loved Henry, and now they felt sorry for him. In 1540 he allowed Cromwell to arrange another marriage, this time to a German princess, Anne of Cleves, a lady he had never seen. He met her on Blackheath, and found her extremely unattractive. The marital problem was quickly settled for Cromwell was arrested in June, and shortly afterwards the marriage was annulled by Parliament.

On the day of Cromwell's execution, Henry married Norfolk's neice, Catherine Howard. (Sometimes his marriages and executions were almost similtaneous.) The unlucky Catherine Howard was executed after two years. His sixth and last wife was Katherine Parr, who married him one year later and managed rather cleverly to survive him.

The truth is that until his death Henry was more loved than feared, especially in the village of Greenwich. The elders had known him all his life. He was not just the King of England. He was the head of the village family, a personal friend, a man who was understood and respected. Had he not created the Royal Navy? Some of his beautiful ships rode at anchor within sight of the royal village, and the villagers loved them as he did.

Henry's son, Edward VI, lived and died in the same palace. His reign lasted only for six years. Then Mary, Henry's first daughter by Katherine of Aragon, soon to be known as "Bloody Mary", rode into London triumphantly, and was met by Elizabeth (Anne Boleyn's daughter) who came to her from the village of Highgate, where she had spent the night.

Both Mary and Elizabeth were well known figures in Greenwich, where both had been born, and today we still have a charming reminder of Henry's two remarkable daughters. It stands in the church of St Alphege, in a glass case—the keyboard of the original organ on which they were both instructed, as girls, by their music master, the celebrated Thomas Tallis. (He was buried beneath the old chancel in 1585.)

Bloody Mary became very unpopular. She died childless in 1558, and the villagers of Greenwich were thankful to see Elizabeth, for whom they felt nothing but love and admiration. The new queen detested executions. Like Henry she loved entertainments and gave them, as he did, in Greenwich Park.

Elizabeth had a way with her which won the hearts of all the villagers. For example, on 19th March 1572, on Maundy Thursday, the queen actually washed and kissed the feet of the poor in remembrance of Jesus washing the feet of the apostles. We are told, however, that the ten women were scrubbed clean before the queen was permitted to touch them. When the washing and feet-kissing was over, Elizabeth gave them each twenty shillings in thirty-nine white and red leather purses. She has been beautifully described in Hentzner's *Itinerarium*, at Greenwich, in a dress of white silk, bordered with pearls of the size of beans, her train born by a marchioness. As she turned on either side all fell on their knees. By this time Elizabeth was in her sixty-fifth year, and the German writer describes her appearance as:

very majestic; her face was oblong, fair but wrinkled; her eyes small yet black and pleasant; her nose a little hooked; her lips narrow, and her teeth black (a defect the English seem subject to from their too great use of sugar). She had in her ears two pearls with very rich drops; she wore false hair, and that red. Upon her head she had a small crown. Her bosom was uncovered, as all the English ladies have it till they marry; and she had a necklace of exceeding fine jewels.

Of course the queen's private life was watched with interest, especially by the villagers. Her greatest favourite was Robert Dudley, whom she created Earl of Leicester. It was known that her lover's wife had mysteriously died in 1560. For this reason Elizabeth could not possibly marry him. And yet, nearly twenty years later, when he married the Countess of Essex, the queen was so offended that he was imprisoned for a time in Duke Humphrey's castle on the hill, in the park. The villagers, who understood Henry's daughter, must have been greatly amused!

As they expected, she forgave him in the end. She kept his last letter, written before his death in 1588, in a casket close to her pillow. It was found there when she died, fifteen years later.

Shakespeare and Drake were among Elizabeth's visitors at Greenwich. So was Walter Raleigh. The famous story of Sir Walter and his mantle (which he gallantly spread in the mud for the queen to walk on), took place on the steps of Greenwich Palace.

Mary, Queen of Scots, was never seen by the villagers, but her death warrant was signed in the palace—most unwillingly—by Elizabeth. She was persuaded by her councillors to do it after many refusals. Then, a few days later, she saw bonfires in Greenwich Park, and was told, to her distress, that Mary had been beheaded.

In 1603 good Queen Elizabeth died, and was probably missed in her favourite village even more than Henry had been. Her home, the red brick Tudor Palace by the river, has now disappeared. We have instead a much more beautiful building, the Queen's House; which was first created by Inigo Jones in the time of King James I.

The beauty and charm of the house, especially when seen from a boat, in the summer sunlight, can be felt as strongly today as when the elegant white building was admired for the first time by the villagers of Greenwich as a gift from their new king to his queen. When it was built it created a sensation. The repentant James gave it to Anne of Denmark, and perhaps it helped her to forget about the Duke of Buckingham and other favourites. (The queen wrote many letters to her charming bi-sexual husband, beginning "My Heart", and showing him great affection.) At any rate, it was Anne who invited Inigo Jones to build her a beautiful house in the Palladian style—a style which later became the fashion for country houses all over England. Inigo Jones had travelled in Italy. To please her, he set about building a unique house—a villa—having at its centre a curious bridge, in this way crossing the main road, from Deptford to Woolwich, which ran, to everyone's amusement, underneath.

It is now considered the most perfect example of English domestic architecture, as well as the focal point of all the historic buildings gathered for kings and queens in Greenwich.

At first the villagers were astonished by the beautiful white house arching over the road. It joined the two parts of the king's estate—

the palace by the river and Greenwich Park, where the king
hunted.

To the disappointment of many, especially in the village, the
queen died before the house was finished. James gave it to his son, the
Prince of Wales, later King Charles I. Building was not resumed
until after his son's accession to the throne, and his marriage to the
pretty Henrietta Maria, from Paris.

Henrietta Maria was a gay little thing, only sixteen years old, and
King Charles was shy, serious, and stiff, suffering with a stammer.
For at least three years the marriage was not at all pleasing to
Henrietta Maria. She had taken a strong dislike to her husband's
favourite, Buckingham, but after the duke's murder, in 1628,
Charles and his wife were seen to be close and sympathetic.

These things were known to the watchful villagers, and everyone
was pleased when dancing and gaiety were restored to the court at
Greenwich. The queen had been married for five years and now, at
last, she conceived. Her son, another Charles, was born in 1630. She
turned with joy to the task of completing the Queen's House.

At this time the king commissioned Inigo Jones to finish his wife's
lovely house, and the queen was frequently there to inspect progress.
She seems to have been quite blissfully happy, with her children, her
entertainments, and a loving husband. It was a period of pleasure for
them both, a delayed honeymoon, and the setting for their
unexpected romance was now always called by them and their family
the "house of delight".

No doubt there was grief in the royal village when all this happiness
came to an end. Henrietta Maria was in England when the Civil War
began, but she escaped to Paris. For a long time the Queen's House
was deserted. She spent years of unceasing effort trying to raise
troops to fight against Oliver Cromwell, and to help Charles.
Finally, on 30th January 1648, she received news of his execution at
Whitehall.

In Greenwich, still known as the royal village, men and women
were shocked by these terrible happenings. They were thankful when
King Charles II at last returned to England. It pleased them to know
that he loved Greenwich, and was planning to make some improvements. Everyone was delighted when he visited the palace. In 1661
the work of repairing and enlarging his mother's house began.

Charles was full of enthusiasm. He decided to beautify Greenwich
by pulling down the old Tudor buildings and creating a model

palace. His decision was found to be right. When the old buildings were demolished his mother's house gained a perfect view of the river. He then started work on the first of the new buildings, to be known as the King's House. It is one of those which all of us admire today.

In Greenwich it was well known that Charles was fond of his Navy, as Henry had been before him, and the villagers could see for themselves that once a week he sailed down the river to visit his ships at Woolwich. In 1661, Pepys writes: "The King hath been this afternoon to Deptford to see the yacht that Commissioner Pett is building which will be very pretty." Evelyn describes the King at the tiller of this same yacht, racing another boat from Greenwich to Gravesend, and back, for a wager!

No doubt all the villagers were greatly excited, in May 1662, when the gay and energetic young king was married to Catherine of Braganza. They knew, like everyone else, that Charles had numerous mistresses. Later they knew that Catherine was extremely jealous. They were not surprised when Henrietta Maria, now living in France, was persuaded to return to Greenwich in the month of July (only two months after the marriage) to pacify the indignant young queen from Portugal.

At this time there must have been a lot of speculation. Old stories about Henry and Anne Boleyn were remembered and repeated by the village elders. Perhaps Charles would become another Henry. How would the two unfortunate queens, his mother and his wife, now talking things over in the Queen's House, be able to manage the king?

Charles, however, was not in the least like Henry, and Catherine loved him all her life, notwithstanding her natural jealousy of Lady Castlemaine and many others. His mother soon comforted Catherine. At this difficult moment in the marriage, to please both ladies, Charles had already begun the task of laying out the park at Greenwich, and Le Notre himself (who designed the gardens at Versailles) had been commissioned to make the designs.

Charles was a lover of architecture and science as well as beautiful women. In 1675 he created, in Greenwich Park, the first official observatory in the world. Christopher Wren designed it. A sum of £520 was raised from the sale of old gunpowder and used to finance the project and pay the workmen. We are told that Christopher Wren had too little money for the stone dressings on the corners of his red brick design, so these had to be made of wood and painted white.

The villagers, some of them working for Christopher Wren, watched and listened and repeated what they had heard, amazed at the introduction of so many new ideas.

Charles, who dreamed up the little and wonderful observatory, which still stands proudly, like a child's toy, in Greenwich Park, died in 1685. He was mourned by everyone around him, his queen, his mistresses, and the villagers of Greenwich, who treated him as others might treat their Lord of the Manor. His unfinished palace—unfinished through lack of money—was now in the hands of Queen Mary, his brother's daughter.

It was Queen Mary (conveniently married to William of Orange) who now took charge, giving her orders to the great Christopher Wren, the man who knew the wishes of Charles and had already designed the Chelsea Royal Hospital for him. He offered his services free.

What Mary wanted was a set of new buildings, to be modest and dignified, on the lines of the Chelsea Hospital, for the use of elderly sailors. To please Charles, she insisted on preserving the King's House, knowing that her uncle had loved it. She also insisted on a strip of land, to be kept clear, stretching from the Queen's House to the river.

Unfortunately Mary died of smallpox, but her dutiful husband was determined to carry out all her plans for the added beauty of Greenwich. Everything must be done as Mary and Charles would have thought right. He even donated £2,000 to the new charity.

As a result we now have the gorgeous collection of white and grey stately buildings, standing by the riverside, like a group of kings and queens, perpetually holding Court. At the centre of the famous group is the most beautiful building of all, and it seems to be the living heart of Greenwich. You can almost see one of the queens of England, emerging from her white house, walking between her maids of honour, attended by her courtiers, descending slowly and gracefully to the wide stone steps, where someone is waiting, perhaps the king, to hand her into the gilded barge.

Perhaps these wonderful buildings were not very suitable as a living place for elderly seamen. It is true that Peter the Great is supposed to have said to King William: "If I were the adviser of Your Majesty, I should council you to remove your Court to Greenwich and convert St James's into a Hospital!"

At this remark Charles would have burst out laughing, but not William, who probably frowned. Today Greenwich Hospital is thought to be one of the finest specimens of classical architecture in the country.

It was used for many years as a Home For Seamen but now it is the headquarters of the Royal Naval College. The Queen's House is the centrepiece of a world famous naval museum. Among other things, it is filled with memories of Nelson and contains numerous souvenirs, including his uniform, worn when he died. In 1960 our present Queen Elizabeth came to Greenwich to open Flamstead House—the original observatory founded by Charles II in 1675. So now we have in Greenwich the finest exhibition of historical astronomy in the world, housed in the same two buildings where it all started. We owe much to Charles. He and his family have given us all that is most beautiful and interesting in the village of Greenwich.

During the Georgian period, the Queen's House was not used like the other buildings as part of the Home For Seamen. It continued in its dignified role as a royal property, and finally became a kind of hotel for foreign visitors—King George I stayed there when he arrived from Hanover on his accession to the throne in 1714.

Owing to bad weather and fog he had to be rowed up the River Thames, arriving at Greenwich after dark, and being led up the steps by torchlight. The Queen's House had been prepared for his arrival, but to George, a critical foreigner, it only seemed unreal and unpleasing. Twenty-five years later, still seeming to the villagers like a foreigner, the king was seen for the last time at Greenwich, on his way home to Hanover. The church warden entered on his expense sheet: "To the ringers when the King embarked, ten shillings".

George managed to die in his beloved Germany shortly afterwards (of a stroke) and his son succeeded to the English throne. George II, like his father, brought with him his German mistresses, installing them at St James's Palace. He had a charming intelligent wife, Queen Caroline, to whom he assigned the lease of the Queen's House. Unfortunately, Queen Caroline seldom used the much loved house, perhaps finding it too English, or too unusual, or both.

It was a time of change, and the villagers were not pleased by what they saw. Greenwich was no longer a royal village. They noticed magnificent houses being built in Blackheath, overlooking the park. In 1710 the little church of St Alphege collapsed in a storm, and the people of the village put their case before Parliament, pleading that the town was "depopulated and deserted by the richer sort". The petition for a new church was granted. Our present church was designed by Nicholas Hawksmoor (a pupil of Wren's) and his beautiful Baroque building was completed by 1714.

At the time of writing, it is still considered fashionable to live in Blackheath, close to Greenwich Park, where beautiful Georgian houses remind us at every turn of the eighteenth century. The famous Crooms Hill leads to the house of Lord Chesterfield (who wrote all those much quoted letters to his son) which is open to the public in summer, and has a restaurant nearby. General Wolfe, the hero of Quebec, lived next door. The Princess of Wales (later the wild and wonderful Queen Caroline) lived at Montague House. Presently she went abroad and became an exile, rampaging round Europe like a wild horse, and her angry husband ordered Montague House to be pulled down.

Even more scandalous was the behaviour of Lady Emma Hamilton, openly in love with Lord Nelson, but still living with her husband, the gentle Sir William. This is perhaps the most extraordinary love story ever told in Greenwich. It beats the stories about Henry VIII and Charles II. Today we can see, in the Greenwich Maritime Museum, a little shabby uniform, so small that it might have belonged to a boy. It was worn in battle by one of England's most glorious heroes, the great Lord Nelson, on the day he died. He was loved in Greenwich during his lifetime, and he is loved still.

Horatio Nelson was a parson's son and a parson's brother. Fifteen of his family in Norfolk were clergymen, and Nelson himself was nearly always guided by his faith in God. In battle he trusted his own judgement (and frequently disobeyed orders) for this unusual reason.

At the age of twenty he was promoted 'post captain', and qualified to command the largest battleships. He became a friend of Prince William Henry (later King William IV) who was then a midshipman in Hood's flagship and saw him as: "the merest boy of a Captain I ever beheld; and his dress was worthy of attention. He had on a full lace uniform; his lank unpowdered hair was tied on a stiff Hessian tail of an extraordinary length; the old fashioned flap of his waistcoat added to the general quaintness of his figure. . . ."

About three months after Revolutionary France had declared war on Britain, Nelson set sail in the *Agamemnon*. His destination was Naples—where he met Lady Hamilton.

Nelson wrote to Fanny, his wife, innocently saying that: "she does honour to the station to which she is raised", having no idea at the time that he had met the love of his life. Her husband was the

British ambassador, Sir William Hamilton, aged sixty-three, in his thirtieth year at Naples. Emma had lived with him for five years, at first as his mistress. He age was twenty-eight. She now acted as hostess and interpreter for Nelson but did not see him again for five years. During this time Nelson became established as a naval genius and a national hero.

At home, in Greenwich, his career was followed with interest. The villagers had been trained for many generations, since the time of Henry VIII, to take a pride in the Royal Navy. Now they had in the village the Home for Seamen, and several hundred elderly sailors, all of them longing for news of Nelson, telling stories of his bravery, drinking his health.

They did not yet know about Emma Hamilton. They only knew he was now Rear Admiral Sir Horatio Nelson. At Santa Cruz, on the Island of Teneriff, a heavily fortified harbour, he mounted a night attack and commanded it himself, losing his right arm as a result. He returned to his ship, the *Theseus*, and said: "Tell the surgeon to make haste and get his instruments. I know I must lose my right arm, and the sooner it is off the better." The only form of anaesthetic was rum, and opium, after the operation, was used as a sedative.

News of the defeat at Teneriffe did Nelson no harm. The newspapers praised his daring (unequalled since Drake) and now there was an empty sleeve to confirm the reports of his courage. But a greater success was to come. In 1798 Nelson fought the famous Battle of the Nile. Of the thirteen French ships of the line that had faced battle the night before, only two survived. Buonaparte had lost his Fleet and more than 5,000 men (nearly six times as much as the British) and he and his army were now stranded in Egypt.

All these triumphs had come to Nelson before his second visit to Naples. A letter from Lady Hamilton prepared him for a hero's welcome.

"Good God, what a victory!" she wrote, "Never, never has there been anything half so glorious, so complete! I fainted when I heard the joyful news, and fell on my side, and am hurt, but what of that. . . . My dress is from head to foot *alla* Nelson. Even my shawl is in blue with gold anchors all over. My ear-rings are Nelson's anchors; in short we are all be-Nelsoned. . . ."

The famous Nelson who returned as a hero to Naples was a little man with a worn tired face, blind in one eye, his hair beginning to turn grey, his empty sleeve giving him a helpless appeal. He was smaller than Emma Hamilton, whose figure was round and full. He wrote to his wife: "I hope one day to have the pleasure of introducing you to Lady Hamilton. She is one of the very best women in the world. How few could have made the turn she has. She is an honour to her sex, and a proof that even reputations can be regained. . . ."

The woman Nelson now loved had been born of working-class parents in North Wales. Her father was a blacksmith. As a girl, she was brought to London by her kind hearted mother. Her beautiful face was painted again and again by Romney, also by Hoppner and Lawrence. By the time Nelson appeared she had managed to establish herself in Naples, a happy wife, a close friend to the Neapolitan queen, Maria Carolina (sister of Marie Antoinette).

Emma was soon presiding over the celebrations for Nelson's fortieth birthday. 800 guests were invited to supper and then to a ball. Shortly afterwards, when Naples fell to troops advancing overland, Nelson rescued the Hamiltons, also the king and queen, sailing them in rough weather to Palermo. Later he returned again to Naples, followed by the king, who was reinstated. For this act Nelson was rewarded by King Ferdinand with the Dukedom of Bronte and an estate in Sicily.

Talk of his love affair with Emma was by this time scandalizing the fleet, and rumours were reaching London, also the village of Greenwich. Most people knew the stories about Emma. For this reason Nelson was called home, and decided to return overland with the Hamiltons—which took five months to accomplish. Perhaps the joy of fathering his first child increased the guilty feelings of Nelson, a man of rigid faith, very much a parson's son. Perhaps that was why he so quickly went back to sea.

At the end of January in the year 1801 Nelson was at Torbay, and there he received the news that Emma had given birth to a daughter— the survivor of twins. He wrote, apparently in a frenzy of passion: "My longing for you, both person and conversation, you may readily imagine. What must be my sensation at the idea of sleeping with you! It sets me on fire, even the thoughts, much more the reality. I am sure my love and desires are all to you, and if any woman naked were to come to me, even as I am at this moment from thinking of you, I hope it may rot off if I were to touch her even with my hand."

He then wrote: "Would to God I had dined with you alone. What a dessert we would have had." He was careful to explain, "with my present feelings, I might be trusted with fifty virgins naked in a dark room."

By this time it was understood by all who knew him that Nelson was serious in his love for Emma. His family, one by one, began to drop their friendship with his wife. Nelson had provided for her generously and now shut her out of his life.

His success in battle continued and the next victory was Copenhagen, on 1st April 1801. In the village of Greenwich, the story was repeated many times. Nelson saw the signal to cease fire and made his famous remark to Captain Foley as he placed the glass to his blind eye. "I really do not see the signal", he said. Of eighteen Danish ships, seventeen were captured, burnt, or sunk, and once again he was England's hero.

He was with Emma long enough to see his daughter, Horatia, christened at the parish church in the village of Marylebone. Meanwhile, Emma purchased Merton Place, near Wimbledon, which was to be their home. Her husband wrote her a stern letter. "I have no complaint to make, but I feel", he said, "that the whole attention of my wife is given to Lord N. and his interest at Merton." Early in 1803 her husband knew he was dying and moved to his large house in Piccadilly. There, with Emma's arms about him and Nelson clasping his hand, he died.

Soon after that the Admiralty announced the appointment of Vice-Admiral Viscount Nelson to command in the Mediterranean. Nelson said goodbye to Emma and Horatia (age five) for the last time in the home they had created for themselves at Merton Place. He took command of the fleet off Cadiz on 28th September 1805, the day before his forty-seventh birthday. This was to be his greatest battle of all—the battle of Trafalgar.

It was said afterwards that Nelson seemed to know his great moment had come. He signed and had witnessed a document leaving Lady Hamilton as a legacy to his king and country. When he left his cabin for the last time he was not wearing his sword as he usually did when about to face the enemy. On the other hand, he was wearing the four stars of chivalry, a thing he never did, for in close action the stars would make him an unmistakable target. Was it suicide? Or was it a desire to offer himself to the god of war? Thomas Hardy, his flag captain, suggested that he change into a plain coat as a normal precaution. Nelson said there was no time—although a messenger could have fetched another coat in an instant.

Signal flags fluttered overhead, giving Nelson's famous message to his officers and men: "England expects that every man will do his duty." During the battle which followed, Nelson and Hardy paced the quarter deck, shoulder to shoulder. Nelson slipped to his knees, then on his side, with his left hand on the deck, supporting his body. "They have done for me a last, Hardy. My backbone is shot through."

He was carried below to the surgeon, his face covered by a handkerchief to prevent panic among his men. Hardy visited him with the news that victory was complete and that at least fifteen of the enemy had surrendered.

"That is well," Nelson said, "but I had bargained for twenty."

He spoke of Lady Hamilton, urging that Emma should be given every care and courtesy, reminded Hardy to anchor after the battle, and then asked Hardy to kiss him farewell. "Now I am satisfied," he said, "Thank God I have done my duty."

To the chaplain Nelson said: "Doctor, I have not been a great sinner." And then he said: "Remember, I leave Lady Hamilton and my daughter Horatia as a legacy to my country. And never forget Horatia."

Three hours after the fatal shot, he died. It happened on 21st October 1805, an unforgettable date for England and the Royal Navy. News of the greatest Nelson victory—two thirds of the enemy fleet destroyed or captured, and not one British ship lost—was less important to the people at home than the death of their hero.

The body was brought home to Greenwich for a magnificent state funeral. It lay, embalmed, in the Painted Hall at Greenwich Hospital. Nelson's chaplain, Doctor Scott, kept vigil beside the coffin for two weeks. Each night the small body of the hero Nelson was removed to the little room which is now known to tourists and visitors as "the Nelson Room".

On Wednesday, 8th January 1806, the Lord Mayor and City Livery Companies assembled for the funeral at Greenwich. The body was reverently placed on a state barge, and the procession rowed slowly up the river to the crack and crackle of minute guns.

Five hundred pensioners, elderly seamen, many of them in tears, had followed the coffin to the river terrace of the hospital, where they stood and waited, as though lost, after Nelson's barge had disappeared. The coffin was landed at Whitehall Stairs and taken to the Admiralty. Next day it was carried in procession to St Paul's Cathedral, followed by the Prince of Wales.

It is sad to recall that Nelson's last wishes were not obeyed or even remembered. A grateful nation honoured his dull brother, and did not forget his wife, or even his stepson, Josiah. Lady Hamilton was ignored.

The love of Nelson's life, who clearly returned his love, was allowed to die, in poverty, about ten years later, in Calais. By then she was a heavy drinker. She was attended by Horatia, too young to understand, who later married a clergyman and became the mother of a large family. So ended a strange story. It comes to mind, like a dream, at the sight of Nelson's uniform, which is still kept so tenderly and proudly in the National Maritime Museum at Greenwich.

The memory of Nelson has been preserved with the greatest care by those who still love him at Greenwich. Today we have visitors and tourists from every part of the world. They arrive in the summer, sometimes by boat from Westminster—which is much the most enjoyable way. They crowd together on the waterfront, studying their guide books, asking questions in many languages, and finally, like a flock of enthusiastic starlings, chattering and twittering happily, they find their way, first to see the famous *Cutty Sark*, and then to the Maritime Museum to see Nelson's uniform. When these important things have been done they probably visit the Queen's House, and then climb the hill to see the Royal Observatory, where they will learn about Greenwich Mean Time and the Prime Meridian.

The *Cutty Sark* made its appearance in Greenwich in the year 1954, and was introduced to us officially, like one of the royal family, by our present Queen Elizabeth in 1957. As most of us know, the *Cutty Sark* is the most famous clipper in the world, the fastest and most beautiful boat of its kind, used in the late nineteenth century on the wool run between England and Australia. Henry VIII and Charles II would have greatly admired the *Cutty Sark*. The boat-loving villagers are proud of it, and the visitors and tourists are mad about it.

There is, by the way, a wonderful walk along the waterfront to a public house called the Cutty Sark, passing a Georgian restaurant called the Trafalgar, which was built in 1837. The latter was well known for the wonderful whitebait dinners and was patronized by Dickens, Wilkie Collins, Thackeray, Marryat, Ainsworth and

Cruikshank. It has an air of dignity, with delightful windows overlooking the water.

Today, unfortunately, Greenwich is spoilt for some of us by the heavy arterial road which cuts through the village, and angers the villagers. The noise, at times, is almost unbearable. That is why so many people now prefer to live in Blackheath closeby. The villagers have been told more than once that improvements are on the way, and it seems there are now definite plans for a Greenwich bypass, a special road for heavy traffic. Already the work has been started.

Meanwhile, there is something delightful which each of us can do when visiting Greenwich. Cross the river by the foot tunnel under the bows of the Cutty Sark. It takes only a few minutes to walk beneath the river to the island gardens on the opposite side. From there we can see the view which was loved by Christopher Wren and Caneletto. We can see perfectly the beautiful white and grey buildings, left to us by our royal families, standing by the riverside as though forever, like a group of kings and queens . . . perpetually holding Court.

GREENWICH LOCAL HISTORY
Recommended Books

The Palace and Hospital or Chronicles of Greenwich, A. C. L'Estrange (Hurst & Blackett, 1896)

Royal Greenwich, Olive and Nigel Hamilton (Greenwich Book Shop, 1969)

A History of Greenwich, Beryl Platts (David & Charles, 1973)

Greenwich Park: Its History and Associations, A. D. Webster Republished 1971 (Conway Maritime Press, 1902)

Note: There are smaller illustrated publications about the main buildings and institutions of Greenwich, from the *Cutty Sark* to the Royal Observatory, which are available locally.

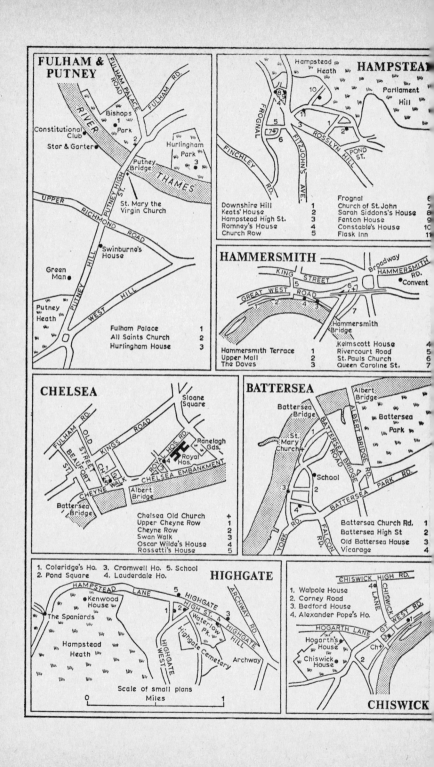

FULHAM & PUTNEY

FULHAM ROAD
FULHAM PALACE ROAD
FULHAM RD.
RIVER

Bishops
Park

Constitutional
Club

Star & Garter

PUTNEY HIGH ST.

Putney
Bridge

Hurlingham
Park

THAMES

UPPER
RICHMOND ROAD
PUTNEY HILL

St. Mary the
Virgin Church

Swinburne's
House

Green
Man

Putney
Heath

WEST HILL

Fulham Palace   1
All Saints Church   2
Hurlingham House   3

HAMPSTEAD

Hampstead
Heath

Parliament
Hill

FROGNAL
FINCHLEY RD.
FITZJOHN'S AVE.
ROSSLYN HILL
POND ST.

Downshire Hill   1
Keats' House   2
Hampstead High St.   3
Romney's House   4
Church Row   5

Frognal   6
Church of St. John   7
Sarah Siddons's House 8
Fenton House   9
Constable's House   10
Flask Inn   11

HAMMERSMITH

Broadway
HAMMERSMITH RD.
Convent

KING STREET

GREAT WEST ROAD

Hammersmith
Bridge

Hammersmith Terrace   1
Upper Mall   2
The Doves   3

Kelmscott House   4
Rivercourt Road   5
St. Pauls Church   6
Queen Caroline St.   7

CHELSEA

Sloane
Square

FULHAM RD.
OLD CHURCH STREET
KINGS ROAD
BEAUFORT STREET
ROYAL HOS. RD.

Ranelagh
Gds.

Royal
Hos.

CHELSEA EMBANKMENT

CHEYNE WALK

Albert
Bridge

Battersea
Bridge

Chelsea Old Church   +
Upper Cheyne Row   1
Cheyne Row   2
Swan Walk   3
Oscar Wilde's House   4
Rossetti's House   5

BATTERSEA

Albert
Bridge

Battersea
Bridge

Battersea
Park

ALBERT BRIDGE RD.
BATTERSEA BRIDGE RD.
BATTERSEA PARK RD.
YORK RD.
FALCON RD.

St.
Mary
Church

School

Battersea Church Rd. 1
Battersea High St   2
Old Battersea House   3
Vicarage   4

HIGHGATE

1. Coleridge's Ho.   3. Cromwell Ho.   5. School
2. Pond Square   4. Lauderdale Ho.

HAMPSTEAD LANE

Kenwood
House

The Spaniards

Hampstead
Heath

HIGHGATE HIGH ST.
HIGHGATE HILL
HIGHGATE WEST
ARCHWAY RD.

Waterlow
Pk.

Highgate Cemetery

Archway

Scale of small plans
Miles
0   1

CHISWICK

CHISWICK HIGH RD.
CHISWICK LANE
GT. WEST RD.

1. Walpole House
2. Corney Road
3. Bedford House
4. Alexander Pope's Ho.

HOGARTH LANE

Hogarth's
House

Chiswick
House

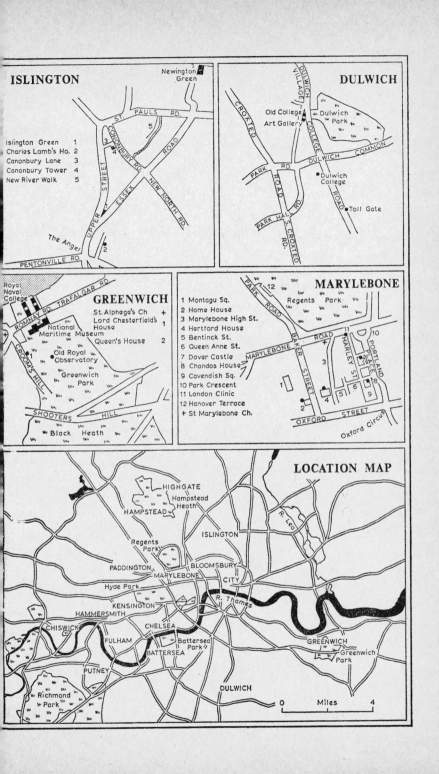

ISLINGTON

Newington Green

St. Pauls Rd.
Conanbury Rd.
Essex Street
New North Rd.
Upper Street
The Angel
Pentonville Rd.

Islington Green 1
Charles Lamb's Ho. 2
Canonbury Lane 3
Canonbury Tower 4
New River Walk 5

DULWICH

Dulwich Village
College Rd.
Croxted Rd.
Old College
Art Gallery
Dulwich Park
Dulwich Common
Park Rd.
Park Hall Rd.
Croxted Rd.
Dulwich College
Toll Gate

GREENWICH

Royal Naval College
Trafalgar Rd.
Romney Rd.
Crooms Hill
National Maritime Museum
Old Royal Observatory
Greenwich Park
Shooters Hill
Black Heath

St. Alphege's Ch. +
Lord Chesterfield's House 1
Queen's House 2

MARYLEBONE

1 Montagu Sq.
2 Home House
3 Marylebone High St.
4 Hertford House
5 Bentinck St.
6 Queen Anne St.
7 Dover Castle
8 Chandos House
9 Cavendish Sq.
10 Park Crescent
11 London Clinic
12 Hanover Terrace
+ St Marylebone Ch.

Park Road
Regents Park
Baker Street
Marylebone Road
Harley St.
Portland Place
Oxford Street
Oxford Circus

LOCATION MAP

HIGHGATE
Hampstead Heath
HAMPSTEAD
R. Lea
Regents Park
ISLINGTON
PADDINGTON
MARYLEBONE
BLOOMSBURY
CITY
Hyde Park
KENSINGTON
R. Thames
HAMMERSMITH
CHISWICK
CHELSEA
GREENWICH
FULHAM
Battersea Park
BATTERSEA
Greenwich Park
PUTNEY
DULWICH
Richmond Park

0   Miles   4

Index